PROXIMITY, LEVINAS, AND THE SOUL OF LAW

Proximity, Levinas, and the Soul of Law

DESMOND MANDERSON

BJ
55
.M36
2006
West

McGill-Queen's University Press
Montreal & Kingston · London · Ithaca

© McGill-Queen's University Press 2006
ISBN-13: 978-0-7735-3041-6   ISBN-10: 0-7735-3041-X
Legal deposit second quarter 2006
Bibliothèque nationale du Québec

Printed in Canada on acid-free paper that is 100% ancient forest free
(100% post-consumer recycled), processed chlorine free.

This book has been published with the help of a grant from the Canadian
Federation for the Humanities and Social Sciences, through the Aid to
Scholarly Publications Programme, using funds provided by the Social
Sciences and Humanities Research Council of Canada.

McGill-Queen's University Press acknowledges the support of the Canada
Council for the Arts for our publishing program. We also acknowledge
the financial support of the Government of Canada through the Book
Publishing Industry Development Program (BPIDP) for our publishing
activities.

Library and Archives Canada Cataloguing in Publication

Manderson, Desmond
    Proximity, Levinas, and the soul of law / Desmond Manderson.

    Includes bibliographical references and index.
    ISBN-13: 978-0-7735-3041-6   ISBN-10: 0-7735-3041-X
    1. Torts. 2. Negligence. 3. Law and ethics. 4. Levinas, Emmanuel – Ethics.
    I. Title.

BJ55.M36 2006   340'.112   C2005-906869-8

Typeset in Sabon 10/13
by Infoscan Collette, Quebec City

To Jackie,
Who has taught me so much about proximity

Contents

Acknowledgments

A book that has taken so long to be born accumulates many debts in utero. For the inspiration to begin this journey, which has introduced me to new areas of scholarship and has changed how I think about the world, I will always be grateful to the marvelous collective of interdisciplinary scholars that met for some years on Friday afternoons in Glebe. There we read and drank and discussed; I was first introduced to Levinas there and first encouraged to take up the idea for this book. To Robyn Ferrell, who jointly convened the Program for Judgment and Expression with me, and to Sue Best, Andrew Murphy, Paul Patton, Colin Perrin, Nick Smith, Nicholas Strobbe, and the passing parade, thanks for an utterly irreplaceable experience of academic friendship and collegiality.

For the enthusiasm to sustain this work even as difficulties mounted and time meandered, I am indebted to those many colleagues and academic friends who read and commented on various chapters, drafts, and papers. I have in mind Peter Cane and Tony Connelly, Rod Macdonald, Nicholas Kasirer, and Shauna van Praagh, Jean Michaud and Richard Mohr, Marinos Diamantides and Simon Critchley, and above all Shaun McVeigh and Peter Goodrich. Thank you for all your suggestions, although I am nothing if not dogged in maintaining my errors.

For the hospitality that allowed me to pursue and complete this task, I have been fortunate enough to have been provided with outstanding institutional support. Research was begun in the Faculty of Law at the

University of Sydney. Most of the writing took place upon my appointment to the Canada Research Chair in Law and Discourse in the Faculty of Law at McGill University, Montreal. In the final (and literal) contractions of rewriting I took advantage of the beneficent environment of the National Europe Centre at the Australian National University and of sanguine research assistance provided by Will Amos and Karen Crawley at McGill. And of course, without the welcoming professionalism of Philip Cercone and McGill-Queen's University Press, this book would have withered on the vine.

A modified version of certain aspects of chapters 1, 3, and, in particular, 7, has appeared as "Proximity: The Law of Ethics and the Ethics of Law" in *University of New South Wales Law Journal* 28 (2005); a modified version of chapters 3 and 4 appeared as "Emmanuel Levinas and the Philosophy of Negligence" in *Tort Law Review* 14 (2006); a modified version of chapter 5 appeared as "The Ethics of Proximity: An Essay for William Deane" in *Griffith Law Review* 14 (2005). I am grateful for the interest shown by these journals and grateful to them for authorizing the use of these articles in this book.

Without all these people and places, this book would not have been written. Without my friends and my family and, above all, if it had not been for Jacqueline Adcock – constant and unfailing support, gentle sceptic – no book of any kind could have been written. My love and gratitude are infinite.

But for all that, responsibility for the work that follows is mine alone. This responsibility has given birth to *me*, singled me out and called me up, and I must accept with it all the undoubted errors, misunderstandings, and shortfalls that go with it. It is often the case that there follows at this point some sentence along the lines that "the law stated is correct as of midnight on 10 March 2005." This has always struck me as bizarre both for its arrogance and for its uselessness, since it is a date on which by definition the book has no readers. Between accuracy and readership there is a null set. So I will confine myself to the following: the law stated is incorrect on any day you happen to be reading it and, if I may briefly foreshadow the long argument to follow, a good thing too.

McGill University, Montreal
March 2005

PROXIMITY, LEVINAS, AND THE SOUL OF LAW

1

Introduction

In fact take my body who will, take it I say, it is not me. And therefore three cheers for Nantucket; and come a stove boat and stove body when they will, for stave my soul, Jove himself cannot.

Herman Melville, Moby Dick[1]

THE QUESTION: DOES LAW HAVE A SOUL?

The Latin word for the soul is *spiritus*, which also means breath. In Greek it is *pneuma*, likewise wind or breath. The Hebrew *ruah* has similar connotations.[2] These words all circle around a cluster of ideas that are neither Christian nor religious. It is surely meaningful to speak of the soul or spirit[3] in order to articulate what we sometimes feel to be a kind of force that animates us, filling us with an *inner* life: "animate" also means to quicken and comes from *anima* – breath, life, soul, mind.

Even someone as implacably materialistic, in his own way, as Michel Foucault granted the psychological existence of something like a soul: "It would be wrong to say that the soul is an illusion, or an ideological effect. On the contrary, it exists, it has a reality, it is produced permanently around, on, within the body … This real, non-corporeal soul is not a substance; it is the element in which are articulated the effects of a certain type of power."[4] But this hardly tells us what we mean when we ourselves speak of and value the soul. The playwright and author Michael Frayn, for example, once said that the soul was to be found in "the little back garden of the English."[5] While suggesting the depths of our attachment to some secret place within us, the image is, to my mind, far too solitary in orientation. "You cannot hide the soul," writes Herman Melville in a key chapter of *Moby Dick*.[6] If the soul is a kind of inwardness, nevertheless we value it because of the way in which it manifests itself in our relations with others. Sometimes we speak of those who care for others as having a soul. Yet the concept of generosity does not go far enough either. In fact the obverse is more nearly true – the soul does not give to others, which would already entail a free choice and a decision, but is rather constituted by a kind of responsiveness and vulnerability to them.[7]

In *Moby Dick* the relationship that Herman Melville explores between his narrator, Ishmael, and the "pagan" Queequeg convincingly and dramatically portrays the sudden love between them in just this way. There is no activity at first, no discovery by them of what the other is or thinks. Conversation – the routine exchange of knowledge or biography, of "who" and "what" they are – comes long after their love takes hold. On the contrary, it is Queequeg's quiet presence that touches Ishmael directly. "I felt a melting in me," he says. "No more my splintered heart and maddened hand were turned against the wolfish world. This soothing savage had redeemed it."[8] We mean by soul the place we hold open, deep within ourselves, for *others* to enter. This openness, this hospitality,[9] does not impose itself on others but allows itself to be redeemed and reformed by difference. Melville knows it is the proof of the soul of both his characters, the cannibal and the sailor alike.

Not to have a soul is to be a self-enclosed fur-ball of ego. The soul allows us to inhale the breath of others. It is vulnerable precisely because it remains open to inspiration – to blow or breathe into, from *spirare*, "to breathe." So inspiration breathes life into something. It comes from outside, or beyond us, arriving unbidden and filling us with a power we never knew we had.[10]

If law has a soul, then for reasons that I hope this book will justify, it is to be found in the law of tort and, more particularly, in the far-reaching doctrines of negligence. Over the past hundred years, the law of negligence has transformed itself and, in the process, transformed our sense of the obligations incurred by all of us in our daily lives – by local governments for the services they provide, by banks and professionals for the advice they give, by drivers on the road, doctors in the surgery, homeowners to their guests or visitors, and even to trespassers who might pay them a call.

Yet what is now compendiously described as "the duty of care" is in some ways an unusual obligation. It is not the outcome of an agreement founded on self-interest, like a contract. It is not a duty owed to the community as a whole and acted on by the State, like criminal law.

It describes a *personal* responsibility we owe to others that has been placed upon us without our consent. It is a kind of debt that each of us owes to others although we never consciously accrued it. Thus, it raises in a distinctly personal way one of the oldest questions of law itself: "Am I my brother's keeper?" What does it mean to be responsible? This is not a question that is easier to answer for us than for Cain. In this book I argue that the idea of responsibility articulated in the law of negligence comes from what might be termed our literal response-ability: it implies a duty to respond to others stemming not from our abstract sameness to others but rather from our particular difference from them. Responsibility is not a quid pro quo – it is asymmetrical, a duty to listen to the breath of others just insofar as their interests diverge from our own. The duty of care emerges not because we have a will (which the law of contract respects) or a body (which the criminal law protects) but because we have a soul.

THE ARGUMENT: TORTS AND ETHICS

This book is in two parts. In the first part I develop a general argument for a relationship between negligence law and the theory of asymmetric responsibility. In the second part, I explore and develop a detailed application of this argument, drawing on, as a complex case study, the specific history of the doctrine of the duty of care in the common law. The starting point, which I develop in chapter 2, is that the common law and its legal theorists have always struggled in attempting to articulate and justify the notion of a duty of care.[11] It received, of course, its paradigmatic expression in *Donoghue v. Stevenson*.[12] Lord Atkin's 1932 judgment contains perhaps the most celebrated passage in the common law:

The rule that you are to love your neighbour becomes in law, you must not injure your neighbour; and the lawyer's question, Who is my neighbour? receives a restricted reply. You must take reasonable care to avoid acts and omissions which you can reasonably foresee would be likely to injure your neighbour. Who, then, in law is my neighbour? The answer seems to be – persons who are so closely and directly affected by my act that I ought reasonably have them in contemplation as being so affected when I am directing my mind to the acts or omissions which are called in question.[13]

Yet the debate on the meaning of this "neighbour principle" has never been entirely comfortable. The law, we are often told, imposes a distinction between the moral and the legal: "The dictates of charity and of compassion do not constitute a duty of care. The law casts no duty upon a man to go to the aid of another who is in peril or distress, not caused by him. The call of common humanity may lead him to the rescue ... A man who, while travelling along a highway, sees a fire starting on the adjacent land is not, as far as I am aware, under any common law duty to stop and try to put it out or to warn those whom it may harm. He may pass on, if not with a quiet conscience at least without a fear of legal consequence ... I do not find such questions easy."[14]

It is perhaps a truism, but nonetheless true for that, that the common law as it emerged from the industrial revolution was framed in terms of individual rights, freedom, and contract.[15] The law of torts, imposing on individuals unchosen obligations to think of others, sits uneasily on this edifice. Further, the common law is not a statutory code that we might imagine as defining people's obligations well in advance of their interactions: on the contrary, judge-made law responds to events and casts judgments on people's actions *post,* if not *ad, hoc.* So we may not even know our obligations before the law deems us to have failed to perform them. Typically, then, the duty of care has been justified either as a kind of restriction on our individual freedom imposed by the State in order to protect our collective well-being or as the articulation of a complex web of implicit agreements amongst us all: either as a multitude of social contracts or as an emanation of social power. Both conceptions stretch back at least as far as Thomas Hobbes. The origin of law as force, the use of that force to require of men that they keep their promises, the use of those promises to enhance the autonomy of individuals by protecting us from each other – all this can already be found in *Leviathan.*

Hereby it is manifest, that during the time men live without a common Power to keep them all in awe, they are in that condition which is called Warre; and such a warre, as is of every man, against every man ... Therefore before the names of Just, and Unjust can have place, there must be some coercive Power, to compell men equally to the performance of their Covenants, by the terrour of some punishment, greater than the benefit they expect by the breach of the Covenant; and to make good that Propriety, which by mutuall Contract men acquire ... And first it is manifest, that Law in generall, is not Counsell, but Command; nor a Command of any man to any man; but only of him, whose Command is addressed to one formerly obliged to obey him.[16]

So according to the orthodox philosophy of the common law, the duty of care stands, awkwardly, as a collective restraint upon that individual freedom which lies, at least rhetorically, at the heart of our legal subjectivity. Instead, I propose in this book to defend a completely different perspective in which the autonomy of individuals is questioned and according to which responsibility is by its very nature unpredictable, unchosen, and asymmetrical. The law of negligence, particularly as articulated fitfully in the common law, would stand on this view not as an oddity but as a paradigm of the idea of responsibility.

My guide in this endeavour has been an immensely influential and somewhat controversial modern writer on ethics, to whose work I offer a preliminary introduction in chapter 3. Emmanuel Levinas (1906–95), a philosopher and Jewish theologian, was until recently mainly of interest to a small but influential circle of French thinkers including Maurice Blanchot, Jean-Paul Sartre, and Jacques Derrida.[17] Now he is rapidly becoming better known. His two main works, *Totality and Infinity* and *Otherwise than Being, or Beyond Essence*, offer a reconstruction of human selfhood away from questions of identity and ego and towards an "ethics of alterity." Forming a vital link between the phenomenology of Heidegger, Merleau-Ponty, and Husserl, on the one hand, and the post-structuralism of Derrida, on the other,[18] his writing is passionate, mystical, and rational, at times bewitchingly erudite and elsewhere bewilderingly obtuse. I cannot promise the reader an easy ride, but as recompense Levinas offers a sustained meditation on the relationship of ethics, responsibility, and law, and – remarkably – he does so using precisely the language of the duty of care. Here then is a philosopher, largely unknown to legal theory, who at last speaks the language of torts.

Neither are *Totality and Infinity* and *Otherwise than Being* removed from the contemporary world. Originally published in 1961 and 1974, these books are haunted by the ashen memory of holocaust, and for the purpose of undermining as powerfully as he could the ego-driven and pragmatic system-building that he believed helped to bring it about. It seemed then, as it seems now, that the most crucial question in the world is the question that the law of negligence has taken on itself: why should we care for others? and how much? In what does our soul consist?

Central to Levinas' meditations is an idea of ethics to which I will have frequent recourse. For Levinas, and for those who have been influenced by him, the word ethics implies a personal responsibility to another that is both involuntary and singular. The demand of ethics comes from the intimacy of an experienced encounter, and its contours cannot therefore be codified or predicted in advance.[19] At least as opposed to the Kantian paradigm of morality as "a system of rules,"[20] ethics therefore speaks about interpersonal relationships and not about abstract principles. Although it has a normative component, ethics explores who we are, and not who we ought to be.[21] At least as opposed to most understandings of rules and law, ethics insists on the necessity of our response to others and the unique predicament of each such response, rather than attempting to reduce such responses to standard instances and norms of general application, norms applicable to whole communities and capable of being largely settled in advance. Indeed, ethics constantly destabilizes and ruptures those rules and that settlement.[22] Furthermore, ethics implies an unavoidable responsibility to another that Levinas exhorts as "first philosophy":[23] by this he means that without some such initial hospitality,[24] or openness to the inarticulate cry of another human being, neither language nor society nor philosophy could ever have got going. At least as opposed to many understandings of justice,[25] there is nothing logical or a priori inevitable about such an openness, except that without it, we would not be here to talk to one another. We cannot derive ethics from universal first principles. Ethics is that first principle.

One of the key questions of this book will therefore be whether and, if so, how such an ethics – spontaneous, uncodifiable, and singular – could have any impact on the law, which seems to be just the opposite of these things. In chapter 4, which serves as the last of the first part of this book, I begin to defend the idea of responsibility offered by Levinas and to show how it makes sense of the central insights of the duty of care: that we must put others first and that this responsibility is not an unfortunate imposition on our naturally individual and autonomous subjectivity but that it is embedded in the idea of responsibility and that it is the *source* of our individuality and our subjectivity. One consequence of such a view is to reclaim tort law as the expression of a distinct philosophical worldview and to emphasize the importance of this perspective as foundational to our understanding of law itself. A more pragmatic consequence is to transform our responsibility for omissions – notably, with respect to the "duty to rescue" – from an anomaly into a core element of the duty of care. On the standard view, the duty to "come to the aid of another who is in peril or distress not caused by him" (picture a drowning child) is at least a hard case and in the view of many writers gives rise to no legal responsibility. On the view I propose here, it is in fact a paradigm case that sums up precisely why we are responsible for others at all. I believe the second view does better justice to our instincts.

Although we shall see that Levinas has very much to say that is pertinent to our thinking about responsibility, neighbourhood, and duty, he is by no means without his problems. Later in the book, particularly in the last two chapters, I will try to come to terms with some aspects of his writing that make his application to legal questions particularly troublesome. These are the very aspects that are the central focus of contemporary scholarship on his work. The present study therefore comes at an opportune time: it speaks to very important debates in the ongoing reception of Levinas.

The first difficulty lies in his insistence on treating the ethical realm, in which responsibility is unique, unbidden, and infinite, as entirely incommensurable with the political realm, in which responsibility is made subject to definite, finite, rules and, moreover, subordinated to the pragmatic demands of the State and social policy. Questioners like Derrida, Rose, and Habermas have wondered how it could ever be possible for Levinas' notion of an ethics of absolute and infinite responsibility towards others to communicate with a political world inevitably governed by regulation, on the one hand, and imperfection, on the other.[26] To compound the problem, Levinas' own limited forays into the application of his ethics to political questions have not been entirely convincing.[27] This question, which asks what a Levinasian "applied ethics" might look like, has been subject to considerable recent analysis.[28] It is a question this book must take up.

The second difficulty lies in Levinas' own relative silence on the question of law itself. In his major works, he says very little about the relationship of law to the ethics of alterity, and what he does say suggests that he thinks of law as a mere arm of politics, on the one hand, and as an entirely positivistic, codified, and rule-bound structure, on the other. In other words, law seems for Levinas to be synonymous with politics and justice synonymous with rules.[29] Yet this conception fails to capture the way in which law serves as a separate modality of thinking about social relations and is not merely politics by other means.[30] As Sarah Roberts writes, "if one takes seriously Levinas' claim that asymmetrical ethical responsibility is the origin of justice then one must also reject Levinas' suggestion that justice [merely] involves viewing persons and responsibility as comparable and symmetrical."[31] Furthermore, as the common law of negligence makes abundantly clear, neither can we simply characterize law as the application of "rules." Jacques Derrida's thinking about law and justice is clearly inspired by Levinas' own writing, of which he is the best-known as well as the most sympathetic critic,[32] but offers a much more elaborate and sophisticated account of their interaction.[33] Drawing on Derrida and on other recent work on Levinas,[34] I wish to offer, most notably in chapter 7, an account of law – particularly in reference to the fluidity and ambiguity that marks the common law discourse on the "duty of care" – that both captures and justifies its distinct form and does so in a way that in fact makes a more convincing case for the possible influence of Levinas' ethics on legal doctrine than his own much narrower conception of law can alone provide.

In order to try and apply Levinas, we have to think more carefully about law. This book therefore makes its contribution to a field of critical legal theory that has over the past few years been steadily drawn to Levinasian ethics.[35] Much of the recent scholarship at this intersection, however, addresses the concept of law and the idea of justice at a very high level of abstraction. In most cases, furthermore, the references to Levinas are allusive and, at the very least, presume a considerable prior acquaintance with the "ethics of alterity" that Levinas presents.

I do not think it unfair to similarly characterize the work of Marinos Diamantides, perhaps the most singular and sustained writer on Emmanuel Levinas and law. In *The Ethics of Suffering* and in several related articles,[36] Diamantides not only takes on Levinas' understanding of responsibility but does so in a specific legal context, namely, in the context of bio-medical law. Yet in some ways the purpose of Diamantides' analysis is to show us the *impossibility* of the relationship of ethics to law. Through a wise and careful reading of cases confronting the margin of life and death, Diamantides insists on demonstrating for us "the structural difficulty with articulating legal principles and norms that would *not* stifle the surprise and anarchy of intersubjectivity."[37]

The point is well made, but I will nevertheless argue in the last chapter that there are in fact structural resources within the common law of negligence, in particular, that allow something of that surprise to endure. My argument responds to a certain view of the hierarchical and systemic nature of "the western juridico-political order"[38] that can, I think, be vastly overstated. But those who have been most guilty of attempting to reduce the discourse of law to a structure of rules in which singularity and response would be largely banished are not so much the scholars as the judges of the common law themselves. What some would see as the problem of "judicial law-making" I see, on the contrary, as its greatest ethical strength. In striving to implicate Levinas' ideas of ethical responsibility right into the body of legal discourse, my approach to the nature of law finds itself in disagreement not only with Levinas and with some of his interpreters but with lawyers themselves.

This marks a further point of departure from the work of others in the field. Diamantides, in particular, shows a particular interest in the affectivity of the judge and its failure to find adequate expression. It is the judges' impatient "attempt to flee from" their emotional response to the unique, uncategorizable, and unassimilable instance before them that interests him.[39] The present analysis is centred less on the phenomenology of judgment than on the constitution of subjectivity. What story does the doctrinal corpus that has grown up around the duty of care tell us about *our* responsibility in the face of this constant surprise of intersubjectivity? The law is above all our story about how our society reattaches commitments to their proper authors. Responsibility is not a judicial auto-da-fé but an influential story as to who we are.

My claim is that this story owes a surprising debt to the perspectives and experiences articulated by Levinas. This is, no doubt, a charitable view of the jurisprudence, and my scholarship is constructivist in the tradition defended by writers as otherwise divergent as Ronald Dworkin, Jules Coleman, or Ernest Weinrib.[40] I aim to construct a view of the law of negligence that provides a persuasive argument by which to understand its key insights and yet that gives us serious critical purchase against which we can test, challenge, and develop it. So, like all good interpretations, my analysis has both a descriptive and a normative dimension. In this, I confess I am an incorrigible optimist. Where others see an abscess in the law, a hole to worry, I see a tunnel, a path to illuminate.

So this book embarks on a project quite different from that of previous scholars. I propose to introduce Levinas to a vast area of legal scholarship that is unlikely to be familiar with him, or he with it. And I wish to explore the relevance of his arguments at the concrete level of legal doctrine in a particular area of substantive law. My question is a simple one: how might Levinas change how we understand the law we have – here and now? And, obversely, how might our understanding of the law change Levinas? This is an effort at translation, dialogue, and a distinct engagement with actual legality. No doubt there will be those who think the muddy process of application demeans Levinas' sublime ideas. Perhaps Levinas himself falls into that category. After all, he insisted, for reasons that will require further discussion later in the book, that "the saying" and "the said" – the first, our spontaneous ethical responsibility for another and the second, our attempts to reduce it to a rule or form of words that might guide our conduct – are irreducible and incommensurable modes.[41] But the peril of such an approach is that it could lead to precisely the sanctified quietism that Gillian Rose accused Levinas of indulging.[42] In fact, if Levinas set his face against one thing all his life, it was *purity*, a hermetic closure that, in defence of sublime perfection, would set itself up as a totality. Ethic purity is no better than ethnic purity. Levinas believed in contamination, in imperfection, and in knotty and chaotic failure. Betrayal, approximation, and ingratitude are necessary to learning.[43] In that spirit, by offering a welcome corruption that aims to keep his words in motion, I take up my interpretive task.

THE STUDY: PROXIMITY

In order to push the limits of Levinas and in order to push the limits of the law, the second part of this book offers a case study in the recent history of the discourse of the duty of care in the common law. My focus throughout is on doctrinal developments that took place between 1984 and 2000 in the High Court of Australia. Chapter 5 is the most detailed and legalistic section of the book, and it provides a careful rereading of this legal history, with a view to understanding its doctrinal to-ing and fro-ing as a mighty struggle between distinct conceptions of the nature of responsibility in the law. Levinas' ideas can help us both analyze and decide between them.

In part, this methodological choice is expedient, since I taught the law of negligence in Australia for several years, and its complex discourse has fascinated me for even longer. It is the case, moreover, that the parallels and borrowings within the Anglo-American common law jurisdictions are closer in the field of negligence than in any other area of law. On the one hand, the connections I am trying to establish between Levinasian ethics and the duty of care could be satisfactorily adapted to the Canadian or English or American jurisprudence, and indeed I refer to this case law periodically. On the other hand, the doctrinal developments in Australia that I explore are well known in these other jurisdictions and will already be familiar to many scholars of tort law.

But there is much more at stake than convenience and coincidence. The French call it the *air du temps*, the Germans *zeitgeist*: both terms

mean the spirit of the times that infuses the intellectual climate. Levinas
was writing about duty and responsibility just as the law, too, was
grappling with them anew. First in the English cases of *Hedley Byrne
v. Heller, Dorset Yacht Co.* and *Anns v. London Borough of Merton*
and then, particularly, in a great line of Australian cases stretching from
Jaensch v. Coffey and *Sutherland Shire Council v. Heyman* to *Gala v.
Preston, Burnie Port Authority v. General Jones, Pyrenees Shire Council v. Day,* and *Perre v. Apand,* the legal understanding of our relationship to others was undergoing a radical, though poorly explicated,
reevaluation.[44] Levinas' work and its reception into English – *Otherwise than Being* was first translated as late as 1981 – suggest the relevance of these questions to many disciplines. Meanwhile, the Australian
jurisprudence on the duty of care offers a truly unparalleled resource,
in both the depth of its discourse and the scope of its reflections, on
the meaning of responsibility in law. These cases are richly imagined
and powerfully argued. They offer an instructive and vigorous debate
on the nature of law, responsibility, and society that wracked the Court
incessantly for almost twenty years. What better body of work could
there possibly be against which to explore Levinas' ideas and to test
their actual relevance to the world of law?

It is not too much to suggest that the High Court of Australia seemed
at times to have been unwittingly inspired by the secret breath of
Levinas. To draw forth these parallels, and to try and provide them
with a more secure basis, recognizes and gives greater depth to the
context that informed the work of the Court. That is the task I attempt
in chapter 5. Chapter 6 takes the argument one step further, exploring
the limits of the duty of care and touching, in the process, on problem
areas such as our responsibility for our words, for the economic consequences of our actions, and over the actions of others. This discussion
will force us to consider in greater depth the following criticism: Levinas'
work, by offering up the promise of an "infinite" responsibility, is incapable of providing us with the substantive limits to responsibility that
law requires if it is to provide us with principles and not just homilies.
Indeed, when confronted with questions requiring political judgment
in his own work, Levinas demonstrated precisely that incapacity. In
order to defend our theory of responsibility from this charge, I will be
forced to develop and extrapolate beyond Levinas' own fragmentary
reflections on law and justice.

In these chapters, the key word that serves as the hinge connecting
Levinas' explanation of the parameters of ethics to the High Court's

explanation of the parameters of the duty of care is the word *proximity*. For Levinas, this word implies a closeness to others, who can be approached but never reached. We are never exactly the same as another person, and in the trauma of that distance lies summoned our soul. "The relationship of proximity cannot be reduced to any modality of distance or geometrical contiguity, or to the simple 'representation' of a neighbour; it is already an assignation, an extremely urgent assignation – an obligation, anachronously prior to any commitment."[45] Our difference and distance from others gives rise to our responsibility for them. Levinas means by proximity something fundamental to who we are and why we have a responsibility to others; something that, furthermore, cannot be reduced to logic or knowledge or rules. Proximity is an experience, emotional and bodily, and not an idea.[46] Incarnate in us all, its implications "exceed the limits of ontology, of the human essence, and of the world."[47]

Astonishingly, in and after 1984 the Australian High Court was on the same track. Particularly in the influential judgments of Justice William Deane, the Court sought to give determinate content to the duty by reference to the concept of proximity.

I have, in *Jaensch v. Coffey* and *Heyman*, endeavoured to explain what I see as the essential content of the requirement of neighbourhood or proximity which Lord Atkin formulated as an overriding control of the test of reasonable foreseeability. So understood, the requirement can, as Lord Atkin pointed out, be traced to the judgments of Lord Esher M.R. and A.L. Smith L.J. in *Le Lievre v. Gould*. In my view, that requirement remains the general conceptual determinant and the unifying theme of the categories of case in which the common law of negligence recognizes the existence of a duty to take reasonable care to avoid a reasonably foreseeable risk of injury to another.[48]

The notion of proximity was a radical and controversial jurisprudential development that led to innovation after innovation in the Court's judgments. When I first read these judgments, it seemed to me that the court was groping towards a new idea of the nature and the legitimacy of our ideas of responsibility. Then when I read Levinas some years later, I came to appreciate much more clearly what they might have wanted to say and why it mattered. The conjunction of these two discourses, in their own ways so uniquely positioned to reflect deeply on the essence of our responsibility to others, and the connections between the language they each used seemed to me so remarkable as to demand a sustained analysis. Out of that shock and surprise this book was born.

Proximity in law, seen as a way of describing those to whom we owe a duty such that "I ought reasonably have them in contemplation as being so affected when I am directing my mind to the acts or omissions which are called in question,"[49] has come in for trenchant criticism. Its vagueness and its irrelevance have alike been attacked.[50] Indeed, following the departure of Justice Deane from the bench, the concept rapidly declined in significance. In 1998, Justice Kirby went so far as to conclude that "it is tolerably clear that proximity's reign in this Court, at least as a universal identifier of the existence of a duty of care at common law, has come to an end."[51] Since this Thermidor and consequent upon several changes in personnel, the Court has sought to limit and even undermine its previous jurisprudence. It has done so in two ways: on the level of substance, by returning to a more limited and voluntaristic conception of responsibility and on the level of method, by attempting to explicitly limit what is sometimes decried as "judicial activism." Proximity was seen as central to both these apparent problems. This book is in part a rearguard action that seeks to understand and defend the idea of proximity against these criticisms and to explain why it might still matter despite the High Court's own dramatic disavowals in recent years.

What Levinas brings to this discussion is a very detailed understanding of proximity as a kind of relationship that gives rise to responsibility, that cannot be codified, and yet that must inevitably find expression in words (legal or otherwise) whose function is to define and to conceptualise. In the period under review the High Court of Australia struggled with and eventually failed to come to terms with the very same paradox, rejecting proximity just because it was "a legal rule without specific content, resistant to precise definition and therefore inadequate as a tool."[52] Yet here Levinas points to the way in which the Court has missed the point. The challenge of this book is to insist on the role of this paradox in the law – the value of an idea that is not reducible to a rule – and to demonstrate that proximity's incapacity of definition does not strip it of – on the contrary, is the very source of – its ethical power. In other words, with the help of Levinas we can begin to see, on the level of substance, the outline of a different idea of responsibility and to see, on the level of method, that the charge of vagueness misunderstands the very nature and role of ethical judgment in law. Furthermore, these two ideas – what it is to be responsible and what it is to judge – are in fact integrally connected.

This argument I develop in chapter 7, where my attention turns away from doctrine and towards the more general implications of the case study. In the first place, I discuss what Levinas calls "the third," which is to say, the problem that arises from the fact that a legal system is not concerned not simply, as T.S. Eliot put it, with our relationships "each to each," but with a world in which we have many responsibilities to many different people. This reality will lead us to consider legally whether Levinas' ideas can offer us any insights into judgments not only of whether a duty of care is owed but whether it has, in a particular circumstance, been breached. And it will lead us to consider philosophically how Levinas attempts to deal with the necessary balancing and limiting of the apparently illimitable obligations of care. Ultimately, we will consider what it means to think of law as embodying something more than a collection of defined "rules" and how ethics might thus be figured in law. As we will see, that will take us beyond Levinas' own conception of law, but not, I will argue, beyond the resources of the common law itself. In rejecting the criticism, which we find in both the current High Court and in Levinasian studies, that proximity is irrelevant to law because it is incapable of reduction to a rule, I will be trying to show that the best understanding of law itself has an ethical component and that proximity is that component. Proximity, like ethics, is no doubt always "asking for trouble." I will contend that that is exactly the point.

Ethics, says Roger Burggraeve, is about scruples, and he reminds us that a scruple was originally a pebble or sharp stone in one's foot that forced us, through our discomfort, to continually keep moving.[53] To be scrupulous, to be ethical, is to be uncomfortable, off balance – and never to stand still. That seems to me a perfect image to describe what proximity does to our own sense of responsibility and to the court's judgments about it too. In keeping the jurisprudence of negligence off balance, proximity also ensures that our law keeps moving. Proximity institutionalizes a kind of permanent revolution in the law and a refusal to be satisfied with the present order. It institutionalizes a constant doubt and questioning that makes justice possible.[54] The High Court's endless struggle with the doctrinal uncertainties of the duty of care have exposed it not only to a different way of thinking about responsibility but to a new way of thinking about its own practice too.

The study of proximity will return an illuminating language to the law of negligence. Levinas' vocabulary provides a particular perspective on important issues in the operation of the "neighbour principle," and suggests both new ways to frame the law and new reflections on perennial problems. Proximity, duty, responsibility, vulnerability. The ideas I wish to explore do not form a complete system; such a system would be anathema to a philosophy in which paradox and incompleteness take their place as fundamental ethical principles.[55] I do not intend to rewrite the duty of care or the law of torts – an act of hubris as arrogant as it would be unwise – but only to suggest how to understand and to develop the asymmetrical obligations it entails and the relationship of those obligations to what we mean by and expect from law itself. Levinasian ethics does not tell us how to end these debates, but it does give us a new place to look for inspiration.

THE METHODOLOGY: INTERDISCIPLINARITY

All law embodies philosophy. The question is, which? In choosing Levinas, I hope to offer the analysis of tort law a novel language that actually captures something of its distinct blend of uncertainty, judgment, and compassion – something of the truth embedded in its unique discourse. Law is emotional and not just logical; its stuttering uncertainty is a failure if what you want from law is efficiency but a success if what you want from it is honesty. Above all, the common law offers us an ethics of *teaching* in which law's instability, its constant reassessment and transformation of its own principles, allows us all, judges and citizens alike, to keep learning from a process that is never entirely settled or rigid.[56] That seems to me the very heart of both the common law and of ethics. Both are essentially exegetical practices and therefore dialogic and responsive, rather than monologic and declaratory.[57] I say this despite law's increasingly anxious and, particularly in the case of the jurisprudence of negligence, hopelessly untenable self-image to the contrary.[58] The notion of ethics, then, as I am proposing to use it here acknowledges and relies on the undeniably muddy reality of law's practices in order to begin to construct a possible justification for them.

Neither do I think that the parallels in language and approach between Levinas and the jurisprudence of the High Court were accidental. In that watershed year 1984, the Court was searching for resources to reconfigure an ethical coherence in law at a unique moment in its jurisprudential history. In legal theory 1984 was the zenith of the school of "critical legal studies,"[59] a brash and relentless outpouring by (mainly) u.s. academics that insisted on the absolute impossibility of the coherence of rules or meaning within the law. Law was power. In philosophy, aspects of the emerging field of poststructural theory (on which cls drew rather clumsily) were also casting doubt on the legitimacy and interpretative stability of institutions of authority.[60] Power was law. In society as a whole, the myth that judges do not "make" law, the bread-and-butter of judicial mythology since the time of Coke and then of Blackstone, had been comprehensively debunked. This had gradually exposed courts around the world to an increasingly virulent criticism, in light of which judges were undoubtedly facing growing pressure from social critics to find new ways to justify and explain their craft. In Australia the appointment of left-leaning politician Lionel Murphy to the High Court was like a red rag to the bull of orthodox theories of judicial legitimacy. On and off the bench, he had, more than any judge, espoused a critical and social-realist approach to law. Yet ironically he had personal reason to come to regret the demystification of the judiciary. Nineteen eighty-four was the very year the "Murphy affair" broke, and there followed the shameless excoriation of a High Court judge in the media, in parliament, and through judicial proceedings.[61] This is not the place to recount that history and that scandal, except to say that Lionel Murphy was pursued as much for his resistance to the conservative norms of the legal and judicial profession as for his own behaviour.[62] Within two years he was dead of cancer. We can well imagine the shattering effect that these events might have had on Murphy's friends and perhaps even some of his colleagues on the bench. Where now was the line between law and politics?

Assailed from without and derided from within, the Australian High Court circa 1984 seems to have been on a quest for renewed goodness in law – trying to explain to a skeptical world why law was a valuable institution despite the fact that it could no longer be defended as simply the robotic "application" of objective "rules." This attempt was perhaps more than a little naïve but, faced with the growing abscesses of cynicism and hostility that encircled it, understandable and even inspiring.

Neither should it surprise us that the push towards the transformation of tort law was initiated by one of the most ethically committed of judges, Sir William Deane, who later, as governor general of Australia, became something of a moral figurehead himself in relation to a range of socially divisive issues. Nor should we be puzzled that these developments flourished in a court led from 1987 by one of the most intellectual of judges, Chief Justice Sir Anthony Mason, who continues to defend the jurisprudence he helped to fashion.[63] Undoubtedly, they detected in the doctrine of proximity, this radical approach to the jurisprudence of responsibility, an ethical sensibility and an intellectual complexity, respectively. This book attempts to illuminate their radicalism by the light of an equally radical philosophy. "A light is needed to see the light."[64]

So the interdisciplinarity of this project is at least plausible. Its aim is to offer a new theory to the common law and a new case study to ethics and to critique each by the application of the other. Ultimately I wish to defend proximity, not privity, as the foundational ethical principle of the law: a relationship built on a pledge *to* and not a contract *with* the other.[65] The language of proximity – even in its imprecision, especially in its imprecision – alludes to a kind of relationship that would justify our responsibility to others neither in terms of an implicit exchange nor as the exercise of sovereign power. Rather, it would build on human experience: the experience of the soul in which from the moment of consciousness, from the very moment in which I experience myself as a self, I am already imbued with the breath of others and already possessed of a responsibility to them. Individual freedom would be the product of, and not the problem with, this responsibility.

Ethics, of course, is not simply law, either in theory or in practice. But justice and law surely *proceed* from the ethical relation found in proximity.[66]

It is not without importance to know if the egalitarian and just State in which man is fulfilled ... proceeds from a war of all against all, or from the irreducible responsibility of the one for all, and if it can do without friendship and faces.[67]

For Hobbes, peace and the force of law are in our mutual self-interest. But how did we ever come to know this? Without the sense of responsibility that awoke us to being, as if from a breathless unconscious, how could we ever have begun to communicate at all? Responsibility establishes both a sense of self and a sense of relationship, and they in turn create the very possibility of agreement, and law, and justice. Thus, the personal pledge on which negligence insists is not some afterthought, some invention of the State. On the contrary, as Sarah Roberts writes, "my relationship with the other in proximity gives meaning to my relationship to all others as 'citizens' ... It is the face-to-face encounter with the other which is the moving force, demanding political justice."[68] If that is the case, then the law of negligence is not only the soul of law but its foundation.

There is another level of interdisciplinarity that pervades this work. The arguments of this book are sustained and justified not just by reference to abstract philosophy and doctrinal law but through the insights into our lives revealed and rendered richly complex by works of art and literature. My scholarly work has always treated law as a cultural practice with closer connections to the arts than to the sciences.[69] I draw on works of art and literature in this way because I believe that they not only provide evidence for the claims about human experience that I will be hoping to elicit from Levinas and from the law. They also provide us with case studies through which we develop a subtler understanding of the ideas and points at issue. In drawing on a Borges short story or a Moore sculpture, I am attempting not to illustrate something but to learn something. And these works, in their complexity and their humanity and their beauty, allow us to establish, on an affective level, a connection between our legal practices and the manifold other ways by which we come both to comprehend and to develop – to value and to critique – our societies. Art and literature are two of the most important ways in which we make sense of the world; so too, and in similar and not less imaginative ways, is law.

In defending what some might take to be an eclectic scholarship, I draw some comfort from Levinas' own approach. It is true that his path wound through biblical exegesis.[70] But it is also true that he defends his use of scripture not "by the dogmatic story of their supernatural or sacred origin but by the expression and illumination of the face of the other human" in them.[71] One might say, therefore, that if there is a god of the Bible then it is also the god of literature, and indeed Levinas elsewhere talks of the convergence of the ethical principles to be gleaned from the great literatures and the great religions alike.[72] All speak with the voice of the other, and this voice is as near as we will ever get to god.[73] In the law, too, we can hear this voice.

2

Tortologies

OF GRAMMATOLOGY

We are friends.
You are threats.
They are our enemies.

It matters how we conjugate the world. The grammar in which one frames an area of law indicates what is seen to be important about it and why. How did law arise and to what end? These questions have generated a variety of powerful myths surrounding the origin of law.[1] Property law, for example, starts from the first-person singular. Its perceived importance derives from the assumed primacy of *I*. Drawing on John Locke and G.W.F. Hegel, the right to the legal protection of property is there constructed as a necessary extension of the ego. There has, of course, been a countertradition of communal rights, of gleaning and commons and usufruct, but since the age of enclosure it has been in retreat. Thus, for Locke the right to property stemmed directly from what it means to be human: to be an individual and to own not only oneself but all that is the product of one's labour.[2] Possession and the individual go hand in hand.[3] "[T]he end of Law is not to abolish or restrain, but to preserve and enlarge Freedom: For in all the states of created beings capable of Laws, where there is no Law, there is no Freedom. For Liberty is to be free from restraint and violence from

others which cannot be, where there is no Law: But Freedom is ... but
a Liberty to dispose and order, as he lists, his person, Actions, Possessions and his whole Property, within the Allowance of those laws under
which he is; and therein not subject to the arbitrary will of another,
but freely to follow his own."[4] As Hegel argues, my capacity to *will*
defines my status as a person and thereby entitles me to the ownership
of whatever is constructed by that will. Appropriation – the law of
property – is constructed on the basis of a fundamental distinction
between legal subjects and legal objects.[5] Conjugated in this way, property appears as the first and necessary law, a perspective strongly supported by writers as diverse as Ernest Weinrib and Robert Nozick.[6]

Contract law lies clearly within this individualism. It assumes the
binding and authoritative nature of our own will. But there is an additional dimension. The law of contract gains its legitimacy from the two
sovereign selves whose agreement the law protects but does not create.
It is law in the second-person singular, or, perhaps more accurately, as
taking place between two *I*s, since it is the two of us that join together
to make a law. This grammar finds its champion in Thomas Hobbes,
wherein the promises that you and I make to each other are the foundation out of which all law emerges. It is a law of nature, he writes,

That men perform their Covenants made: without which, Covenants are in
vain, and but Empty words; and the Right of all men to all things remaining,
we are still in the condition of War. And in this law of Nature, consisteth the
Fountain and Original of JUSTICE. For where no Covenant hath preceded,
there hath no Right been transferred, and every man has right to every thing;
and consequently, no action can be Unjust. But when a Covenant is made,
then to break it is UNJUST: And the definition of INJUSTICE, is no other than
the non Performance of Covenants.[7]

The force of law comes into being only to ensure the performance by
you of your promises and thus to preserve to me the property and the
life that are mine.

Yet if contract seems the first law, in Hobbes' grammar it is a promise
made against a background of mutual distrust.

Therefore before the names of Just, and Unjust can have place, there must be
some coercive Power, to compel men equally to the performance of their
Covenants, by the terror of some punishment, greater than the benefit they
expect by the breach of the Covenant; and to make good that Propriety, which

by mutual Contract men acquire, in recompense of the universal Right they abandon ... So that the nature of Justice, consisteth in keeping of valid Covenants: but the Validity of Covenants begins not but with the Constitution of a Civil Power, sufficient to compel men to keep them: And then it is also that Propriety begins.[8]

Distrust and fear takes us to criminal law. For in Hobbes, as in Freud,[9] contract – you and I – lies deep in the heart of law, but the violence of other men – "they" – lies deeper still.

And therefore if any two men desire the same thing, which nevertheless they cannot both enjoy, they become enemies; and in the way to their End, (which is principally their own conservation, and sometimes their delectation only) endeavour to destroy, or subdue one another ... Again, men have no pleasure, (but on the contrary a great deal of grief) in keeping company, where there is no power able to over-awe them all.

Hereby it is manifest, that during, the time men live without a common Power to keep them all in awe, they are in that condition which is called War; and such a war, as is of every man, against every man ... And the life of man, solitary, poor, nasty, brutish, and short.[10]

Hobbes' powerful and influential vision thus also conjugates the law in, and more precisely against, the third-person plural. The need to control *them* is the foundation for the apparatus of the State and the insignia of the police, death penalties, and prisons and all the panoply of order. Vulnerability is therefore key to the operation of a myth of origin, which, as Fitzpatrick has so convincingly demonstrated, has been accepted as true all the way down to H.L.A. Hart and beyond.[11] The primordial vulnerability of *I* in the face of *they* justifies law and the State. It is an old story and articulated no better than by Creon the king in Sophocles' *Antigone,* who insists that the power of law to impose order is a necessary condition to all justice and all other laws.[12]

There is a countertradition here – a myth of origin in the register of the first-person plural. Law, from Aristotle onwards, comes out of a family, a community, a *we*. Indeed, the legitimacy of this *we* is a central step in the reasoning of much mainstream jurisprudence. Ronald Dworkin, too, uses the family as his model for the State, arguing that we owe both of them our respect and our obedience for the values we all share. Dworkin's "law as integrity" and Stanley Fish's "interpretive community" both insist on a shared (social or legal) community of values in order for law to exist and to function.[13] The difference between them comes down to reflection. For Dworkin, we can reflect consciously on the goals of our community; for Fish, they are as natural and as closed to self-consciousness as the air we breathe.[14] For both, they are the necessary fountainhead of law.

Constitutional law is the same, writ large. "We, the People" begins the United States Declaration of Independence, instituting a State and an insurrection by begging the very question of grammar – who is this *we* that, already constituted, claims a right to constitute itself?[15] This is and always has been the essence of state-building and self-determination. The Constitution's claim to be the originating and legitimating *grundnorm* of any legal system, given its most comprehensive elucidation in the work of Hans Kelsen,[16] derives from the social legitimacy of a certain geographic entity and the people's rights to make laws for "themselves."[17]

On the one hand, then, the justification of law begins from the first-person singular, as variations on a theme of individualism. Both *you* and *they* are conceived as threats to this *I,* whose interests are safeguarded by structures of consent and institutions of force. Thus, contract is conceived as advancing and criminal law as protecting individual self-interest. On the other hand, law begins with the first-person plural, as variations on a theme of community. The collectivity is understood as a group of selves who are already broadly the same and who together advance towards certain goals.[18] While the *I* protects itself against difference, *we* overcome and absorb difference. The former is the cautious rhetoric of isolationism, the latter the triumphal language of assimilation. But we have not really moved away from the first person. *I* and *we* are both grammars that see the world from different ends of the same telescope; which is to say, they are both grammars that telescope everything into sameness – mine, on the one hand, or ours, on the other.

The justifications of tort law have largely proceeded by means of this limited grammar. One scours the literature and finds barely the murmur of an alternative approach. Are these, then, our only choices: to begin law either from an assumption of individualism grounded in mutual fear or from an assumption of shared values that seems less and less plausible? How do we come to share values? How does the stranger become a friend? Clifford Geertz writes, "The problem is that so drastic a contrast, cleaving the world into ... the House of Observance and the House of War, not only leaves law the most powerful where the least needed, a sprinkler system that turns off when the fire gets too hot ... If law needs, even 'in a society like our own,' a well-stitched social fabric in order to function, it is not just a nostalgic whimsy, it is through altogether."[19] Where is *he or she* in all this? Not yet *you* or *we* but more than only *I*? The third-person singular would surely be the grammar proper to the conceptualisation of tort. Singular, since tort law concerns itself with a judgment on each case as a unique set of circumstances, and not with rules of universal application. In the third person, since it is concerned with duties to others and not with individual rights, our relationships rather than our agreements. To speak of *you* or *thou* already implies a dialogue and a choice: I choose to address you and in that address is already an agreement, an agreement of language and an agreement to contract. But torts, and the law of negligence above all, considers my dealings with *him,* to whom my relationship is as a neighbour – unchosen, contingent, and unavoidable. "Who is my neighbour?" asked Lord Atkin, a question that has since consumed the law.[20] In an incisive footnote, Levinas explains that "a neighbour concerns me outside of any a priori."[21] The relationship is prior to contract. *He* or *she* is an other, not because of us or one of us, but next to us.[22] Levinas continues, "perhaps because of current moral maxims in which the word *neighbour* occurs, we have ceased to be surprised by all that is involved in proximity and approach."[23]

To think of *s/he* as the origin of law would somehow place our relationship with the other before the self. It would place our unchosen obligations before our agreements and elections.[24] If law grew out of our encounter with the other, like the inspiration of a soul, before consent, before community – and even before the self – this would require a leap of imagination. Yet this is precisely the philosophical grammar in which Levinas works.[25]

PSYCHOPATHS AND SOCIOPATHS

For Levinas the construction of the world according to the grammar of the first person presents us, like *zugswang* in chess, with a duality – singular or plural – but no real choice.[26] Either way, it is a logic posited on the primacy of being, the self's immediate presence to itself, a concept embedded in the very word "in-dividual," a fundamental particle incapable of further division. "For our logic rests on the indissoluble bond between the One and Being ... Being qua being is for us monadic. Pluralism appears in Western philosophy only as a plurality of subjects that exist ... The Plural, exterior to the existence of beings, is given as a number ... Unity alone is ontologically privileged."[27] The self is philosophy's *grundnorm*. To be or not to be, asked Shakespeare; *cogito ergo sum,* answered Descartes.[28] Being and thinking originate with the self, to which alone we have unmediated access and from which all our knowledge must be derived. This closed circle in which everything is related to the unitary self or to the collective unity of those selves, Levinas characterizes as "totality." But there are different ways to experience this totality. In fact, most contemporary commentators combine them, merging the homogeneity of the economy with the heterogeneity of persons. This is the "hybrid totality of modernity," but the purport of the argument is that far from being polar opposites, *I* and *we* are two sides of the same coin, two expressions of the totalizing essentialism of the self.[29] Our oscillation between these two poles has blinded us to other possibilities: possibilities without which our understanding of the law of negligence, the unbidden responsibility for the other, must be seriously incomplete.

If philosophy is an "egology"[30] – just a way of talking about the self – our relationship to others becomes a crisis, a problem to be solved, for how is something outside this closed circle of knowledge and experience possible? "Totality has no outside; the subject receives nothing, learns nothing, that it does not or cannot possess or know."[31] What then does one do about our relationship with other people? The two answers would appear to be either "to totalize the Other at an adequate distance" and thus to institute a discourse of separation and difference or "to engulf the Other in a communion" and thus to introduce a discourse of union and sameness.[32] Either their difference condemns them to remain forever outside my comprehension, or their sameness reduces them to a factor in my equation. The former, for example, can be recognized in deontological liberalism, or the philosophy of rights, since it preserves the integrity of others just because their interests cannot be measured against mine. The latter may be recognized in teleological liberalism, or the philosophy of utilitarianism, since it preserves the equality of others just because their interests *can* be weighed up and summed across society as a whole.[33]

In either discourse, our ability to comprehend another person *as* other is, and must be, fatally compromised: since the totality of difference (conjugated in the first-person singular) rejects the possibility of any comprehension by me and since the totality of sameness (conjugated in the first-person plural) rejects the possibility of their otherness from me. Once the self is taken as the natural starting point from which we build all our understanding of the world, it is inevitable that one will succumb to one or other of these psychoses.

I use the word advisedly, for one might conceive of the philosophies of separation or absorption to which the primacy of the self leads in terms of their psychiatric correspondences. Admittedly, diagnostic labelling has shown a considerable fluctuation in terminology over the years; those who once were called psychopaths or sociopaths are now said to suffer antisocial personality disorder. Indeed, the two terms are frequently used interchangeably or to express differences in degree only.[34] Nevertheless, it seems to me that there is a distinction worth pursuing here. As I would use the terms, the psychopath knows of no interests beyond his own. He requires, erected between himself and others, an impermeable shield to protect him from intrusion and them from annihilation. This is the self as nothing but boundaries and edges; everyone outside the self is a stranger. Psychopathic thought is a philosophy of *I*, its law the delimitation of boundaries and rights. The essence of rights, after all, is to protect each of us from the others. It is also the law of contracts, since the undertaking of a responsibility involves the dissolution of boundaries between selves that only a freely given consent can justify. The self must *get* something in order to justify any sacrifice of its interests. Consideration must be received if consideration is to be shown. Altruism is inconceivable. Indeed, this is precisely Levinas' point about the alienation to which autonomy leads. "To be good is a deficit, waste and foolishness in a being ... Ethics is not a moment of being; it is otherwise than being, the very possibility of the beyond."[35]

Conversely, the sociopath imagines we are all the same as him and conceives therefore of no boundaries between his interests and those of others. He assumes, he presumes, he imposes, he indulges: since everybody outside the self is just like him, he naturally universalizes his preferences. Sociopathic thought is a philosophy of *we*, its law the law of the community and politics and of the unproblematic balancing of different interests across society as a whole. Note that on neither construction is there any room for the neighbour: he who is neither a friend nor an enemy.

Yet our very experience of relationship is betrayed by this assumption that other people are defined in relation to us, as if every relationship would have to derive from and be justified by this self as a point of reference. "You are like me" and "you are unlike me" are both just ways of talking about me. The totality – or comprehensible whole – about which the psychopath and the sociopath reveal different aspects implies in different ways the same omission of the other and therefore embodies at its core an impossibility. Levinas explains this paradox through the idea of desire. On the one hand, desire "tends to bring the object 'close enough' to be engulfed" by the self and by assimilation (or sameness) therefore destroys the sensation of incompletion that generated the attraction in the first place. We cannot communicate with ourselves but only with something outside us. This desire is like a parasite; it consumes the host that makes it possible. On the other hand, desire "is the tendency to place the object at a distance adequate to phenomenality" (so that we can study and observe and know and perhaps even adore but in any case objectify it). By this movement of segregation (or difference) we destroy the possibility of any connection between exterior and interior that might consummate the attraction. This is desire that, like Sisyphus, postpones indefinitely the point of fulfilment. As Joseph Libertson concludes, "Thus totalization in *either* sense would be the destruction of communication (either too close or too far) and therefore the destruction of separation. The desire for totalization always tends toward the 'absolute loss' of indifferentiation or continuity at the same time."[36] Either way, then, there is "a reduction of difference to negation and dispersion, and a reduction of proximity to communion."[37]

The failure that I am trying to get at here stems from binomial thinking. Any explanation of the other person y is expressed as a function of x. But y is not a function of x, nor yet of not-x. Here is the problem for Levinas: if you are a kind of me, what is to stop me (or society, or the state) from using you or sacrificing your interests in a grand plan that is objectively to our greater co-prosperity? But if you are utterly different from me, why should I be obliged to take your interests into account at all? Either way, I express you in my terms, in the coinage of an economy with which I am already familiar and as a limit on the free expression of my self that must be justified in terms amenable to that self. In neither discourse can responsibility to another person be posited, except if it is consented to by the self, the reference point for all freedom and the justification for all constraint. Consent may be treated as being fundamentally individual and explicit, as in the case of contract law, or social and implicit, as in the case of criminal or constitutional law, but in either case the concept of the self reduces responsibility to one species of quid pro quo or another.

No totality can explain how the self comes to be in the first place or what would justify it in any care of or responsibility for another except in its terms. It is of course quite circular to suggest that the reason I owe you a duty of care is because you would owe me a duty of care if the positions were reversed. An absence of duty would suffice to satisfy the conditions of perfect equality just as well. So what must be explained is why I should owe you a duty of care quite apart from whether you owe such a duty to me. There is an assymetry here that cannot be fully accounted for from within the logic of a system.[38] We can explain it only if we stand back from the assumption of the priority of the self, which already taints our conclusions. "Why does the other concern me? What is Hecuba to me? Am I my brother's keeper? These questions have meaning only if one has already supposed that the ego is concerned only with itself, is only a concern for itself."[39] Levinas writes, "To be or not to be – is that the question? Is it the first and final question?"[40] The nature of this first question is crucial above all to the law of torts and the concept of responsibility with which it is intimately concerned, for it determines the quality and extent of the answers that are possible. One asks for reasons as to why and how we ought relate to others, but reasons on what basis and in whose terms? What would count as a satisfactory justification? To assume the priority of the self *begs* the very question we should be interrogating. "Not 'Why being rather than nothing?' but how being justifies itself."[41]

Totality is incapable of addressing our relations with others; its impoverished language can speak only by comparison with the sameness or difference of the already-known. Within the discourse of the self, the other is capable of being only "its property, its booty, its prey or its victim";[42] no "non-allergenic" encounter is possible and neither, argues Levinas, is justice. "The totality of Being is flawless and all-encompassing; because it incorporates alterity within the empire of sameness, the Other is only other in a restricted sense. Totality has no outside; the subject receives nothing, learns nothing, that it does not or cannot possess or know."[43] The problem remains, however, whether we *can* move beyond the totality of *I* or *we*. *Cogito ergo sum*, said Descartes: *I* think therefore *I* am. What would a theory of the self that was not self-centred look like? Can such a thing really exist?[44]

Levinas gives an answer to this question under the rubric "infinity."[45] Infinity is a way of experiencing otherness and other people that is not bound to the movement of an economy, since infinity provides us with a model of something we can experience but cannot know. Infinity is not a concept, since it is by definition beyond our ability to conceptualize. It must therefore indicate a presence that is in us but not amenable to cognition or knowledge. It thereby betokens the possibility of a relationship or connection that does not already take place on the ego's terms. Levinas' defence of a relationship that is not based on knowledge will be important in our future discussions about responsibility and proximity. "In thinking infinity the I from the first *thinks .more than it thinks*. Infinity does not enter into the *idea* of infinity, is not grasped; this idea is not a concept. The infinite is the radically, absolutely, other ... It is experience in the sole radical sense of the term: a relationship with the exterior, with the other, without this exteriority being able to be integrated into the same."[46] Clearly there are problems here. Even the word "in-finite," though presented by Levinas as a positive experience of incommensurability, or "otherness," in fact seems to be understood negatively. It means that which is *not* finite, that which is understood as surpassing understanding. Infinity, not yet a positive term, continues to be defined by its relationship of absolute difference from the knowable.[47] Levinas protests that "the *in* of infinity is not a *not* like any other; its negation is the subjectivity of the subject, which is behind intentionality."[48] This is central to the argument, but it is unclear just how convincingly Levinas can make the claim. Indeed, throughout *Totality and Infinity*, infinity seems still to be thought of as the absence of totality.[49]

In his well-known discussion – seen by some as a critique and by others as an elaboration[50] – Jacques Derrida makes a similar point with respect to Levinas' whole project. Firstly, wasn't Levinas a writer? If language is the reduction of meaning to the terms of a preexisting system, the epitome of totality as a science of comparative epistemology, how can he hope to explain his meaning from within the inevitable confines of language itself? Secondly, wasn't Levinas a philosopher? If philosophy is and always has been nothing but the analysis of this circular system of thought, how can he hope to explain himself from within its stranglehold? One might wonder, in short, if it is ever possible to stand outside a totality that on Levinas' own analysis is "flawless and all-encompassing." If "totality has no outside; [if] the subject receives nothing, learns nothing, that it does not or cannot possess or know,"[51] then exactly where does Levinas propose to stand?[52] Derrida at his harshest accuses Levinas of enacting a dream of "pure thought of pure difference. We say the *dream* because it must vanish *at daybreak*, as soon as language awakens."[53] According to Davis, "the contortions through which [Levinas'] text passes, and much of the difficulty of *Totality and Infinity*, derive from the endeavour to avoid describing the encounter with the Other in terms that would implicitly restore primacy to the Same."[54] Levinas' undoubted obscurity is part of his attempt to avoid the awkward trap he has set for himself.

Concerned as we might be with the circularity of Levinas at this point, it is absolutely imperative to insist that he on no account aimed to dismiss human subjectivity as a mere social construction, à la Foucault.[55] He aims to defend the human subject, the self, without basing it on selfishness.[56] Instead, Levinas proposes a self that has been formed from the outside in, a "denucleated" ego.[57] The trajectory is announced at the very beginning of *Totality and Infinity*. "This book then does present itself as a defense of subjectivity, but it will apprehend the subjectivity not at the level of its purely egoist protestation against totality ... but as founded in the idea of infinity."[58] For Levinas, in short, our subjectivity and our unique individuality matter very much but they derive from our responsibility to others, and not the other way around.[59]

SAMENESS THEORY

The totality trap and its twin psychotic registers can be found throughout the literature of tort theory. The language of the self falls far short of explaining the very notion of responsibility to others that must lie at the heart of any satisfactory theory. Let us begin with the totalization proper to sameness, the sociopathic law of the *we* – distributive justice. It is described in Aristotle's *Nichomachean Ethics* as the proportional entitlement of persons to "any distributions of honour or money or the other things that fall to be divided" according to some allocative criteria.[60] Justice consists in the logic of the criteria, whether it be to each according to his need, or merit, or birth, or rank, or effort;[61] and its proper application across society. Distributive justice implies, therefore, the evaluation of the claims of many people in terms of a norm against which they can all be measured. It focuses on the best social outcomes in general, even at the cost of some sacrifice to individual entitlements. Thus, income tax, a classic regime of distributive justice, may take more from the rich than the poor precisely in order to pattern

the allocation of social resources in a fashion that is deemed equita-
ble.[62] Of necessity, therefore, any concept of distributive justice must
be built upon the idea of an economy in which it becomes possible to
treat your interests and mine, and everyone's, as comparable in terms
of the criteria that have been set up. Law is, in the ancient words of
Sir Edward Coke, "a golden mete-wand and measure to try the causes
of the subjects."[63]

The law of torts invariably involves a loss, some damage that we
attempt to measure in monetary terms. The question is, to whom
should this loss be allocated? Should the loss stay where it falls? Should
those who caused it be made to pay? Should the community as a whole
bear the burden through no-fault liability or insurance? In short, when
will a loss that an injured party suffers be shifted and to whom? In
one sense, the whole of tort law is of necessity a system of distributive
justice. But in another sense, only those interpretations qualify that
treat the interest of the person who has suffered the loss as commensurable to and measurable against those of the rest of society (including
the person or persons who occasioned the loss). On such a view, at
least according to the more severe versions of utilitarianism, an injury
to one person that made two people happy would (everything else being
equal) make society better off and would be presumptively just. The
equality of persons – indeed their intrinsic arithmetical sameness –
arises, in the words of Jeremy Bentham, not from any absolute invio-
lability of persons but rather from a society in which "each count for
one, and none for more than one."[64]

One rarely finds such extremism countenanced nowadays, but a
similar calculus animates much of the economic analysis of law.[65] Given
that utilitarianism is built upon the idea of an economy of persons,
this is not surprising. For Ronald Coase, whose work has been of
unparalleled importance to the law and economics movement, there is
no such thing as a harm inflicted by one person on another. The problem
is by its very nature "reciprocal."

The traditional approach has tended to obscure the nature of the choice that
has to be made. The question is commonly thought of as one in which A inflicts
harm on B and what has to be decided is: how should we restrain A? But this
is wrong. We are dealing with a problem of a reciprocal nature. To avoid the
harm to B would inflict harm on A. The real question that has to be decided
is: should A be allowed to harm B or should B be allowed to harm A? The

problem is to avoid the more serious harm. I instanced in my previous article the case of a confectioner the noise and vibrations from whose machinery disturbed a doctor in his work. To avoid harming the doctor would inflict harm on the confectioner.[66]

Coase looks at the best *outcome* of a conflict for society. The implications of this analysis are that the concept of causation becomes strictly speaking irrelevant. Our goal ought to be to minimize the costs of accidents and to increase the overall efficiency of society. If my invasion of your space is more efficient than avoiding it, then so be it. As Coase argues, "The reasoning employed by the courts in determining legal rights will often seem strange to an economist because many of the factors on which the decision turns are, to an economist, irrelevant. Because of this, situations which are, from an economic point of view, identical will be treated quite differently by the courts. The economic problem in all cases of harmful effects is how to maximise the value of production."[67] The effect of this approach is to treat the doer and the sufferer of harm as equal and to evaluate the overall social costs on both parties. Richard Posner describes this as "the social function of negligence" and argues that the moral indignation we experience when A carelessly injures B is merely an expression of an underlying social and economic judgment. It is not that A has caused harm to B that upsets us (since Coase would say that in economic terms, each must harm the other) but merely the fact that the harm could have been avoided at less cost – a fact we lay at the foot of the "cheapest cost avoider," whose behaviour we label careless. Thus, "because we do not like to see resources squandered, a judgment of negligence has inescapable overtones of moral disapproval, for it implies that there was a cheaper alternative to the accident ... Indignation has its roots in efficiency."[68]
   Crucially, therefore, the economic point of view is about social welfare, and since we are all the same, the benefits of one person's behaviour can be weighed against the costs it imposes upon others. Such an approach necessarily appropriates the other as a mere factor in a calculus of overall utility. This commitment to the equation and balancing of interests is an essential ingredient of distributive justice and law and economics alike. While Posner rightly describes utilitarianism as mandating the "sacrifice" of individual injury "on the altar of social need," his own approach simply substitutes a utility principle based on measuring and totalling happiness with a utility principle

based on measuring and totalling economic effects.[69] Although perhaps less indeterminate, it is no less totallizing. Now we are to be sacrificed on the altar of social wealth.

Neither is it only in the nether reaches of law and economics that one finds such functionalism. In the seminal case of *United States v. Carroll Towing*, which contains the classic formulation of negligence law in the United States, Justice Learned Hand articulated the issues in just this way:

The owner's duty, as in other similar situations, to provide against resulting injuries, is a function of three variables: (1) The probability that she will break away; (2) the gravity of the resulting injury, if she does; (3) the burden of adequate precautions. Possibly it serves to bring this notion into relief to state it in algebraic terms: if the probability be called P; the injury L; and the burden B; liability depends upon whether B is less than L multiplied by P: i.e., whether $B<PL$.[70]

The implications of this judgment are unequivocal. The inconvenience of my avoiding the injury is placed on the same scales as your risk of harm; whether the risk is worth running will be calculated *as if we were the same person.*[71] The self and the other have thus been assimilated into elements of the same structure; our needs and interests are not the same, but nevertheless they are to be treated as if they were commensurable. Justice weighs the scales blindfolded, using the social language of reasonableness, and determines where the loss most efficaciously lies. As Jules Coleman puts it, "if precaution costs are foregone opportunities to engage in an activity the injurer values, then the measure of those costs is given by the value of the activity to him. The degree of security the victim is entitled to is fixed by the evaluations of the injurer in violation of the criterion of fairness."[72]

This distributive approach, whether market or social, derived across individuals or collectives, omits an intrinsic truth of human relations. I am not merely an object in your calculations, a creature for your appropriation. In *Totality and Infinity* Levinas treats this as merely the first phase of a coming to awareness. In it, we experience ourselves through enjoyment, by which he means the infantile desire to consume something, make it part of ourselves, and convert it to our use. We enjoy our food, our playthings, our very breath, and in the process enjoy our mastery of the environment and our capacity to take something and render it subject to our will. The sociopath even enjoys people in this way, as an object for his commodification. "All enjoyment is in this sense alimentation."[73] The external world becomes (literally) internalized and therefore ours. "What we live from does not enslave us; we enjoy it. The human being thrives on his needs; he is happy for his needs ... If enjoyment is the very eddy of the same, it is not ignorance but exploitation of the other. A being has detached itself from the world from which it still nourishes itself! ... Animal need is liberated from vegetable dependence, but this liberation is itself dependence and uncertainty ... Needs are in my power; they constitute me as the same and not as dependent on the other."[74] Thus, "in the satisfaction of need the alienness of the world that founds me loses its alterity; in satiety the real I sank my teeth into is assimilated, the forces that were in the other become my forces, become me."[75] Representation adds a further dimension to the process of enjoyment, since language gives us a conceptual, as well as an elemental, ownership of the things around us and gives them a stability, an identity, a name.[76]

But there is necessarily a remainder to this process, an aspect of our relations that escapes capture or commodification. The return of things to their elements – of bodies to food, of beings to objects – fails in its work of appropriation. Thus, as Levinas reminds us most vividly in French, we say *du vent, de la terre, de la mer, du ciel, de l'air.*[77] We partake *of* the world and its bounty, but we cannot ever fully take it over. Representation, too, whether through language or images, offers me only "a side of being while its whole depth remains undetermined."[78] The imperfection of the process is inevitable. Indeed, as Levinas says, the sense of ourselves that alimentation creates generates an anxiety for an ever more perfect and impossible fulfilment alongside the satisfaction it permits. The very sense of our difference from others, the heteronomy we all experience, "incites to another destiny than this animal complacency in oneself ... The possibility of rising from the animal condition is assuredly thus described."[79] According to Levinas, the abyss between "interiority" – our sense of an inner life – "and economy" cannot be resolved from within the language of hunger, of enjoyment, of consumption, or of distribution. Even knowledge is just a kind of assimilation. Totality cannot explain what it means to relate to others in a society, because by reducing everything to a great calculation, we find ourselves ever more alone. Other people, in short, cannot be consumed, distributed, calculated, or assimilated.[80]

Levinas' language in this phase of the argument is unusual and corporeal, even sensual. But his central point has much in common with many other French writers, all of whom can be said to draw upon the insight he develops. *Jouissance*, or surplus, in Jacques Lacan, *dépense*, or waste, in Georges Bataille, and *différance*, or supplement, in Jacques Derrida.[81] All invoke terms to suggest that there is something about our relations with others that cannot be reduced to a systemic structure of equivalences.[82]

What is left over from our relentless attempts to systematize the world, to treat it as one great differential equation, is alterity: the otherness of others.[83] This essential remainder Levinas epitomises through the experience of the human face, which "differs from every represented content" of it.[84] The face cannot, in fact, be possessed.[85] "The other person pushes back, as it were, does not allow himself to be consumed in the egoism of my enjoyment. The other resists consumption. The other person is not capable of being known, but 'is encountered as a felt weight against me.'"[86] The face of the other. Murder attempts to negate the face, but even murder cannot obliterate resistance. Indeed, the whole rage to murder wells up with the realization that another being will in some sense never be entirely subject to my appropriation. This fury expresses itself as a final desperate effort to eliminate that resistance, but even when it succeeds physically, it fails psychologically. Death, far from being the apotheosis of consumption and appropriation, manifests its final impossibility. "To kill is not to dominate but to annihilate; it is to renounce comprehension absolutely ... This infinity, stronger than murder, already resists us in his face, is his face, is the primordial *expression*, is the first word: 'you shall not commit murder.' The infinite paralyses power by its infinite resistance to murder, which, firm and insurmountable, gleams in the face of the Other, in the total nudity of his defenceless eyes ... There is here a relation not with a very great resistance but with something absolutely *other*: the resistance of what has no resistance – the ethical resistance."[87] And recall that murder, this futile effort at obliteration and the haunting that inevitably succeeds it, was not an abstract concept for Levinas. Indeed, the one fragment of writing that dates from his time in a Nazi prisoner-of-war camp addresses precisely this question: it is an elaboration on the theme of ghosts, of the power that cannot be contained or captured even after the body is destroyed.[88] We can kill the other, but in that very moment they escape their subjection once and for all and haunt our dreams forever.

A face demonstrates for us the impossibility of totalization: no balancing of interests, no accountant's ledger of pros and cons could ever wholly sum it up. It marks the inadequacy of accountability. Most importantly for law, it also marks the nature of responsibility. The concept of responsibility is incoherent without some distance between me and you. We are not the same as each other; we are not absorbed into some collective utility. And this is just what makes responsibility possible, since otherwise I would be responsible only for me or for us. But responsibility implies a *response* to you at the very point at which and only inasmuch as our needs differ. There is no responsibility without "a distance more precious than contact, a non-possession more precious than possession, a hunger that nourishes itself not with bread but with hunger itself."[89] Our respect for this distance, not its elimination, allows us to be responsible "for the other." It is the *for* of the relationship.[90] There can be no responsibility without such a divergence between us, without a conflict of interests that demands from me some small or large sacrifice.

If that divergence is merely expressed as two differing but mutually measurable interests within a greater unity that declares itself entitled to arbitrate between them, as theories of distributive justice postulate, then the distinction between us has been eviscerated with a mere sleight of hand. Distributive justice is a theory of the totality, because it purports to solve the problem of difference, and thus to dissolve it. Any theory that reduces *you* and *I* to like terms in an algebra, building on the abstract equivalence and convertibility of our interests, cannot recognise the prime ethical movement of negligence: towards responsibility, that is, towards and in recognition of the material and embodied otherness of the other.

DIFFERENCE THEORY

The intuition expressed in the previous section is intrinsic to the law of negligence. Negligence has always looked to the actions of individuals and sought thereby not just to provide compensation or to maximize welfare but to attribute responsibility within relationships.

Nevertheless, under the influence of orthodox legal theory, common law courts in recent years have striven to emphasize that the terms and expectations of that relationship will be determined by the parties' own choices and understandings. Responsibility is, to adopt a frequent turn of phrase, "assumed" – meaning willingly accepted – by the parties themselves.[91] If anything, therefore, the courts have turned away from a notion of responsibility imposed by society to one grounded in free will and personal choice. So we have only moved from sociopaths to psychopaths. It is not *we* the community who determine what will constitute the ambit of my obligations, but *I* myself who decides.

Let us turn then to the totalization proper to difference, the law of the *I* – corrective justice. It proceeds from a principle of autonomy according to which human beings are first and foremost independent and "fully accountable choosing agents."[92] The preservation of this abstract independence is the goal of corrective justice. As Aristotle explains it in the *Nichomachean Ethics*, it requires the rectification or annulment of any wrongful gains I have secured at the expense of your independence and of any wrongful losses I have imposed upon that independence.[93]

Corrective justice therefore resists the subjection of the individual to any communal good or social interests; if I damage your property in an accident, it makes no difference whether you or I can best afford to absorb the cost. My intrusion on your autonomy demands rectification regardless of our substantive positions and regardless of its impact on general welfare. In this sense then, it respects and preserves a space for the unique face of the other person: there is no calculus here, no weighing up of interests. This commitment to the value of autonomy has attracted an impressive range of thinkers to it. But the argument for corrective justice stems from the right to independence of the self, and not from the needs or vulnerability of the other person. It is fundamentally *my* autonomy that is protected by the principles of corrective justice: yours is what I give up in exchange for it.

The key question, however, remains: for what are we responsible? If we were responsible for something, then we would be wrong not to do it. Words like "cause" or "property," "wrong" or "loss," cannot by themselves answer the question but can only provide us with different ways of articulating the conclusion to which we are drawn. In answering this question, the scholars of corrective justice, Epstein and Coleman, Weinrib and Benson, despite their differences, all share certain assumptions that constrain the answers they are prepared to offer. The themes of autonomy and self-hood, the totality proper to *I*, dominate their register. If the self is defined in terms of its utter individuation from all other selves and in terms of its "free will" to act entirely in accordance with its wishes, one might wonder how we came to owe any responsibility – a burden on our freedom – to any other person at all.

The answer, according to this approach, is twofold. First, the autonomy of each of us is protected in terms of the autonomy of all of us. The other person's inviolable self is to be protected in like fashion to mine. There is, then, both an egoism and a symmetry that governs this understanding. Responsibility flows from the self to the other only to the extent that I have acted upon that other person. There is no inevitability of interaction or relationship; responsibility emerges only when I have by word or deed brought myself into contact with another. Silence or inaction cannot, without more, generate responsibility.

Second, we may expand this natural "force field" of responsibility beyond the mere limits of bodily integrity if and only if we choose to do so. The great common law cases that expanded the concept of the duty of care from the 1960s on were dominated by just this understanding. Responsibility might, in the language of the time, be "assumed." An agreement by a bank to give specialist advice;[94] a school that opens its gates early to permit children to play in the grounds;[95] a government department that undertakes the management of delinquents or orphans;[96] a public authority that builds change rooms by a swimming hole.[97] All these have by their consent or by their behaviour assumed a new and "affirmative responsibility" – a duty to act. Fundamentally, it is their free will that has placed these duties of care upon them. Choice brings one into relationship with others, and choice can likewise curtail it.

In fact, on this model the assumption of responsibility assumes nothing: it is born of an act of will. Responsibility is undertaken by us, not imposed upon us. It is for that reason that "rescue cases" have been so often considered outside the ambit of corrective justice.[98] I have no duty of care to save a drowning child, even in circumstances in which the rescue throws no burden or risk on me, because this would impose a responsibility in relation to an other that violates *my* autonomy when I have not violated theirs. Neither my actions nor my consent have brought about this relationship: accordingly, no principle of corrective justice could justify the violation of autonomy that responsibility imposes. What have *I* done that needs correcting? In what way has this demand, this relationship, become *mine*? In short, because all responsibility is understood to be a problem, a transgression on our autonomy rights, it must be positively justified.

Corrective justice, then, becomes in effect a species of implied contract: an agreement to take care constructed in order to preserve our agency and extended by the exercise of that agency. So much is explicit in a writer like Richard Posner; tort law is necessary "to overcome the adverse effects of transaction costs on the operation of free markets."[99]

So, too, Charles Fried, in an oft-cited passage, insists that the promise is the "moral basis ... by which persons may impose upon themselves obligations where none existed before."[100] Tony Honoré, in a series of articles recently republished, is relentless in his insistence that the purpose of responsibility is to give recognition to our sense of agency, choice, action, freedom, identity, promise, and control. It is necessary for us to be responsible, he argues, because it is necessary for us to have a sense of "people as the authors of their actions."[101] Responsibility, he argues, comes with agency and with the ownership of actions. It is, in fact, an assertion of our freedom, our control, and our consent – an act of will. "Consider the ways in which we take on responsibility," he writes. "Most of them involve assuming control of some situation or purporting to control it ... our responsibility for what we do is connected with the control we have over our conduct ... Responsibility [therefore] involves a combination of actual or assumed control and risk."[102] Responsibility for our actions is a condition of being a self with independent control over events in the world. We "take on" responsibility by an exercise in free will. "It is outcomes" – the things we choose to do and, by our actions, for which we accept responsibility – "that in the long run make us what we are."[103]

This argument is at one with the consistent approach taken to responsibility within much of analytic philosophy. Mackie dogmatically asserts the "straight rule of responsibility: an agent is responsible for all and only his intentional actions."[104] Michael Smith characterizes responsibility as deriving from "rational self control." Our control over our *selves* allows us to make choices to which the idea of responsibility holds us. Philip Pettit, too, provides an "agent-centred" analysis. We hold persons responsible "for a given action" because "they could have done otherwise." Again, then, the notion of choice by and agency of the self governs his approach.[105] Stephen Perry likewise constructs the idea of responsibility as deriving from our ability to control our behaviour, and this in turn derives from "our status as moral agents." Responsibility is imputed to – and only to – those acts we do and those states of affairs we bring about.[106] Perhaps John Gardner puts it best and most simply: "We are what we do – complete with results."[107]

This consistency is extraordinary, since it makes so little sense of the legal approach to responsibility, at least. Peter Cane points out with considerable force that "responsibility in civil law is always responsibility *to* someone ... In civil law, the nature and quality of relevant outcomes and their impact on the victim are at least as important as, and often more important than, the nature and quality of the conduct that produced the outcome."[108] Cane's latest work develops this argument at greater length. As he points out, the idea of vicarious liability – of the responsibility, for example, of an employer for the negligent acts of his or her employees in circumstances in which it we cannot easily describe the employer as having intended in any sense to bring about the action *at all* – would make little sense were "the rule of responsibility" really so straight.[109]

More fundamentally, the very notion of a duty of care is personal and relational. Even before we are responsible *for* our actions, we are responsible *to* certain people because of their relationship with us. In negligence law, this is the first and foundational step of the analysis of responsibility. One asks the question, to whom am I responsible? before one asks, what have I done? Duty, as Justice Benjamin Cardozo reminded us so eloquently in the celebrated case of *Palsgraf v. Long Island*, is a term of relation not a term of intention: "'Proof of negligence in the air, so to speak, will not do' ... The argument for the plaintiff is built upon the shifting meanings of such words as 'wrong' and 'wrongful' and shares their instability. What the plaintiff must show is 'a wrong' to herself, i.e., a violation of her own right, and not merely a wrong to someone else, nor conduct 'wrongful' because unsocial, but not 'a wrong' to anyone ... Negligence like risk, is thus a term of relation. Negligence in the abstract, apart from things related, is surely not a tort, if indeed it is understandable at all."[110] Faced with the two assertions we have so often seen – that responsibility is inherent in personality and that personality is inherent in agency – Cane rejects both. Responsibility is not a "natural fact" but a "heterogeneous context-specific practice."[111] "All moral and legal personality and responsibility is human artefact," he says, and law simply evidence for one contingent form of that artefact.[112]

It is at this point that it becomes possible to sever the two propositions at the heart of the "agent-oriented" paradigm we have been considering. One, as against Cane, I maintain that our understanding of responsibility does derive from what it means to be a human subject. In this sense, responsibility is by no means a contingent "artefact." Legal structures give expression to more than themselves: they are sketches of an essential ethical principle. But two, it is a mistake to assume that the essence of the human subject inheres in its agency and will. That is precisely the self-centred construction of the person outlined and critiqued in the first part of this chapter. It is possible to believe that responsibility is intrinsically linked to human subjectivity without taking the second step and linking it to the idea of choice and of free will. That is just what the idea of a responsibility to someone, rather than for something, highlights. *Responsibility is relational because personhood itself is relational:* responsibility is therefore not a consequence of our agency or will or choice but prior to it. Levinas goes further. Responsibility does not derive from our personhood; on the contrary, it produces it.

THE ONTOLOGY OF THE WOLF

What is particularly striking in the debates over tort theory is the constant presentation of justice as if there were only two choices available. Corrective justice *or* distributive justice: the two Aristotelian options, which correspond to two psychoses, are presented as if that was all there could possibly be. The assumed and therefore invisible insistence on this dualism is quite remarkable.[113] The question is whether the completeness of this philosophy, its solidity, is really just its rigidity.[114] In their a prioris concerning the individual integrity and agency of the human being and in their reduction of responsibility to the term by which this self is protected from interference, these are distinctions without a difference. *Zugzwang* again.

The construction of human beings as radically different and separate from each other fails to capture something intrinsic to the person and to the very idea of personality. Just as we saw the totality proper to sameness fail to respect incommensurability in humans, the totality proper to difference fails to account for our capacity for connection. Both are systems of totalization unable to comprehend anything actually outside of themselves: the sociopathic by including everything within the boundaries of the self, the psychopathic by excluding everything from it.

If one *is* only "in and for oneself" then responsibility must be explained in those terms. "Am I my brother's keeper? These questions have meaning only if one has already supposed that the ego is concerned only with itself, is only a concern for itself. In this hypothesis it indeed remains incomprehensible that the absolute outside of me, the other, would concern me."[115] Thus, the language of agency, will, control, and freedom becomes inevitable. Omissions and rescues become problems. The duty of care becomes an imposition or an artefact. The morality of the promise founds it. And the whole of tort law is reducible to a footnote in the ideology of contract. In the next few paragraphs, I want to begin to show how Levinas points to the priority of the other (not in a normative but in a conceptual or philosophical sense) before the self. Once we can accept that the self is not the bedrock and given term from which we must derive all our reasoning, then a notion of responsibility as founded on our duty to others becomes far less problematic to initiate.

Now, the conceptual form of a relationship, any relationship between any two things, we call knowledge. Under conditions of totality, all knowledge (including the knowledge of justice or the knowledge of others that we call a personal relationship) emerges as a process of calculation on the basis of what is already known. Levinas frequently speaks of knowing as a way of "grasping" or incorporating something into the empire of the same, the sovereign self. Knowledge, then, is a kind of reaching out and bringing in, through reference to the already familiar, that arises from a voluntary movement. "If the other could be possessed, seized, and known, then it would not be other. To possess, to know, to grasp, are all synonyms of power."[116]

Thus, if the self exists prior to the limitations incurred by its responsibilities and if it exists *as* autonomy and freedom, then the exercise of one's will over others is a natural state and war not just a "permanent possibility" but the condition that best expresses human "being."[117] Then responsibility itself – even the responsibility not to violate the freedom or integrity of others – becomes the consequence of a social contract that, whether out of convenience or necessity, acts to *restrict* our natural grasp.[118]

One response to this argument might be empirical. Actually existing human beings necessarily depend on others and in all cases need relationships. On a sociological and psychological level, this is undoubtedly true. Moreover, from the day of our birth (and even before) our personalities are constructed out of our relationships with others, rather than emerging fully formed, parthenogenetically, as it were. The self does not in fact exist before it has relationships but comes to fruition with and through them.

Yet this is altogether too easy a response. The question remains as to the origin of those relationships. Do we acquire them out of the depths of our autonomy, or are they somehow intrinsic to what it means to be a self? This is a question of ontology, which is to say, of the nature or essence of things, and one that accordingly requires a more abstract answer. It matters because, as we have seen, the autarchy of the self at the moment determines the justification and extent of our responsibilities. What is the state of nature? – "The war of all against all" or "the irreducible responsibility of the one for all"?[119] "It is extremely important to know if society, as currently constituted, is the result of a limitation of the principle that man is a wolf for man, or if on the contrary it results from a limitation of the principle that man is *for* man."[120]

Let us consider the logic of the wolf a little more closely. In the section that follows, I propose to work in layers through the assumptions about selfhood that the orthodox model of responsibility takes as bedrock and thus to show what lies behind these assumptions. I want to argue that the autarchic self cannot be the "original position." So there must be something – some relationships – that stands before this supposedly primordial and autonomous existence. In making this argument, my aim is to critique the ontological claims of the autarchic conception of self and responsibility from the inside, as it were. Against these claims, I will argue that "selves" are relational through and through: not just in fact but in theory, not just derivatively and contingently but necessarily.

Peter Benson is, in the clearly expressed and categorical nature of his assumptions, a good example of lupine logic. For Benson, we exist first and foremost as separate selves; our relationships come *after* our original "self-relatedness," and are experienced as conflict or choice. Responsibility derives from, imposes upon, and is limited by our essential "moral independence."[121] "At this point in the analysis, subjects are represented as persons who are both identical to and separate from one another."[122]

This is the central claim of corrective justice: that selfhood must be understood in terms of "identical" and "separate" persons. The nature of our responsibility to "one another" stems from this initial assumption. But how do we know this? Benson's first assumption is that selves already exist. Not only do they exist, but they can be identified and distinguished from things that are not selves. Objects, for example, are forms of property. "Being without the form of self-relatedness," he writes "they can therefore, consistent with this standpoint, be used merely as means to something else."[123]

How could this distinction ever have emanated from within the depths of a purely self-related being? How exactly can a self tell another self from a thing (indeed, the psychopath cannot)? Some relationship with others, then, is already implied even at the moment when Benson wants to demonstrate the primordial independence and purely self-relatedness of selfhood. Some knowledge of the other, some insight into the other's being, must be found and cannot be located from solely within the self.

Portraiture in Western art has long striven to acknowledge the fact that a self is not an object like any other. A person has a depth, a secrecy, which is untrue of any still life. The successful portrait conveys something of the personality of the sitter, the sitter's internal makeup, which cannot be explained simply in terms of the sum of that person's features. Certainly we can reduce a person to a collection of likenesses – the shape of the face, the colour of the eyes or of the hair – but who would argue but that objectification misses the person altogether?[124] Leonardo Da Vinci's *Mona Lisa,* so clichéd now as to be virtually beyond redemption, is nevertheless the most famous portrait in the history of painting for a reason. Its greatness subsists in precisely this: that we see there depicted a woman with a secret, an inner world that Da Vinci has managed to convey to us without disclosure. Da Vinci has shown us *consciousness as such.* And the essence of consciousness is the mystery of the inner worlds of others that we sense but to which we can never gain access. The gaze of the Mona Lisa is an annoying little smile that tells us that there is something going on behind those eyes that we will never entirely fathom. In fact, Da Vinci's use of *sfumato* gives the painting itself a blurred and misty surface that further intensifies this sense of mystery. Even the five or six layers of plexiglass behind which the painting is now shrouded only serve to add to this sense of distance and opacity. In conveying consciousness, the face of *La Gioconda* dramatizes the separateness of the other's being, which no proximity, however close and transparent we get, can ever efface. In this, it is the very epitome of portraiture.

When Benson assumes that we recognize other selves as our alter egos, he assumes that we have already been touched by them in a way that cannot be defined by any inventory of objects or external features. Nothing on the surface would permit us to distinguish a subject from an object. The distinction already requires the recognition of a secret world. Relationship, then, is the way in which the self first comes to recognize selfhood in others and in itself.

The second assumption is this: not only can other selves be identified and distinguished, according to Benson, but they can be represented. Representation requires language of some kind – a system of signs. And signification implies not just difference but sameness or, strictly speaking, relatedness. Language works by the sharing of a currency between people, a sharing that never identically reproduces its content.[125] Language without any sameness could not be communicated but would die ephemerally in an eternal present – it could not be re-presented. But language without an awareness of difference, which the self by itself cannot provide, could not express any content, concept, or thing. So if the self already has, on this analysis, a representational capacity, it must already exist in relationship with others. It is not alone.

The self represents, but, we might ask, to whom? At the very least, to itself. That is what "self-relatedness," or to put it another way, consciousness, the very core of the self, means. But consciousness is always consciousness of something.[126] It involves an ability to think of oneself as apart, in a fashion that treats oneself as an object of contemplation, even if it is only one's future self or past memories that are distanced in this way. Even if one is only thinking "here I am, thinking" – the worst kind of Cartesian bore – one has opened up a "knot" in the fabric of being, a "diremption," or breakage, in which we must experience ourselves discontinuously if we are to experience ourselves at all. So it would be wrong to say that the other appears as an object to our established consciousness. Some otherness, some outside, is necessary for that consciousness to have come into existence. "The same has to do with the other before the other appears in any way to a consciousness. Consciousness is always correlative with a theme, a presented represented, a theme put before me, a being which is a phenomenon ... [But] subjectivity is the other in the same ... The other in the same determinative of subjectivity is the restlessness of the same disturbed by the other [and] ... signifies an allegiance of the same to the other."[127] We must have experienced some difference, some outside within us or ourselves as part of that outside, in order to have experienced ourselves at all. As Adriaan Peperzak, one of Levinas' most devoted interpreters, puts it, "self-consciousness discovers itself as an original and irreducible relation to some 'other' it can neither absorb nor posit on its own."[128]

All knowledge, therefore, since it too is dependent on "consciousness of" something, requires in the first place this self-distance and therefore a primary relationship with otherness. A relationship that is not ethical would either assimilate or exclude the other and therefore reduce it once more to a species of the same. It would be unable to move outside itself. That is what it means to speak of "ethics as first philosophy."[129] There can be no philosophy or knowledge – indeed no self-consciousness –

without this recognition of and commitment to maintain the difference of another.

Let us take one more step into the ontology of the wolf. Its third assumption is that the self is capable of representation not only to itself but also, it would appear, to other selves. I speak to you and, for the theorists we have been looking at, our communicative agreement is the very foundation of any acceptance of responsibility. Such a theory, therefore, requires a discourse. Again, exactly how this could emerge from amongst a collection of autarchic selves, "a sheer unity of self-consciousness ... not yet the more complex 'we,'" is not explained.[130] For this step requires not just language and self-hood in the abstract; it also requires a capacity to talk *to* each other. Language is not just the description of the world as object. Before I can speak to another person of anything at all, there must be an initial trust, a promise to offer something of myself and to listen to you. There is nothing straightforward in this if one starts from the proposition that a self first exists for itself alone.

Thomas Hobbes saw the problem very clearly. His social contract is founded on a law of nature: "that men perform their covenants made; without which covenants are in vain, and but empty words; and the right of all men to all things remaining, we are still in the condition of war. And in this law of nature consisteth the fountain and original of justice."[131] If we could not at least start from the supposition of the truth of what people say to us (and the default position is that every conversation is backed by a promise that I mean what I say), then no discourse would be possible.[132] This "offering of the world ... first opens the perspective of the meaningful."[133] There can be no understanding without an initial trust as an opening gambit.[134]

Thus, before words can depict things or opinions, they must present a relationship of trust between people. And here we get to the point at which Levinas can be seen to diverge from these philosophies of autonomy and of community. For Levinas argues that this trust alone makes communication possible and hence that I start off, even before my conscious self exists, obligated to respond to another person. This initial, unfounded, and unauthorized obligation makes discourse possible, prior to the world of meaning and expression, idea and agreement. Any consciousness or "inward dialogue" is "beholden to the solidarity that sustains communication."[135] Language is ethical before it is epistemological.[136] It is a gift before it is a commodity.[137]

In *Otherwise than Being*, Levinas develops this idea further through the contrast between *dire* and *dit*, "saying" and "said." Before any proposition or concept, before language as a collection of nouns, language is a verb, a "saying" that cannot by definition be justified by reference to anything said. The saying stands as promisor to the said and has nothing but the person to back it up. Above all, there is nothing equal or contractual about the saying. I do not open myself up through speech in return for your promise to do likewise. That would already be in the realm of the said and already presuppose the existence of a credible discourse. I must begin unilaterally, offering myself nakedly through language. What I say does not matter. The fact of saying is already a relationship. Communication and self-consciousness begin from a pledge to and not a contract with another.

There is a rhetorical difference here in Levinas' analysis. In *Totality and Infinity* this initial movement is described as a gesture of welcome and hospitality to the other.[138] In *Otherwise than Being* it has become a vulnerability, an exposure, a trauma.[139] The saying is even at times described as "exposed like a bleeding wound."[140] "The body," he writes, "is neither an obstacle opposed to the soul, nor a tomb that imprisons it, but that by which the self is susceptibility itself."[141] Either way, as vulnerability *and* as opportunity, language begins, like all trust, with inequality. It is not an agreement to be secured but a fine risk to be run, with no promise of a return.

A THIRD WAY?

This argument suggests a way of thinking about who we are and how we relate to others that is quite different from the modes of corrective or distributive justice, with their shared premises of autonomy, symmetry, and choice. Levinas' argument at this point has nothing whatsoever to do with the morality or goodness of such premises. He insists on their logical and factual inadequacy. He says, this is just not what it means to be a human subject, and working from those premises human subjectivity – neither selfhood nor consciousness nor language nor philosophy nor law – could never have emerged.

There is nothing perverse in such a view. It is part, I think, of our understanding of many things, including how we make friends and how we experience responsibility. Responsibility, too, comes from our exposure to others and is not due to the unfettered exercise of our agency. It does not come from our intentions but prevails upon them.

It is not an active but a passive experience. It has nothing to do with the symmetry of a promise or the free will of an autonomous agent. Such is Levinas' view, and it seems to me to capture something pervasive in our lives. Even in those circumstances in which we have agreed to a responsibility, surely it is the case that, by and large, our feelings of responsibility exceed and surprise those expectations. Is not responsibility always a kind of surplus of experience over our intentions? This is what Levinas means in distinguishing the obligation to a neighbour from a contractual obligation and in distinguishing the closeness that just happens to us (which he calls proximity) from the closeness we choose to bring about (which we might term privity). For Levinas, human experience always commences with proximity not privity. Responsibility, he argues, "obliges beyond contracts; it comes to me from what is prior to my freedom ... The sober coldness of Cain consists in conceiving responsibility as proceeding from freedom or in terms of a contract. But responsibility for another comes from what is prior to my freedom ... It does not allow me to constitute myself into an I think, substantial like a stone, or like a heart of stone, existing in and for oneself."[142]

We see here the beginnings of an argument to suggest that the responsibility that comes from sheer proximity is in fact the foundation stone without which the agreements that come from privity will not long stay intact. Alas, the warriors of the world, in the Middle East or Northern Ireland, the Balkans or Somalia, do not understand that law is initiated perilously. They wait for trust to be guaranteed before embarking on it; they wait for the conditions of discourse to be agreed upon before beginning. They think of speech as an exchange of propositions, a miraculous contract. They wait for "a *sign* of good faith" – how often have we heard that in recent years? – when good faith is what makes signs possible. They will be waiting for a very long time. For without the risk that comes from trust, there can be no covenant made at all.

Could it be otherwise? Is it possible to understand responsibility and subjectivity in a way that does not derive from the primary freedom of the self, but instead "precedes every free consent, every pact, every contract?"[143] The answer is yes if we understand responsibility as the description of an ethical relationship and ethics as preceding philosophy and knowledge of the world and (as we have already begun to appreciate) making them possible.[144] In that case, our responsibility to others would not be our choice but our condition. This is what might lead us to begin to think of responsibility as asymmetrical.

What Levinas suggests is a kind of third way. This approach does not take as its baseline the socially constructed or practical inequality of circumstances that distributive justice addresses, justifying its demands by virtue of a theory of collective will and the priority of community interests (*we*). Neither does it take as its baseline the theoretical or absolute equality of beings, which we have seen corrective justice posit, justifying its demands by virtue of a theory of individual will and the priority of autonomy interests (*I*). Where is the third-person singular in all this, the grammatology of the other person? On the contrary, responsibility is best understood as proceeding neither from collective action nor from our autonomy but as preceding both these possibilities.[145]

Instead, we are being asked to take the theoretical and absolute *in*equality of beings as the starting point of our analysis of responsibility. Such obligations are not an expression of reciprocity. They do not arise because someone else ought to do the same for us but because acts of responsibility are ethical regardless of what any other person might do. Our responsibility is singular and personal, and not a social construct. Unlike the humanism of rights, the "humanism of the other man"[146] starts not from our autonomous choices but from the demands that the other, already connected to us from the moment of our consciousness, makes of us.

To sum up, Levinas wishes to defend a view of responsibility that provides what Coleman describes as "agent specific" reasons for care – and in this he is opposed to models of distributive justice (*we*). But these reasons do not necessarily derive from the agent's prior choices and actions – and in this he is opposed to models of corrective justice (*I*).[147] What such a perspective might offer us is the subject of the next chapter.

3

Before the World

Or [if I] ask if all be right
From mirror after mirror,
No vanity's displayed:
I'm looking for the face I had
Before the world was made
W.B. Yeats[1]

THE COMEDY OF ETHICS

In this chapter I want to say a little more about the general tenor and outline of Levinas' approach to ethics, precisely because his ideas here will be important throughout the rest of this book. In particular, I want to explore what Levinas means by "assymetric" responsibility and why he perceives ethics as a necessarily unstable force irreducible to a code or system of rules. In the first of Levinas' two major works, *Totality and Infinity*, Levinas' approach is broadly speaking phenomenological and metaphorical. He asks us to think about experiences in our life that belie the assumptions of totality – of the self as the origin of all knowledge and the justification for all morality. He then treats these aspects as instances that point towards a new way of thinking about what it means to be a human subject that is not self-enclosed. We are asked to deduce the existence of "infinity" from the ghostly shadows and reflections it has left around us. This other way of thinking about the self becomes necessary in order to explain the life experiences upon which Levinas remarks.[2]

Herein lies one of Levinas' abiding strengths. Obscure as his writing undoubtedly is, he speaks about the stuff of life as if it mattered.[3] Suffering, pain, and love are not secondary to his philosophical hypotheses any more than they are to our own: they are precisely why thinking and living matter. Emmanuel Levinas was a survivor of holocaust, to whose victims *Otherwise than Being* was dedicated. He began to think in the context and the wake of great trauma and violence.[4] And his purpose is this: to explain it and to explain above all why the suffering of others ought to matter to us. Only in a world of infinite responsibility would future oppression prove inconceivable. And it was to this end that Levinas dedicated his own fortuitous survival.

If there is pain and guilt in Levinas, it is perhaps understandable. And if there is severity in his criticism of philosophy after the war as business as usual, then that is readily understandable too. "Totality" has two ways to justify the infliction of suffering: one, because it is in *our* long-term interests and, two, because it is not *my* concern. It is not that the logic of the totality inevitably issues in a politics of oppression but, rather, that while politics and philosophy are understood in this way, a politics of oppression remains, like war, "a permanent possibility."[5] This is not an argument against politics or logic, but it is an argument for their insufficiency. We need politics, but we also need something more – a supplement that, whether expressed in terms of ethics or justice, cannot be reduced to its terms.[6]

By "ethical," we mean a relationship that allows communication without appropriation. Ethics is not the application of a discipline such as philosophy or politics. Neither is it a distinct body of knowledge like law or sociology. On the contrary, "ethics is an optics" – a way of seeing and relating to others. It is, moreover, primary, because without it there could be no objective knowledge of anything. "The establishment of this primacy of the ethical, that is, of the relationship of man to man – signification, teaching, and justice – [acknowledges] an irreducible structure upon which all the other structures rest."[7] Levinas is therefore not arguing that we *ought* to think more about ethics or that we *ought* to care more about others. As if there were not already enough encomia in the world! This is why his roots in phenomenology are crucial.[8] Levinas wishes us to see that we cannot adequately explain our own experience and existence without reconfiguring our understanding of the relationship of selves to others, which is, to put it another way, the relationship of being to what lies outside or "otherwise than" being.

We have already seen two central moments in which things are able to affect us outside of our possible knowledge of them: the face (*visage*) and language (*dire*). Both share the features of nudity or vulnerability, on the one hand, and inequality or asymmetry, on the other. The face, as I have noted, "*is* by itself and not by reference to a system."[9] Because the face is irreducible to its contents, because it stands beyond representation, recollection, or possession, it presents itself to us as an entreaty.[10] The face resists appropriation, but it does so in a totally passive way, as a pure vulnerability.[11] Its very muteness and its inability to explain or define itself constitutes the first and singular demand placed upon us. Unique, unfathomable, and indefensible, the first encounter with a face is a moment of crisis. Destroy or trust? This is the question before and beyond all words that every face asks of us. It is the foundation of responsibility.

There is a remarkable artwork by Antony Gormley that captures the ethical demand of the face. *Field* comprises almost forty thousand clay figurines in a vast room.[12] They are hand baked and of the crudest formulation. Nothing but a rough shape, elongated and bulbous, with two indentations, probably fashioned by skewering them with a stick before they were baked. But it is enough. Just the presence of the two points makes eyes. Just the presence of the eyes makes a face. Just the presence of a face makes a figure. These are beings, although perhaps not human. They are small – maybe knee-high – and infinitely, though subtly distinct. The clay and the different firing conditions have given them slightly varied colourations. The heads are each slightly different, the eyes different distances apart, different sizes, angled differently.

To enter a large room, crowded, crowded to overflowing, with a city of little people, clumsy and naked, is an overwhelming experience, and I do not use the word lightly. Forty thousand unique beings *look* at you. And in that gaze there is something else: an ethical entreaty. Just by looking, they are calling for help, because that is what a face is. It looks at you. "The face is not a metaphor. It is not a figure."[13] It just *is* this demand: "twenty-five tons of clay, energised by fire, sensitised by touch and made conscious by being given eyes ... a field of gazes which looks at the observer making him or her its subject."[14] This is what is meant by a responsibility that emerges before knowledge or reason, not in the logic of the community or in the autonomy and symmetry of individuals. On the contrary, it is the surprise and inequality we experience – our capacity and their incapacity – that founds the relationship. This surprise and inequality, which standard theories of the law of torts fail to capture, seems to me precisely what the duty of care expresses. It's not something you think about – the duty of care just happens to you. Before you know anything at all about another

Antony Gormley, *Field for the British Isles* (1993). Reproduced by kind permission of the Arts Council Collection, Hayward Gallery, London, and the artist.
Purchased with the support of the Henry Moore Foundation and the National Art Collections Fund. Copyright Antony Gormley 1993.

being, before language or any connection whatsoever, and indeed *in* the ineffable otherness of a being, there resides already a demand. Others are not objects of our comprehension, and before they can be subjects for us, we must be subject to them. Our consciousness comes to pass under the scrutiny of a gaze that is both incommensurable and vulnerable. "The dimension of irreversibility in the relationship, that by which alterity ... remains other, was what Levinas named illeity. Illeity is that by which the you is not the simple reverse of the I. The irreversibility is essential to the whole analysis: there can be command, imperative obligation, contestation and appeal put on me, only if the other is not only not derivative of me, but not equivalent to me."[15]

The gaze of something unique and strange cannot, in other words, be accommodated or rationalized. It cannot be subject to a preexisting rule or principle, since its unique otherness, its "illeity," would prevent any reconciliation with anything already known and accounted for. There can be no meeting of minds, no contract. Beyond our ability to apprehend it, therefore, the face of the stranger can only pose a question. And the question it poses is, How will you respond? "For the ethical relationship which sustains discourse is not a species of consciousness whose ray emanates from the I; it puts the I in question. This putting in question emanates from the other."[16] This is what Levinas means by the phenomenological primacy of the ethical. It initiates language and consciousness itself, but the relationship does not come as a free decision from me towards you. On the contrary, it emerges precisely as something that comes from the other to me, as a way of putting me in question, as a shock. I am not a free and spontaneous being. I am being called to account, prior to my freedom of choice: asymmetrically, involuntarily. "One calls this putting into question of my spontaneity by the [mere] presence of the Other, ethics."[17]

What transpires from this encounter is language, again understood by the initial inequality and vulnerability that I noted previously. *Le dire*, "saying," is not a sentence or a proposition and neither therefore is ethics; it is the foundation of all such propositions – a promise of authenticity and openness not made in return for anything but simply as a gesture of faith, without which there could be no communication. "The face and discourse are bound together. The face speaks ... It is discourse and more exactly, the movement of response and responsibility which is this authentic relation."[18]

During a helpful series of interviews broadcast on Radio-France, Levinas and Philippe Nemo clarified this point succinctly.

EL: *Le dire* is a way of greeting an other person, but to greet him is already to respond to him. Of course we speak of some *thing*, of the rain or the fine day, it doesn't matter, but to speak is already to reply.

PN: ... Yes, in some cases. But in others, on the contrary, the encounter with another is in the mode of violence, hatred, or disdain.

EL: Sure. But [this analysis of the face] comes first. It's the presupposition of all human relations ... It's that original "after you, sir" that I've tried to describe.[19]

The combination of *visage* and *dire* constitute relationship prior to any system of meaning or structure of signification. In both, what is accomplished is not the destruction of reason or objectification or self-consciousness but their possibility.[20]

The crucial point for Levinas is that the constitutive shocks of face and speech must be understood as events that, while they are unassimilable to the already-known, are yet able to reach us. It is only because we can experience this connection with incommensurability without reducing it to something with which we are already familiar, some system of comfort and nourishment, that this is possible. The self comes to consciousness, therefore, not as a movement from the inside out but, surprisingly, from the outside in – as a quickening of the soul. This movement is the opposite of safety, since the opening to the outside cannot, of course, be subject to any safeguards or protection or prior rules of engagement. "The unblocking of communication, irreducible to the circulation of information which presupposes it, is accomplished in saying. It is not due to the contents that are inscribed in the said and transmitted to the interpretation and decoding done by the other. It is in the risky uncovering of oneself, in sincerity, the breaking up of inwardness and the abandon of all shelter, exposure to traumas, vulnerability."[21] The face, in its nudity and expectation, demands a response. The response is in the form of a "risky uncovering of oneself" that "unblocks communication" and allows the process of self-discovery and world-unfolding to at last begin. Neither are accomplished by a system of meaning of which we are already the master. On the contrary, they can be accomplished only by a process of *infection*, or *infestation*, in which we discover the seeds of this connection already lodged within us.

But in what other ways can we see this infestation, or this non-correlation, or this diachrony, operative? In *Totality and Infinity* the instances of asymmetry Levinas provides are positive in orientation. The speech and the face are two. The erotic is a third. Now, there has been a substantial feminist critique of Levinas' work. No doubt his discussions draw too readily, under the guise of phenomenology and metaphor, on clichés such as the male builder and masculine activity, against the female homemaker and feminine passivity.[22] Perhaps on the other hand such references do not signify a gendered distinction but refer instead to elements within each of us – a familiar strategy of feminist redemption and revisionism.[23] Nevertheless, it seems to me that his discussion of love and attraction remains illuminating. Erotic love or attachment is not an appropriation of the other but on the contrary the experience and the maintenance of distance. Not a finite distance, of course, but an infinitely close distance. As close as possible, but still apart: proximity. We seek to join with each other in love but never to consume each other. As Levinas so perceptively remarks, "nothing is further from *eros* than possession."[24] This is why domestic violence stems from narcissism and only masquerades as love. Because the violent partner seeks to control and possess the object of his affections, co-dependence may endure but never love. Love rejoices in difference and reaches out to experience it, not to domesticate it. Indeed the fantasy of unity does nothing but destroy love: there *can* be no attraction without a distance.

The paradox, then, of the erotic is that it exists as a continual movement towards the other that can never and ought never to be satisfied. On a smaller scale, a caress captures just this moment. A caress is the opposite of a grasp that attempts to reduce to possession.[25] To grasp is active and controlling: it seeks to explore and hold and still. It is a way of obtaining knowledge and an act of colonizing the world. A caress is the gentlest of touches, the meaning of passivity, the most nonpurposive of gestures.[26] It means nothing but itself. One might say that to be conscious of a caress is already to destroy it by the reduction of closeness to an act of intention or the object of knowledge. We caress precisely *without meaning*, and that is the contact it makes.[27] "The tenderness of skin is ... a disparity, a non-intentionality, a non-teleology."[28] Above all, to caress something is to feel the limit of skins, to feel the infinite distance that separates us, and to feel it not as a problem but as a pleasure.

For Levinas, desire and ethics are intimately connected. First, desire is ethical because it breaks up our solitude and drives us to the risky business of others. The ethical is a desire because it exists prior to and above rational argument. "Ethics is not a moment of being; it is otherwise than being, the very possibility of the beyond."[29] Both are risks to be run. They reward us not by fulfillment but, paradoxically, by emptiness. Goodness does not "fill me up with goods, but compels me to goodness."[30] Desire does not fill me with objects, but compels me to desire. Ethics and desire are experienced precisely as this yearning and seeking. They are neither of them rule-bound and predictable. Instead, they challenge our complacent expectations and push us in new directions.

Second, desire draws us out, as if we were being pulled from the outside. We are bent towards the other, towards our desire, as metal drawn to a magnet. That is the meaning of attraction! – it is not either from us or to us, but out of us. Desire is therefore not a way of "being," since it exhibits a weakness and an unnecessary waste for a being, a foolish excess. Neither intentionality nor need exhaust the movement of desire. It is instead a way of "otherwise than being," a way of finding in ourselves an enlivening force external to our control that transforms our intentions and goes beyond our needs.[31] The essence of Levinas' argument is that all relationship – speech, face, eros, responsibility – is a phenomenon of desire and shares with desire the nature of an experience that we do not choose. Rather, it chooses and impels us outwards. Desire is the *midwife* of ethics.

The *I* to which these things happen – since, as we saw in the last chapter, the very idea of an *I* already presupposes the experience of an ethical relationship with others – is therefore not captain of its own identity. The other is already in me, questioning me with his vulnerability, enticing me with desire, dragging me out of myself. In *Totality and Infinity* Levinas expresses this engorgement from beyond by reference to a language both immediately familiar and immensely positive in its connotations. "Enthusiasm" comes from the Greek *en-theos*, to be possessed by a God.[32] We certainly know that to be possessed by an enthusiasm is a gift or, if you will, a contamination that seems to take hold of us. One speaks of enthusiasm as infectious. So, too, "inspiration" comes from the Latin *in-spirare*, to breathe into. An inspiration is a breath from outside that fills our lung with new air.[33] And again, "eccentric" comes from the Greek *ekkentros*, off centre. For Levinas, we are all eccentric beings, because the centre of gravity of our orbit is outside us.[34] If it were not, we would have no weight at all.[35] Gravity, after all, as Einstein told us, exists only intersubjectively.

This is, of course, the converse of what Milan Kundera called the unbearable lightness of being.[36] For Levinas, it is only by the goodness aroused through and as desire that we are possessed of an "irremissible weight of being that gives rise to my freedom." Kundera's unbearable lightness is a direct function of the empty autonomy he describes. Only the exteriority postulated by Levinas saves us from such a bottomless pit of self-absorption. This ghastly nothingness, in which we just exist without purpose or relation, Levinas explored in greatest depth in an earlier book, *Existence and Existents*. But his first meditations on it can be found in the prison fragment that was written while he was confined to a German prisoner of war camp during World War II. This is hardly surprising. The camps, and even more so the concentration camps, which Levinas was fortuitously spared, seemed to him, as they seemed to others, the reduction of human beings to a world of pure survival in which relations with others ceased to have meaning and in which, in the process, their very subjectivity was destroyed. What was for some a glimpse into a dystopic future was for him a glimpse into a long ago past, a time without time and without responsibility in which a shapeless existence was all there was.[37] The incapacity of human beings to behave responsibly in such a slave environment was the loss of their humanity.

THE TRAGEDY OF VULNERABILITY

In the second of his two major works, *Otherwise than Being*, Levinas investigates similar themes in a distinctly minor key. Perhaps one might even say that whereas his early work was comedy, his later work moved towards tragedy. But the recognition of the tragic in our lives is by no means a denial of truth. The shift can be observed in the theme of hospitality. In *Totality*, hospitality is the welcome we provide to the other's residence in us and the other's calls upon us.[38] It too is an obligation prior to all agreement, like the guest who arrives hungry and unbidden. Hospitality is a key ethical trope. But of course not all guests are welcome, and few (just for the record) remain so indefinitely. This, too, formed part of Derrida's critique of *Totality and Infinity* in "Violence and Metaphysics," and again we can read *Otherwise than Being* as Levinas' careful response. In his second major work Levinas recognizes the reality of the risk we run in being touched by the other. Not all infections are benign. The host may at any moment become the hostage. In the vulnerability of this interaction we may find ourselves harmed or exploited. But Levinas' point is that the danger is necessary and inevitable. On the one hand "the self is through and through a hostage, older than the ego, prior to principles." Yet on the other, "It is on the condition of being hostage that there can be in the world pity, compassion, pardon and proximity – even the little there is, even the simple 'after you, Sir.'"[39]

Because an ethical relationship with another is prior to any condition or formulation that might govern or control it, we find ourselves both host to the demands that the other levels at us and hostage to them. How on earth could we find ourselves held hostage by another's vulnerability? This is, of course, the very essence of conscience. In fact, the experience is quite everyday. Ask a parent. Ask a child. Ask a friend. Ask a teacher.[40] Here we might have the definition of what is sometimes termed a calling: a relationship with the vulnerable that calls *us,* that cannot be circumscribed in advance, and that therefore inevitably places demands upon us that we may not wholly welcome and do not wholly expect. The infinite demands of this initial relationship – its inevitable but unpredictable difficulty – are therefore not the end of the story of social organization. It is for that reason that we develop limiting principles of law and justice, which I will explore in later chapters.[41] But it is enough to note here that law thereby limits a relationship that is initially maximal and unchosen, rather than justifying a relationship that is initially minimal until chosen. So the premise of human responsibility is reversed. In Hobbes, one starts from the wolf, and asks, Why? In Levinas, one starts from the hostage, and asks, Why not?

In Hobbes, responsibility is justified as an exchange of hostages: it comes into being as a quid pro quo. For Levinas, as for the law of torts, it does not.

EL: Subjectivity is not one for myself; it is, one more time, initially for the other. To say: "here I am." To do something for an other. To give.
PN: But the other one, isn't he equally responsible in the face of my gaze?
EL: Maybe so, but that's *his* business. The inter-subjective relation is not symmetrical. I am responsible for the other without waiting for any reciprocity.[42]

Again, the establishment of some equivalence comes after and as a limitation upon obligation and not as the condition of its establishment. From a theoretical point of view, nothing could be more important. "It is without words, but not with hands empty ... here I am! The accusative [*me* voici!] here is remarkable: here I am, under your eyes, at your service."[43]

But to say *me voici,* and thus to establish the possibility of discourse by offering, lies somewhere between bravery and foolishness. If the language of *Totality* is dream-like and idealistic,[44] the language of

Otherwise is closer to a nightmare. The openness to others is characterized here sometimes as nakedness, "exposing [even] the exposedness which might cloak it,"[45] sometimes as a "bleeding wound" that will not heal.[46] "The one is exposed to the other as a skin is exposed to what wounds it ... exposing oneself to outrage, insults, and wounding."[47] Above all, in a remarkably physical turn of phrase, Levinas speaks of the self as "in one own's skin." But this is not a metaphor for comfort and homeliness. On the contrary, to have a skin is to be itchy, uncomfortable, ill at ease, irritable.[48] The claustrophobia of skin prevents us from being entirely at our ease and propels us outwards to others. "In its own skin. Not at rest under a form, but tight in its skin, encumbered and as it were stuffed with itself, suffocating under itself, insufficiently open, forced to detach itself from itself, to breathe more deeply, all the way, forced to dispossess itself to the point of losing itself."[49] There is, then, a similarity with the Hobbesian outlook, wherein other people do indeed appear as threats to our vulnerability. As "the weakest has strength enough to kill the strongest," we live "in continual fear, and danger of violent death."[50] The difference is that whereas Hobbes therefore strives to guard against the perils of relationship and creates a Leviathan or State to do it, Levinas argues that it cannot be avoided. Instead, he seeks to create an initial indebtedness of one to the other for that very selfhood. Our dangerous propensity for being wounded by others becomes, like the pain of childbirth, a bond that issues in subjectivity and not a scission that destroys it. The relationship is personal not social, constitutive not derivative.

The examples that we find in *Otherwise than Being* are darkly hued. Pain, trauma, and suffering, whether of illness or of labour or old age, demonstrate precisely that there is more to us and in us than we know. They provide us with another illustration of how things *happen* to us, coming into us as if from elsewhere. To be in pain is both to be intensely conscious of the body and to have nothing else to do but experience it. There is a sense in which pain makes us most aware of our life: every breath hurts and every second leaves its mark upon us as it passes. In pain we are the passive recipients of something that is both deeply and uniquely ours and yet not subject to our control.[51] It is both our pure presence to "the irremissibility of being" and our pure passivity in face of it.[52] To be in pain is to experience the loneliness of an inescapable subjectivity that seems to come from outside of us.

All this and much more are intended as a lesson in the way in which our relationship to others cannot ever be reduced to assimilation or exclusion, to structures of distributive or corrective justice, or to rules and procedures by which we get what we bargained for and choose who we are. On the contrary, we have constant experience of the things that contact and affect us but cannot be subject to our appropriation. Pain. Death. The passage of time. These are not marginal to our life; they "mark this life in its very living. Life is life despite life – in its patience and its ageing."[53] Both the virtue and the inevitability of this passivity points to a mode of experience that is not a mode of apprehension.

Our relationships to others and the responsibility we have for them fall into just this category. At the same time as we do undoubtedly experience a world of knowledge and control and a psyche subject to the authority of the ego – a world that the standard articulations of responsibility and justice take as their alpha and their omega – we also inhabit this very different world, beyond, or as Levinas sometimes says, "on the hither side" of, being.[54] "Hither" (meaning "nearest"), because it is closer to us than our ego and older than our self. In this other world, we do not choose the mode and experience of our subjectivity. We are singled out from the outside: as death singles us out irreplaceably and as does the original entreaty of the other. Each are the midwives of our subjectivity or our responsibility. Whether this proves a boon or a bane will depend upon the nature of our response, but here too we do not have an option to decline the burden. One way or the other, it cannot be ignored. Once the nucleus of the atom has been split apart by its exposure to exteriority, there is no glueing it back together again. Levinas sometimes refers to this is a *denucléation*, or hollowing out, of the ego.[55] The wind of death, the storm of desire, the breath of others has blown over us once and for all.

A SYNOPSIS OF RESPONSIBILITY

Responsibility is the outcome of this analysis of the nature of human subjectivity and human experience. The "condition of being hostage"[56] to the gaze of the other compels a response from us. The obligation to respond to the eyes that look at us in nudity and expectation is not our choice but our condition. This is precisely the meaning of the word "responsibility": the capacity to respond to the predicament of another person. About this Levinas makes the following points.

First, responsibility is inherent in the first encounter between persons. The obligation to respond is intrinsically prior to any specific response and, therefore, any preexisting rules of limitation. That is the "irreducible paradox of intelligibility." Levinas explains this both in terms of sensibility, or phenomenology (through the world-revealing exposure of *le visage*) and in terms of the logic of language (through his analysis of *le dire*). Responsibility is in some ways the fusion of these two primordial calls.

Contrary to some rather severe criticism that is at times directed at him, Levinas is not simply condemning the realm of the said or logic or rules.[57] Rather he attempts to demonstrate the conditions necessary for their appearance. And fundamental to those conditions are both an openness to discourse – *me voici* – and an awareness that something within us and critical to our existence is not ours and not reducible to our interests.[58] It is not sameness or difference, both of which, as we have already seen, refer everything to *me*, but what Levinas sometimes calls "non-indifference"[59] that founds the symbolic order.

I am summoned to this assignation without choice or predeliction. Responsibility is the opposite of contract or commitment: I do not agree to it but *find* myself responsible; it is not a way of advancing the ego's purposes, but, rather, it disturbs them. "Strictly speaking, the other is the end; I am a hostage, a responsibility and a substitution supporting the world in the passivity of assignation, even in an accusing persecution, which is undeclinable. Humanism has to be denounced only because it is not sufficiently human."[60] This is the fundamental aspect of responsibility towards which all Levinas' demonstrations about the irreducibility of subjectivity to choice are directed. It is, I think, obvious by now but nevertheless of central importance to the business of legal justification: responsibility is not a choice. This "unexceptionable responsibility, preceding every free consent, every pact, every contract"[61] is not a tragedy or an unpleasant necessity. On the contrary, it lies at the very core of those experiences that constitute us. It is not as if we were free and then a responsibility was imposed upon us against our will. Responsibility emerges with our selfhood, with relationship, with desire.[62]

Second, responsibility is not reciprocal.[63] It has nothing to do with social contracts or legal policies. It arises simply from the vulnerability with which the other approaches us and which places a demand on us and in us. In some sense, then, this responsibility always remains incalculable and hence cannot be measured against any responsibilities that the other might owe to me or that I might owe to others. Now Levinas is forced to admit that this creates a problem in any society in which many different and over-lapping relationships are implicated.

It is troubled and becomes a problem when a third party enters. The third party is other than the neighbour, but also another neighbour, and also a neighbour of the other, and not simply his fellow. What are the other and the third party for one another? What have they done to one another? Which passes before the other?[64]

The fact that we are all responsible for each other renders law and justice necessary as a practical matter: "comparison, coexistence ... order" – some measurement or limitation must be placed on the infinite demands of infinite others.[65]

This is a matter that may readily be conceded and that will concern us in chapters 6 and 7, when we consider how Levinasian ethics affects legal concepts. In fact, the relationship between Levinas' ethics and the political and legal world, of which judgment, balance, and compromise are necessary features, is one of the most fraught aspects of contemporary scholarship. Levinas insists on the distinctness, and indeed the utter incommensurability, of the paradigms of ethics and law; and yet at the same time he seems to want to say that ethics can contribute to the kind of political or legal processes we instantiate. There seems a paradox here about which Levinas is, at the very least, imprecise. For some writers, the paradox of "an ethics without law ... a language without phrase"[66] condemns his project to fantasy.[67] For others, it is enough to observe the paradox, or even to suggest that it stems from Levinas' own horror of the brutal nature of his own political experience.[68] For still others, and clearly for this book, the effort to think through the ways in which legal principles and political practices can be touched by the breath of ethics without abandoning their own mundane and pragmatic tasks is a vital aspect of the task of the translator.[69] But the initial point, the fact of our responsibility and its philosophical form and origin are not undermined by these later problems of limitation. To begin with, my responsibility for another person does not depend on any reciprocity of obligation. He may be responsible for me too, but as Levinas curtly remarks, "that's *his* business."[70]

Third, it follows that in the challenge with which responsibility confronts us, we are singled out. This means to be made individual – "the very subjectivity of the subject." We are called to account – we are called to respond – as unique and irreplaceable beings by someone who asks for or needs *our* help. There is no deferral. No one else will do. How we respond cannot be hidden behind some rules or principles: it is all up to us and up to now. I think the experience of charity brings home the point. When I meet a beggar on the street, I cannot escape the moment. There is no point saying "I gave at the office" or "I don't believe you." No rule of my own devising can protect me from the demand of an immediate decision that is mine and mine alone. I can give, or I can not give. But no one can do this for me; no one (no prior rule nor even a government or a social service) can take my place. This is what Levinas means when he says that the relationship with another "is not a species of consciousness whose ray emanates from the I; it puts the I in question. This putting in question emanates from the other."[71] The demand from the other that puts me on the spot likewise constitutes me as a unique subject, a self. "Uniqueness signifies through the non-coinciding with oneself, the non-repose in oneself, restlessness … For it is a sign given of this giving of signs, the exposure of oneself to another."[72] So in stark opposition to the standard view, responsibility is not the outcome of individuality. It is the cause of it. The demand of the other individualizes *me*. It is achieved for me, not by me. Responsibility is therefore not only the foundation of all relationships. It also constitutes our subjectivity. And this responsibility is never abstract, never conceived and predictable in advance. It is always a specific and contextual experience, and this contextuality must also find its place in our law.

We are not just a being, a thing among things. Our existence expresses human be-*ing*. But here we are faced with a problem. We know what running looks like, or singing or enervating. We can see these actions as they take place. But what does be-ing look like? "As Plato noted, besides the eye and the thing, vision presupposes the light. The eye does not see the light but the object in the light … A relation with what in another sense comes absolutely from itself is needed to make possible the consciousness of radical exteriority. A light is needed to see the light."[73] In *Totality and Infinity* the face and speech, and then in *Otherwise than Being* responsibility, turn out to be that light. The face of the other calls us into question and in the process shines on us the light that allows us to discover our be-ing.[74] If we are to understand responsibility in law as a necessity, even as a welcome and constitutive event, and not as a problem – as the law of torts surely does – then this is why. It is the torchlight held by another that, shining on us, allows us to come to see ourselves.

Finally, the exercise of responsibility is not finite. As desire, which draws us forth towards others, responsibility deepens with practice and awareness. This, too, it seems to me, describes very well the actual experience of responsibility. The relationship of responsibility "is not a return to oneself" but, on the contrary, "disengages the *one* as a term, which nothing could rejoin."[75] Responsibility is a rent in the fabric of being, an interruption to the ceaseless monologue of the self. Once undone, the knot that rejoins us to ourselves nevertheless preserves the discontinuity as part of us.[76] Furthermore, since we are *constituted* through responsibility, which is external, challenging, and unpredictable, no formula of words, no system or rules, could entirely determine the conditions of its future exercise. We always remain open to future and unknowable obligations of responsibility because this "question mark" of duty is our hither side, our soul, and our inspiration. The necessarily responsive nature of responsibility is a problem for law, which after all seeks to write down the "full stop" of duty. But at the same time it provides a justification that other models do not address for the flexibility and change that imbues the common law of negligence. Indeed, most articulations of the law do not even recognize that responsiveness and responsibility are connected. If the principles of responsibility are simply rules laid down in order to stabilize expectations and put our social interactions on a more predictable footing, then the constant reassessment that marks the jurisprudence of the duty of care can only be seen as a failure. But, as Levinas suggests, such fluidity and openness are necessary to the very idea of responsibility.

THE GARDEN OF EXILE

In the argument so far I have attempted to found the legitimacy of an obligation, prior to all commitment, towards another whose interests are incommensurable with my own. It has been argued that this obligation is necessary to explain critical facets of human experience and to account for the emergence of consciousness, language, and subjectivity.[77] I have tried to show that orthodox analyses of obligation and justice fail to account for these elements and that therefore Levinas' perspective offers a major new contribution to legal theory. The argument fundamentally inverts the unstated assumption as to the priority of the self adopted by most explanations of responsibility. That the *alter* is a form of *ego*, and not vice versa,[78] turns out to be the central begged question in all conventional theories of duty. In Levinas' two main works, published in 1961 and 1974 and translated into English in 1969 and 1981, he attempted to argue, paradoxically, that being was itself dependent on "otherwise than being." This otherwise, this living for the other at the very heart of humanity, may be described as hospitality or as responsibility. Ethics inhabits a realm before, and is constitutive of, philosophy; just as responsibility lives before and is constitutive of freedom.[79] This responsibility is not willed by the self. But neither is it imposed by society, as an act of collective will. On the contrary, it is a personal relationship owed directly from me to the other and deriving immediately from my desire to respond to the vulnerability of the other.

There can be little doubt that our culture could do with such an argument. Resurgent economic liberalism appears to have deprived government intervention of much of its social legitimacy at the same time as it appears to have defined individual action almost exclusively in terms of self-interest. It is true that there is talk of a "new philanthropy," but if this is to be construed as a dimension of voluntary action, an exercise in kindness, it only further enforces the idea of autonomy and freedom as foundational to our sense of self. If charity is reduced to something else we might deign to spend our money on, like shoes or cars, we are in deep trouble. We have need of a *tertium quid*, not between these poles, in the form of a compromise, but beginning from different premises altogether. The paramountcy of the ethical, and the derivation of responsibility from this alternative framework, would afford such a new direction. An ethical understanding would be neither socialist nor individualist but intersubjective: the orbit of our responsibility would be traced through the gravitational pull exerted by the presence of other bodies around us.[80]

The bankruptcy of much social policy and political debate stems precisely from ignorance of the distinct register of ethical, as opposed to political, considerations. Politics is the realm of totality par excellence. It weighs and calculates – literally, totalizes – different interests on the scale of social utility, or preference, or, from time to time, just votes. One way or another, it inevitably adds us up and subtracts us (and in the process sometimes divides us). This balancing act from within a framework of equivalence is necessary, but it is not adequate. Neither is morality, understood in the Kantian sense as a system of universal principles derived from reason. Immanuel Kant argued that only a rational being could be a moral agent.[81] Emmanuel Levinas turns this argument on its head too[82] – only a moral agent has access to reason. Ethics must find a place for a response to need removed from both calculation on the one hand, and from predetermined abstractions on the other. It must find a place for responsibility. As for us, we do not have a say in the matter. Responsibility is not a choice but a predicament in which find ourselves, already, the chosen people.

This shift suggests some of Levinas' own inspirations. Levinas is at times ingenuous about the informative relationship between his theology and his philosophy. He has insisted on the distinction between his "philosophical" and his rabbinical, or "confessional," texts.[83] But at the same time it is clear that Jewish experience has fundamentally directed the course of his investigations and that the Talmud is never far from his thoughts or his examples.

As we have seen, the experience of Holocaust governed the specific problem of ethical responsibility to which he dedicated his life. His "biography ... is dominated by the presentiment and the memory of the Nazi horror."[84] Thus the dedication to *Otherwise than Being*: "To the memory of those who were closest among the six million assassinated by the National Socialists, and of the millions on millions of all confessions and all nations, victims of the same hatred of the other man, the same anti-semitism."[85] Through a critique of Western philosophy and its omissions, Levinas wants to demonstrate that antisemitism is in fact misanthropy.[85] The Bible is and remains the constant companion of his philosophical reflections, and its stories are given the status of archetypes and evidence throughout his work.[87]

Levinas' work can be understood as part of a distinctly Jewish tradition, or, rather, as an attempt, in a way, to translate Jewish insight into the language of the Western philosophical tradition.[88] While this is undoubtedly an easily overdrawn distinction – and Gillian Rose, for one, attacks it remorselessly[89] – it is not entirely without merit. "It isn't true that my thought isn't Greek. On the contrary, everything that I say about justice comes from Greek thought, and Greek politics as well. But what I say, quite simply, is that it is, ultimately, based on the relationship of the other, on the ethics without which I would not have *sought* justice."[90] The question points to another important debate within Levinasian studies. If writers such as Derrida, and even Levinas, have hesitated before placing themselves in an intellectual ghetto, we should perhaps be sympathetic to their reasons. Even as late as Habermas and Rose, "Jewish" – whether attached to ethics or to deconstruction – was a shorthand for "mystical," illogical, anarchic and, in short, not worthy of serious philosophical attention.[91] Is it surprising then that Derrida should insist not on the distinctiveness of "Jewish thought" but rather on the prior contamination of each great tradition by the other? The point for Derrida, and it is surely Levinas' too, is that our concepts are already mixed and touched by the other. The stranger has already inspired us. "Are we Jews? Are we Greeks? We live in the difference between the Jew and the Greek, which is perhaps the unity of what is called history ... Are we Greeks? Are we Jews? But who, we? ... Jewgreek is greekjew."[92]

This mixity is profoundly true and true, moreover, to the spirit of Levinas' argument, which is all about a fertilization that does not appropriate. Yet it remains the case that as against, for example, the Aristotelian tradition of justice, Levinasian ethics has particular resources and resonances that are well worth drawing out. Levinas has remarked that "We are faced with the great task of articulating in Greek those principles of which Greece had no knowledge. The singularity of the Jews awaits its philosophy."[93] This task is not only a function of the narrative tradition to which he makes frequent reference – discussion of the stories of Moses and Abraham, Cain, Jacob and Esau are seminal references in his writing[94] – nor even the weight he gives to these narrative arguments and interpretative method.[95]

Rather, the idea of responsibility here depends on a series of conceptual reversals with which Judaism is well familiar. First, for Levinas the ethical precedes the political. Far from being an accomplishment of the State, a genuine society built upon care makes government possible.[96] While this may come as a shock to the orthodox thinking of many, it will not be so to Jews, since they lived and flourished as a community for thousands of years in the absence of a state. Until the foundation of the state of Israel, Judaism faced the problem of how to constitute a legitimate and authoritative normative culture without any of the apparatus of nationhood. The answer, as both Levinas and other theorists like Robert Cover[97] have recognized, was through powerful and interrelated traditions of both textual exegesis and of the ethical relationships in which the interpretative tradition is embedded. *Haggadah*, the meat of law, and *aggadah*, the wine of lore, operate together to cement and protect a community in the absence of spatial jurisdiction or governmental force.[98]

No less significantly, this pre-political interpretative practice mandates a certain necessary openness in relation to the textual tradition too. Without any of the institutional mechanisms that H.L.A. Hart characterizes as "secondary rules" that facilitate orderly legal change and

ensure effective legal enforcement, "Talmudic hermeneutics demonstrates an interpretative process that allows for polysemy without indeterminacy."[99] The nature of this exegesis essentially involves not a
stripping down of meaning but a building up of layers. The unitary
text is seen to offer multiple resources. And not least, such a close and
organic textual study invites the engagement and "existential self-
transformation" of the reader and not their mere subservience.[100] Ethical responsibility, with its notions of change and surprise and transformation, is not only read in these texts but is part of the process of
reading itself. Interpretation is not then a science, discovering universal
truths that can then be applied thereafter, but an ongoing process of
self-discovery.[101] Such an exegetical interpretative practice offers an
alternative paradigm that can already be recognized as being intimately
connected with the common law. "The doctors of the law will never
have peace," goes an old Talmudic saying, "neither in this world nor
in the next ... for there is always more to be discussed."[102]

The second of these conceptual reversals is that responsibility
precedes choice. Again, this provides remarkable resonance with a religion that is, after all, founded on "the chosen people." It is easy to
read this phrase as a mere claim of honour. But of course, it is far more
complicated than that. "The biblical teaching does not consist of praise
for a model people. It consists of invectives ... It is not through pride
that Israel feels it has been chosen ... The civilization is defined in terms
not of prerogatives but of responsibilities."[103] To be chosen, whether
by god or otherwise, is a burden – a responsibility. But being the subject
of this chosenness and bearing the demands that god chose them to
accept is what constitutes Jews as people and as a people.

Third, home precedes homelessness. The Western tradition has
always prioritized the experience of "dwelling" and "home." Intellec-
tually we attempt to synthesize all ideas and all experience into a coherent web of logical connections and in that way, too, attempt to relate
everything to a framework in which we are already at home. The home
and the familiar become the sole point of reference by which everything
else is judged. We thus attempt to make an economy – a unified and
coherent system of exchanges – out of our lives. According to Levinas,
this tradition reaches its apotheosis in the work of Heidegger, for whom
possession and dwelling form the very meaning of being.[104] To dwell
in a world of the familiar – arrived home at last from our travels, like
Ulysses – is our goal and our destination.[105]

Not for Levinas. Dwelling is a complacency that never allows us to grow or to learn. If it allows others into our lives and our thoughts only on our own terms, then it does not really allow others at all. The solution is to eschew forever a world of psychological or intellectual comfort in favour of "the exteriority of absolute exile." "As in a desert, one can find no place to reside. From the depths of sedentary existence a nomadic memory arises."[106] Levinas wishes us to remain always unsettled and restless, "driven from the outside," being "in exile in itself."[107] To be at home, to possess our thoughts and our experiences as we would possess a comfortable armchair, is the prelude to solitude and to a violence in which we protect "our" possessions through the totalities of appropriation, assimilation, or conquest. Levinas is fond of quoting Blaise Pascal: "'That is my place in the sun.' That is how the usurpation of the world began."[108]

Levinas defends a life spent wandering in the desert. We can be open to others and allow their pluralism to affect *us* only if we resist all the accumulation of intellectual furniture. Internal exile alone makes both communication and responsibility continually possible. More, it allows us to be influenced by those around us without possession or control. Merely to speak in this language demonstrates the enormous metaphorical power of the history that is drawn upon here. There is an ambiguity in Levinas: this ideal of ethical freedom is uncomfortably juxtaposed with his commitment to the political freedom that the founding of the State of Israel promised; for what is Israel but, at last, a home? Levinas struggled with the tension between Zionism and Talmud, place and book, all his life, and his writings, I think, cannot readily be reconciled.[109] Yet it is clear that although the political exigencies of Statehood are always powerfully felt, he never ceased to recognize and give ethical import to the diaspora and exile that characterized the experience of the Jewish people for millenia. Theirs has been a history of wandering, of guiding stars not hearths. For Habermas, this intellectual rootlessness is precisely the defect of deconstructionist thought, otherwise known dismissively as Jewish mysticism.[110] "They wander ... lost in the discursive zone."[111] Levinas turns a vice into a virtue. To defend nomadism not just as an intellectual virtue but as an ethical necessity clearly argues for a singular cast of mind constituted by Jewish experience.[112]

The final conceptual reversal comes from the fact that the Jewish God is comprehended as an absence. He has no image. His name is not to be spoken, his temple is destroyed, and the Ark of the Covenant contains nothing but the imagination of the commandments. This absence, says Levinas, is infinity and is God.¹¹³ And again Levinas sets up the very idea of the space respecting and protecting this absence as central to the openness of the soul to others. For in his philosophical and his confessional texts alike, Levinas glorifies the infinite over knowledge, absence over presence, wandering over possession, and away over home.

Of many meditations on this theme, the most vivid to me has been the experience of visiting Daniel Libeskind's Jewish Museum in Berlin.¹¹⁴ This poetic space, one of the most remarkable architectural projects of the last century, embodies within itself both the experience of exile and the experience of the void. One path within the museum leads directly to diaspora and the so-called garden of exile. Another literally shrinks and contracts around us until we find ourselves trapped in a shocking black tower in lieu of a holocaust memorial. But a third, one senses, is to be found by paying attention to a range of internal spaces that the museum's trajectories criss-cross, but to which there is in fact no access. These "void bridges," as Libeskind calls them, are spaces that can never be reached. They connote the idea of the Jewish God as an absence or an otherness. One experiences here not only a sense of great traumas and of a silence walled up but also a sense of what it means to be proximate to some power or presence that constitutes us but that cannot be directly grasped. Here is the void within us that can be neither assimilated nor annihilated. Here is the soul, the keystone of our psychic architecture, depicted precisely as a "negative space" outside our control.

4

From Philosophy to Law

Law must live in the middle, between two incompatible logics; "the need to be saved and the need to be satisfied."[1] It cannot do without practical results and compromises, without balancing the interests of selves. It cannot live only in the realm of ethical purity. But neither can it live only in the realm of bartered pragmatism. This would give law no identity apart from politics. Law strives to gain a mess of pottage without betraying its birthright.[2] So the normative foundations of law matter, though they are by no means the final word. Having introduced the reader to what I take to be an alternative justification for responsibility, I want now to begin to explore how it might throw light on various aspects of everyday law. The first two sections of this chapter address two of the most thorough critics of Levinas, both of whom have argued, from quite different directions, against the possibility of such an application or translation. The rest of the chapter then defends a limited engagement between ethics and law and begins to demonstrate at the most general level some ways in which this understanding of responsibility matters in tort.

AN ETHICS WITHOUT LAW? ...

Can such a translation on the basis of Levinas' ethics even be attempted? Gillian Rose thought not.[3] For Rose, ethics must be understood as embedded in social practice and its institutions. It is the middle way, between detached faith, on the one hand, and pragmatic works, on the other. This middle is always "broken," because it is situated in an imperfect world, but there is no choice but to participate in it. Rose believes that Levinas surrenders the task in favour of the extreme unction of sacrifice and, in fact, invites a return to theology under the guise of what she calls "holy sociology."[4] First, the very contrast between West and East, "old Athens and new Jerusalem,"[5] the city of reason and the city of god, is too crude and evasive to be of real value.[6] Judaism is not the "sublime other" of modernity; its complex history and present cannot be so dichotomously misrepresented.[7] There is undoubtedly much truth in this response. In particular, Levinas' own reading of the contrast between Greek and Jewish thought and, more specifically, between *halacha* and *aggadah* in Talmudic law is idiosyncratic and overdrawn.[8] Clearly it is right to say, as Rose insists, that "the modern city intensifies these perennial diremptions in its *inner* oppositions."[9] This is Habermas' critique of the postmodern turn too.[10] But to appreciate the inner oppositions that are already at work within our traditions is, as we saw in the previous chapter, precisely the purpose of these characterizations. It is not Levinas and certainly not Derrida who wish to separate the Jew from the Greek but, rather, Habermas and Rose. It is they who wish to preserve the purity of "their" tradition against those who would question its established intellectual dichotomies – science versus literature, logic versus rhetoric, philosophy versus psychology.[11] Against these dogmatic dichotomies, the trope of "Jerusalem" is deployed by Levinas "not as a Dionysian motif or theological foundation but as a semiological concept that marks the breakup of identity."[12]

At the same time, it is not an overstatement to understand "Jerusalem" and "Athens" as two contrasting approaches to identity and responsibility. Neither does it seem to me implausible that these two traditions have by and large addressed interestingly different questions over a great span of years. That is what a tradition does: it sustains a pattern of questions, not answers, over time.[13] Of course within the register of a tradition there is much room for different harmonics to reverberate. We would not expect the contrast to be complete. Their intersection makes the kind of translation Levinas has attempted possible, but their distinction makes it worthwhile.

Second, Rose argues that in dismissing the work of the Enlightenment, as she takes Levinas and his companions in "Messianic deconstruction"[14] to do (and note that she, too, rather overdraws the distinction in order to make the point), we are left with no recourse: no place for dialogue and negotiation, no ability to progress by small and steady steps. No compromise is possible between the realms of ethics and politics (or law). Interestingly, the argument at this point echoes that of Derrida. In "Violence and Metaphysics" he, too, was skeptical of how Levinas could actualize his infinite responsibility, and distinctly scathing on the subject of the "Messianic" tendencies of his philosophy.[15] The critique of rationality foreshadows its impossibility. In its place, according to Rose, Levinas proposes a naïve sacrifice of self to other, which is both mythic and unfeasible.[16] Hostage – substitution – wound – trauma – sacrifice. Levinas' language, particularly in *Otherwise than Being*, chills Rose to the bone. It betokens the complete elimination of reason in favour of revelation and the constitution of an absolute responsibility (meaning what exactly?) by rhetorical fiat. "This holiness corrupts because it would sling us between ecstasy and eschatology, between a promise of touching our own-most singularity and the irenic holy city, precisely without any disturbing middle ... Because the middle is broken – because these institutions are systematically flawed – does not mean they should be eliminated."[17]

Rose therefore argues that Levinas' rhetoric wills away the very problem it poses. His "evasive theology, insinuated epistemology, sacralized polity"[18] attempts to overcome the violence of law or the violence of disinterest but substitutes instead a new and even more powerful violence built, without any source of justification, upon myth and sanctity.[19] This violence is not lessened by being directed inwards, at ourselves. Levinas' version of the messianic surrenders reason and knowledge in favour of a mere utopia or dystopia that is by definition both impossible and unintelligible.[20] "New ethics," since it eschews all relationship with law, can accomplish precisely nothing. Its hortatory excess incites only institutional inertia.[21] If we are all "infinitely responsible," she argues, then in practice we are none of us really responsible. Without rules and choices and criteria for judgment, Levinas will give us a reason to feel guilty about everything, but no reason to act about anything. Rather, Rose urges us to continue our work with and not against the broken middle of our institutions, "to aim – scandalously – to return philosophy from her pathos to her logos. In this way, we may resume reflexively what we always do: to know, to misknow and yet to grow."[22]

The problem with this analysis is that it is built on a misreading of the terms, the status, and the consequences of Levinas' argument. As to terms, Robert Bernasconi convincingly argues that Derrida (and Rose too) dramatically overstates the role of some messianic or eschatological element in Levinas' writings, arguing that his use of this rhetoric is late and aberrant.[23] Furthermore, the use of these words in Levinas does not imply a resolution of the conflicts between the ideal and the real by some miraculous apparition, some deus ex machina that will, one of these days, usher in a new order, purify the political realm, and put an end to time and politics. If such was the case, then it is assuredly true that Levinas would have given up on the relationship of ethics and politics, assigning it to some utopian future. But this is just not so. Levinas explicitly says that "I could not accept a form of messianism which could terminate the need for discussion, which would end our watchfulness."[24] The "beyond" or the "outside" is, as is always the case for Levinas, not a question of a different time or place but of a different register or way of seeing the world we live in now: "*within* the totality and history, *within* experience."[25] Levinas understands totality and infinity not as a progression towards the future but as two actually existent but incommensurable orders that compete for our attention and haunt our memory. For Levinas the messianic and the eschatological, like the ethical itself, of course, invite "not a question of the future, but a disturbance or interruption of the present."[26] The Messiah is not a postponement into the distant future of a current problem: on the contrary, "le Messie, c'est Moi."[27]

As to status, I mean the kind of argument Levinas is making about the origin and nature of ethical responsibility. Rose systematically dismisses the role of myth in the institutional worlds of the "middle." Ironically, Levinas would appear to agree with her.[28] But I do not think that his argument can do without the idea of myth understood as a series of constitutive narratives.[29] Levinas' argument is a story of origins that tries to make sense of our relationship to the world and to others: just like Hobbes', or Freud's, or Rawls'. Just like these, Levinasian ethics provides us with a standpoint from which to view and to judge our human affairs: an "optics." And neither can Rose do without some such set of stories as to the nature of relationship or responsibility. Law, after all, is not just "in the middle": it is in the middle of something. One way or another, we cannot do without origins and eschatology – Genesis and Revelations – for they form the polestars of our thought. Indeed, although Rose insists on the need for "mediating institutions" like law,[30] she is little better than Levinas when it comes to actually telling us how and by what standards this mediation ought to take place. Her own arguments are also more comfortable in the realm of myth – of law's imagination – than of practicality.

As to consequences, I mean just what Levinas has in mind by the relationship of the infinite to the world of the totality. Rose is simply mistaken in believing that Levinas wants to give up on knowledge or reason (or for that matter rules or law) altogether.[31] On the contrary, the notion of diachrony that is so central to his work insists that we live in these two worlds, the worlds of totality and of infinity, at once. He is here attempting to show the structure of relationships that lies behind the world of knowledge and law and on which they critically depend. These relationships must be reduced to the "said" of doctrine and rules, and in the process something of the "saying" – law's spirit – will be betrayed. But a trace will remain, hidden interstitially in the fabric of the law, and it is our duty to listen to it and act on it.[32] This involves, among other things, a recognition of our responsibility to others and a duty of respect for their absolute difference to my interests. Such a trace, or ghost, affects the humility of our "saying" but not the logic of the "said," putting an interval between them.[33] It therefore invites our otherwise arrogant systems to stutter, as it were. Stuttering is a consciousness of distance, the physical symptom of "a philosophy of hesitation."[34] It appears to be what happens when one becomes acutely aware of the feedback loop between the saying and the said. It is the sound of diachrony. To know that we speak only provisionally does not deprive us of the power of speech altogether, though it may affect what we say and how we say it. So, too, the ethical relationship that "sustains discourse" is not a knowledge but contaminates knowledge, "putting the I in question" from moment to moment.[35] While the rules and systems that law makes must betray this ethical consciousness of the imperfection of rules, by reducing and limiting it, that does not thereby deprive it of relevance altogether: it remains like a stutter or a feedback loop.

Indeed, Levinas is really quite painstaking in insisting that an ethical optics is both the starting point for knowledge and consciousness and the condition of ethics, rather than its completion. The whole language of "hither side," "prior," and "otherwise" is intended to insist on this relationship. Levinas wishes to show us how the experience of ethics can be detected through the phenomenology of caress, love, language, and so forth. It is not a knowledge but it is capable of "disrupting" that knowledge – not superceding, disallowing, overcoming, or corrupting it.[36] If law and ethics were as utterly "dirempted" or sundered as Rose claims, then no "middle" could ever heal their rift. What we need is some way of recognizing that law already has something to do with ethics, that each of us already has some responsibility for each other, and at the same time that these relationships are and must remain irreducible to codes and abstractions. To know and yet to grow, what we need, in short, is Levinas.

In conclusion, Rose asks, "how can Levinas ... refute the consequence that justice, as he conceives it to be social not sacred, will nevertheless be utopian? Its intelligibility can only be ideal, for it involves setting aside the character of the modern state, which he describes as 'the alliance of logic and politics.'"[37] Her question misses, on the one hand, the importance of ideals for the character of any actually existent state and, on the other, the relationship between ethics and the State that Levinas by no means sets aside. Levinas' point is made on the very page from which Rose quotes too selectively. His critique of the "political character of logical rationalism" "does *not* ... signify the possible breakup of structures" in the way that Rose imputes to Levinas' position but only signifies that this alliance is "not the ultimate framework of meaning."[38] Ethics thus takes its place – and this has been the purport of much recent work on this question – as a motivation, a trajectory, and an optics by which to judge law.[39] Admittedly, for Levinas, as for Derrida, justice cannot therefore be codified or reduced to rules.[40] It remains a singularity, a treatment or judgment that resolutely refuses to determine people according to the formulaic application of a pre-existing system. Justice remains skeptical of the alliance of logic and politics. This creates a space of uncertainty within the workings of the legal system or the political system and accounts, perhaps, for a certain discomfiture amongst lawyers and politicians when the question of justice is raised as an alternative standard against which law or government might be judged. The logical necessity of this stuttering moment no doubt induces anxiety. But "who will claim to be just by economizing on anxiety?"[41]

... OR A LAW WITHOUT ETHICS?

The contamination of law by ethics is not something to which Levinas pays much attention. We see here in fact not contempt for law (as Rose alleges) but an uncritical and unelaborated respect for its function: "Violence calls up violence, but we must put a stop to this chain reaction. That is the nature of justice ... Humanity is born in man to the extent that he manages to reduce a mortal offence to the level of a civil lawsuit, to the extent that punishing becomes a question of putting right what can be put right and re-educating the wicked."[42] The problem, of course, is how one gets from a responsibility to every other, to a responsibility that must invariably choose between others. "Am I my brother's keeper?"[43] is the quintessential question not only of ethics but of law. In the seminal case of *Donoghue v. Stevenson*, the practical limitation of the call of the other is most explicitly conceded: "But acts or omissions which any moral code would censure cannot in a practical world be treated so as to give a right to every person injured by them to demand relief. In this way rules of law arise which limit the range of complainants and the extent of their remedy. The rule that you are to love your neighbour becomes in law, you must not injure your neighbour; and the lawyer's question, Who is my neighbour? receives a restricted reply."[44] By "lawyer's question," Lord Atkin reminds us not only that this is a question asked of lawyers but that it was originally asked in the Biblical text *by* "a certain lawyer," too.[45] If there were only two of us in the world, there would be no need of a restricted reply. Levinas: "If proximity ordered me to only the other alone, there would have not been any problem ... It is troubled and becomes a problem when a third party enters. The third party is other than the neighbour, but also another neighbour, and also a neighbour of the other and not simply his fellow ... It is of itself the limit of responsibility and the birth of the question: What do I have to do with justice?"[46]

In other words, we live in a world of multiple face-to-face encounters, not just between you and me but involving many third parties. No initial postulate of responsibility could determine which would have the priority. For I cannot be absolutely responsible for everybody all the time. Responsibility may be infinite, but I am not. Neither could a simple proposition determine how we might decide the responsibility I owe to the other or the responsibility an other owes to me. Again Levinas explicitly concedes this necessary limitation on his initial insight: "To be sure – but this is another theme – my responsibility for all can and has to manifest itself also in limiting itself. The ego can, in the name of this unlimited responsibility, be called upon to concern itself also with itself. The fact that the other, my neighbour, is also a third party with respect to another, who is also a neighbour, is the birth of thought, consciousness, justice and philosophy."[47] Levinas indeed goes further, much further, in arguing, at least at times, that justice "is rendered to the totality." "It is an illusion or hypocrisy," he goes on, "to suppose that, originating outside of economic relations, it could be maintained outside of them in a kingdom of pure respect."[48] "If the radical difference between men ... was not surmounted by the quantitative equality measurable by money, human violence could be repaired only through vengeance or pardon ... It is to be sure shocking to see in the quantifications of man one of the essential conditions for justice. But can one conceive of a justice without quantity and without reparation?"[49] It would appear, then, that the law of negligence, the quantitative compensation for physical suffering, is here presented as the model of the sacrifice of infinite ethics in order to achieve finite justice. "Thus we need laws," he insists, "and – yes – courts of law, institutions and the state to render justice."[50]

There is a danger here that in defending Levinas against the charge of utopian idealism, one might end up impoverishing him altogether. Have we come full circle? Are we left with a justice of the totality and the economy that exists simply in its own, and no doubt familiar, terms? This is perhaps Rose's weightiest and simplest charge: his ethical extremism *cannot* be translated into the "real world" and becomes utterly irrelevant to the cities of the middle. But such an argument fails to come to terms with the "trace," which is to say, with the ghostly marks that the "saying" and the "face of the other," which are irreducible to the logic of our everyday lives, nevertheless leave upon us.[51] This stutter is "like knots in a thread tied again"; though it rejoins the linear passage of our life, nevertheless it continually reminds us of our broken and hostaged subjectivity.[52]

The trace is the voice of ethical "otherness" that infects being, haunting the system with which it is not commensurable. That is, after all, the nature of haunting: the scarcely perceptible slippage between two incommensurable worlds that we sense but cannot ever capture by the light of day.[53] The concept of the trace has become a key term throughout the literature of deconstruction. Justice, as Derrida will say, exists precisely as the trace, or "ghost of the undecidable."[54] It is perhaps the most significant conceptual development between Levinas' two testaments.[55] Indeed, Derrida's own critical response to *Totality and Infinity* led Levinas to draw out more explicitly the elements of this approach.

On this point, Derrida's concern was precisely opposite to that of Rose.[56] While Rose wished to know how Levinas' ethical norms, so removed from logic and politics, could possibly effect the "broken middle," Derrida wished to know how Levinas' language and tradition, so steeped in logic and politics, could possibly effect to break with it. In

"Violence and Metaphysics" Derrida points out with rigorous sympathy that Levinas' critique of language as a totalizing system takes place within language, just as his critique of "philosophy as egology" takes place using the very resources that it seeks to renounce.[57] How can Levinas describe the prephilosophical face from within philosophy? How can Levinas explain the ethical nature of our initial "signifyingness" using only conventional preexisting significations? "By making the origin of language, meaning and difference," concludes Derrida, "the relation to the infinitely other, Levinas is resigned to betraying his own intentions."[58] The whole project was, in the words of the subtitle of *Totality and Infinity*, "an essay on exteriority."[59] Levinas yearned to stand "outside," once and for all: outside his skin, outside language, outside the self.[60] But Derrida argued that it can't be done – there is no outside.[61] Infinity, the outside of knowledge, cannot be thought, except negatively. Rose criticized the possibility of revolution by arguing that Levinas eschewed any relationship with the modern world. Derrida, on the contrary, criticized the possibility of reform by arguing that Levinas remained trapped in it.

Ironically, the "trace" that Levinas elaborated in *Otherwise than Being* forms his response to both these criticisms. Because it is the hinge that links infinity to totality, the trace allows the political and the legal to limit ethics and at the same moment allows the ethical to shine through the political, while remaining irreconcilable with it. As Simon Critchley demonstrated, this was an enormously significant step that permitted Levinas to avoid the charge of impotence that, though they approach the problem from opposite directions, both Rose and Derrida levelled at him. "The language of thematization that is being used *at this very moment* is only made possible by the essence of language revealed in the relation to the Other ... This language is, *at this very moment*, only made possible by the ethical relation which constitutes the essence of language."[62]

Nothing on the subject of the trace is clearer than Levinas' original explication in his essay on "Meaning and Sense."[63] A trace plays the role of a sign: the detective seeks out clues, the hunter tracks, and the historian relics. All provide us with hints of a vanished presence.[64] But a trace is "not a sign like any other," precisely because it offers these clues in relation to an order of meaning not just absent but in fact incommensurable with our own. Though they cannot exist together, they nevertheless contaminate one another. The burglar, for example, does not just leave; he attempts to wipe out his presence. But in the process he cannot help but leave other marks of his passing. "He who left traces in wiping out his traces did not mean to say or do anything by the traces he left. [But] he disturbed the order in an irreparable way ... These signify something on the basis of a past which, in a trace, is neither indicated nor signalled *but yet disturbs order.*"[65] In this sense, "every sign is a trace." It betrays the existence of something radical and irreversible behind its simple meaning. Though it cannot therefore be reduced to a mere sign,[66] which is to say, incorporated into the present system of meaning or logic or politics, et cetera, our sense of its invisibility nevertheless disturbs us in much the same way that relativism disturbs us or ghosts disturb us. A trace is a question mark that hovers over us, capable neither of being answered nor ignored.

Much has been written on the idea of the trace by – and with respect to its place in the work of – both Levinas and Derrida. It is probably the better view that "Violence and Metaphysics" stands not as a rejection of Levinas but, rather, as a thorough-going exploration of the consequences and difficulties of Levinas' ideas, with a view to encouraging Levinas to follow his train of thought wherever it might lead.[67] The oscillating movement between unpacking the internal logic of an argument and pushing against its limits and assumptions is very much Derrida's method. Thus, when Derrida describes the trace as "unthinkable, impossible, unutterable," he should not be seen as criticizing Levinas so much as instructing us on how something incoherent within an intellectual tradition could nevertheless survive to influence it.[68] Somehow, we can think the unthinkable, utter the unutterable, if only for a moment. So Derrida writes, "we are not denouncing here an incoherence of language or a contradiction in the system. We are wondering about the meaning of a necessity: the necessity of lodging oneself within traditional conceptuality in order to destroy it."[69]

Indeed, Derrida's initial scepticism concerning the idea of the trace and the subsequent importance that it nevertheless came to have in his later work, particularly on law and justice, might stand for just this process of haunting, influence, and contamination.[70] In an oft-quoted line, Derrida asks, "how could there be a play of the same if alterity itself was not already *in* the same?" Clearly this too stands not as a rejection of Levinas but in fact as an elaboration of the very possibility he imagines.[71] The "other *in* the same" is just what Levinas means by *in*-finity.

This possibility is neither the segregation of ethics and politics or law, as Rose suggested,[72] nor their assimilation, as Derrida feared, but the force field generated by their continuing *proximity.*[73] Although the incommensurable orders of ethics and politics cannot therefore be married, one can nevertheless interrogate or haunt the other.[74] Thus, although every philosophy and every discourse, including not least law, must inevitably reduce the "ethical Saying" to the rules that govern and constrain the "Said," still, the former continually "interrupts" the latter and prevents forever its self-sufficiency, which is the danger of any system or logic.[75] This stutter, which occurs not within language but behind it, between it, and as its condition, is the undying theme of *Otherwise*. The "residue" of saying is never entirely lost within our legal and political orders. Ethics is not domesticated or appropriated, which would indeed be a betrayal, but contaminates it – the preservation of a realm of purity is never Levinas' way.[76]

Even on those occasions of Derrida's most severe criticisms we see the trace of a deeper and more sympathetic reading. Derrida is right to say that we cannot *stay* with Levinas, because he offers us "an ethics without law."[77] And this point Levinas freely concedes, agreeing that ethics "becomes a problem with the entry of the third party,"[78] requiring political calculations of us: balance, proportion, and limitation. We cannot stay with an ethics apart from law. This is the necessary instability of ethics: it is not a place or an abode or any promised stability of rules but something rather more uncomfortable: the scruples under our feet that keep us on the hop.[79] But although ethics is not therefore reducible to a legal system or a politics – *pace* Rose – it can still be informed and questioned by it – *pace* Derrida. The result is a "certain creative antagonism"[80] in which the political life that thinks only of the social whole and weighs things only in its own terms and by the use of its own self-sufficient calculus or grammar is held up to (and held up by) the self-questioning gaze of our particular relationship with each and every other.[81] Law is not ethics, certainly; ethics is rather the scruple that constantly discomforts law and impels it to move.

THE ORIGIN OF RESPONSIBILITY IN TORTS: A CASE STUDY ON ILLEGALITY

We will see in chapter 7 that there is a double movement here: as Levinas responded to Derrida by trying to explain what he meant by "the force of an alterity *in* me," Derrida and others responded to Levinas by applying that very notion to our institutions as well as our selves and arguing for the force of an ethics *in* law.[82] But let us assume for the moment the separate realms of ethics and law. If ethics founds but cannot maintain justice – if justice, indeed, is the social limit placed on ethics[83] – what then? Surely the starting point we take, our initial orientation before this understanding of justice as *logos* is applied, still matters.[84] From within the orthodox common law tradition of negligence, responsibility must be justified by something within me: my conduct, my consent. But for Levinas, responsibility comes from something outside me: his gaze, his vulnerability. While conceding that absolute responsibility must be limited, one immediately has, therefore, a different premise. "It is then not without importance to know if the egalitarian and just State in which man is fulfilled (and which is to be set up, and especially to be maintained) proceeds from a war of all against all, or from the irreducible responsibility of the one for all, and if it can do without friendship and faces."[85] This argument legitimates personal obligations in tort with reference neither to social policy nor to any theories of contractual bargaining. Negligence law reflects not some imposed limitation on our initial freedom but our initial indebtedness to "a neighbour." It is, in fact, a profound statement of the human necessity of what has come to be known, broadly, as the duty of care. Tort law captures something that "obliges beyond contracts." Its essence is its one-sidedness: it is an oath, not a contract, "anachronously prior to any commitment."[86] Levinas tells us how this could be and why it matters.

This provides us with an attractive justification for the nature and concerns of tortious obligation and particularly of the duty of care. It suggests the philosophical origin of these obligations in terms that speak persuasively to our instincts and emotions and that draw on vital elements of the human experience that matter to us and about which many contemporary theories of law are oddly silent. Levinas' theory of responsibility connects law to ourselves, our feelings, and our relationships even as it calls on us to strive gladly towards goodness and not to flee from it.

Neither is the question of law's origins of only theoretical interest. On occasion, the law finds itself – somewhat, perhaps, to its own surprise – required to seriously reflect on those origins. As an example, consider negligent acts committed in the course of illegal conduct. Common law jurisdictions have often had cause to reflect on the conditions under which a "criminal" can sue in tort. No doubt "there is no rule denying to a person who is doing an unlawful thing the protection of the general law imposing upon others duties of care for his safety."[87] But the court has had more difficulty with the issue of what

is called "joint illegality." The problem has been to determine the
boundaries of illegal conduct. On the one hand, it would hardly seem
fair to prevent a plaintiff from suing a defendant for negligent driving
just because both were disqualified drivers at the time or because the
driver was unlicensed to the knowledge of the passenger.[88] Although
both parties are engaging in illegal conduct – "joint illegality" – this
seems no reason to deny them the protection of the normal law of
negligence. On the other hand, to give an oft-cited example, it would
seem invidious for the courts to decide whether one bank robber was
negligent to another as they prepared to blow a safe. But how are we
to distinguish the types of illegality in these cases? What allows us to
permit the first cause of action and strike out the second?

   In the High Court of Australia, to whose approach I will later
compare that of the Supreme Court of Canada, the problem came to
a head in *Gala v. Preston*.[89] A group of young men stole a car after
an extended bout of drinking. They headed off up the Queensland
coast around 8:00 in the evening. Some hours later, while the plaintiff
was asleep in the back seat, the car crashed into a tree. Tragically, one
of the passengers, Ray Simms, was killed, while Preston was injured.
"If it were not for the joint criminal activity of the four young men
who were unlawfully using the vehicle, there would be no doubt but
that the first defendant as driver owed a duty of care to the plaintiff
as passenger."[90] Yet the court held unanimously that the boy could not
sue. The majority of the court focused on the extent to which the illegal
context would affect the Court's ability to determine the relationship
between the parties. It may be, for example, that the illegal enterprise
"absolves the one party from the duty towards the other to perform
the activity with care for [the other's] safety."[91] A getaway driver can
hardly be sued for driving dangerously when that is the point of the
relationship.[92] But in contrast, the fact that the drivers in *Jackson v.
Harrison* were unlicensed did not impinge upon the expectation of
safety that the passenger surely demanded. The "joint illegality" in
such a case, concluded the Court in *Gala v. Preston*, "had no bearing
at all on the standard of care reasonably to be expected of the driver."[93]

   The problem was that this case, as with *Smith v. Jenkins* before it,[94]
fell somewhat between the two extremes. The boys were not on the
run in circumstances in which dangerous driving was only to be
expected. On the contrary, the dangerous driving took place some
hours after the car had been stolen, under no pressure, and with the
plaintiff simply asleep. It is self-evident that the boy reposed his trust

in the driver to get him to Gladstone safely, notwithstanding that the car was stolen. Nevertheless, the Court decided that the relationship between the parties was subsumed by the illegality that gave rise to it.

The joint criminal activity ... gave rise to the only relevant relationship between the parties and constituted the whole context of the accident. That criminal activity was of its nature, fraught with serious risks. The consumption by the participants ... of massive amounts of alcohol for many hours prior to the accident would have affected adversely the capacity of a driver to handle the motor vehicle competently ... Each of the parties to the enterprise must be taken to have appreciated that he would be encountering serious risks in travelling in the stolen vehicle.[95]

The majority therefore concluded that there was no duty owed by the driver to the passenger because "it would not be possible or feasible for a court to determine what was an appropriate standard of care to be expected" without reference to their criminality. This the court in *Gala* refused to do.[96] Accordingly, "there was no relationship of proximity" between the parties.[97]

Merely to express the argument in these terms is to expose the fragility of its logic. It is simply bizarre to try and claim that there was no "proximate relationship" between the parties. On the contrary, the relationship of two people in a car is a textbook example of such proximity.[98] Indeed, it is apparent that the majority is confusing whether a duty of care existed with the "standard of care," that is, with the factual assessment of how a reasonable driver might be expected to act in all the circumstances. Even if we accept that sometimes the relationship will be so bound up with the perils of illegal conduct that we cannot say that there is any expectation of safety at all, this is surely not the case here. Although the majority emphasizes the "actual relationship between the parties," it does not make a convincing case as to why this relationship does not import a duty of care, or why its determination "would not be possible or feasible."[99]

The majority consciously eschewed an analysis based on "public policy" in relation to illegal conduct in favour of an attempt to demonstrate that a lack of responsibility was inherent within the terms of the relationship itself. But as we have seen, this argument is difficult to maintain. To shore up its position, the majority judgment emphasizes the drunkenness of the boys even though, and for reasons that need not detain us, the law has long recognized that a drunk driver normally still has a responsibility to drive safely.[100] The effect, nevertheless, was to characterize the boys in terms of their (undoubted) irresponsibility so as to sustain the public-policy argument, which was implicit but necessary.[101]

This argument found direct expression in the concurring judgments of Brennan and Dawson JJ. Both indicate that the duty of care founders not just because the boys were behaving illegally but because of the type of illegality. Thus, Brennan suggests that to allow the plaintiff to recover for their injuries in such a case, or indeed in a case such as *Gala v. Preston*, would "condone a breach of the criminal law."[102] "It is only where the admission of a duty of care impairs the normative influence of the law creating an offence that the civil law can be said to condone a breach of that law. In such cases, it would be contrary to public policy to admit a duty of care."[103] Justice Dawson's argument is similar. The recognition of a duty of care "gives validity to the criminal enterprise by using it as the foundation for erecting a standard of care."[104] This is clearly the policy of the Court, and it is only by reference to such a policy that the decision makes sense.

Underneath all the analyses of the Court lie two simple propositions. One is that it would be undignified for the courts to acknowledge the relationship between two criminals, even long after they were in flagrante delicto, as it were. The second is that the normative value of the criminal law takes priority over the purely instrumental value of tort law. Crime trumps tort. In support of these ideas the courts are prepared effectively to outlaw certain persons or at least to withdraw from them the support of the law of torts. In this case, for example, a nineteen-year-old boy with serous injuries was denied any compensation or support. The High Court appears to think he deserved it;[105] so, it must be said, do a lot of my students.

I disagree. There are two relevant relationships in a situation like *Gala v. Preston*: the relationship between the boys and the State was breached by criminal conduct (and will, we imagine, be punished accordingly), and the relationship between the two boys themselves was breached by negligent conduct and is no less deserving of recognition. These relationships operate in different registers, "diachronously," as Levinas might say. The High Court of Australia suggests that to give respect to the relationship between the parties would amount to "condoning a breach of the criminal law." In what sense, condoning? One might as well suggest that the present interpretation of the law, by throwing out the action in negligence, is condoning a breach of the civil law. Each action is independent of the other. Should we continue to be blind to the actual suffering and needs of the plaintiff and to the actual relationship that gave rise to it? The Court seems to think here that it must make a choice between "real" law – crime – and the expendable superstructure of civil compensation. They have chosen, in other words, to accept a theory of responsibility that draws on Hobbes and that imagines civil responsibility for another as basically a convenient social fiction and nothing more.

In *Hall v. Hebert*, the Supreme Court of Canada was faced with a broadly similar situation involving "a souped-up muscle car" that exuded, in the ironic commentary of Cory J, "a compelling seductive charm that would attract young men of all ages."[106] An accident on Graveyard Road (no less) took place when the defendant allowed the plaintiff to drive while drunk. Yet the court in that case rejected the idea that to recognize a duty of care in such circumstances would some-how undermine the criminal law. Justice McLachlin compared those circumstances to situations in which one might seek to enforce an ille-gal contract or a secret trust in the courts[107] or, as in the celebrated U.S. case of *Riggs v. Palmer*, to probate a testament after having mur-dered the testator.[108] In those cases, the "fabric of the law" is compro-mised because it is being used to allow someone to profit from their illegal conduct. But a negligence action is not about profit: it is about responsibility for harm actually suffered.

The hypothetical burglar in the midst of a job might be placed within this category of profit. One might convincingly argue that with respect to the getaway driver there is no expectation of safety and therefore no duty of care. As Justice Brennan suggests, the situation of the safe-cracker is rather different.[109] There are probably well-understood safe-guards and practices to reduce the risk of injury, and it would not be beyond the wit of the legal process to uncover them, though the experts who would be called to give evidence would present quite a spectacle. Nevertheless, to ask the Court to make such a judgment might, in some cases, amount to laying down standards of "reasonable crimi-nality." This is what the Court in *Gala* means when it points to the impossibility of determining a standard of care that "would require modification by reference to the criminal aspects of the venture,"[110] as in situations "necessitating secrecy, subterfuge, or haste."[111]

There is a difference between asking the court to define standards *of* illegal conduct and asking it to define standards of general conduct that take place illegally. The Court in *Gala v. Preston* was not being asked to lay down standards of "reasonable joy riding," just to acknowledge the normal standard of care for driving. To sustain the action would not have encouraged, condoned, justified, or validated the boys' criminal conduct. It would merely have recognized that there was also, and no less significantly, a personal relationship between them that did not disappear the moment they transgressed the margins of the state. This responsibility is not conditional on good conduct or posited by the State only as a reward for law-abiding behaviour. My argument has been that it deserves our respect regardless of the circumstances. The duty of care expresses our recognition of a kind of ethical relationship between two persons that exists prior to law and is of the utmost and foundational importance to it. Suppose that in an illegal injecting room set up by a charitable organization somewhere in defiance of the law, a doctor or a nurse were negligently to inject a user, inducing an overdose. The personal duty of care is surely real and intimate in such a circumstance. It does not do any good to deny it or to deny the injured person long-term support in consequence of that denial. The Australian courts, presumably, would deny it.

On the High Court's view, the criminal law is the first creation of the State; a tort action would be an appeal for the assistance of some invention of the State by one who has otherwise felt free to disregard it. Yet, as McLachlin J argues in the Supreme Court of Canada: "Tort … does not require a plaintiff to have a certain moral character in order to bring an action before the court. The duty of care is owed to *all* persons who may reasonably be foreseen to be injured by the negligent conduct … This follows from the fact that the justice which tort law seeks to accomplish is justice between the parties to the particular action."[112] McLachlin J goes on to insist that because it derives from distinct normative foundations, the civil law does not outlaw wrongdoers, recalling in the process the old Latin term for an outlaw, *caput lupinum*, or "wolf's head."[113] Levinas, it will be recalled, remarks that "it is extremely important to know if society, as currently constituted, is the result of a limitation of the principle that man is a wolf for man, or if on the contrary it results from a limitation of the principle that man is *for* man."[114] *Gala v. Preston* establishes the proposition that a criminal is no longer entitled to the limitation imposed by the civil law and returns to the state of a wolf. But Levinas argues that our personal responsibility to others *is* our state of nature. It is personal, ineluctable, and itself the origin of a social legal system. It is a mistake to believe that law has invented this responsibility and finds itself at liberty to withhold such recognition at will. Law is an attempt to express this responsibility, on which the foundations of its legitimacy depend. The gravity of the approach adopted by *Gala v. Preston* becomes clear once we appreciate that by creating outlaws we are withdrawing not just an instrumental convenience bestowed by the State but an ethical principle that sustains it.

Ironically, the joint majority judgment in *Gala v. Preston* does not despise this principle. The judges dismissed the lure of public policy and sought instead to found the pertinent legal principles exclusively in the internal logic of a duty of care itself.[115] They did so because, in a celebrated series of cases over several years, the Australian courts had recognized the importance to be attached to the independent normative edifice of negligence principles. Under the intellectual leadership of Justice William Deane, the Court's defence of "proximity" insistently (though not always successfully) sought to define what it was about particular relationships that necessarily attracted legal responsibility – not just because the law says so but because our ethical instincts demand it. But in *Gala v. Preston* the Court concluded that "the requirement of proximity ... will include policy considerations."[116] These policy considerations, foremost among them the Court's protection of the primacy of the criminal law, then proved so determinative that "the parties were not," by judgment's end, "in a relationship of proximity to each other" after all.[117] Such a conclusion would seem to be a nonsense. It has received considerable well-directed criticism because in the process the word "proximity" – "a closeness to others giving rise to responsibility" – lost all meaning.[118]

Many critics have concluded, therefore, that proximity itself is surplus to reasoning.[119] But, on the contrary, the case demonstrates an insufficient respect for the value of the ethical relationship between the boys, which their proximity is meant to describe. The majority did not go far enough. First, rather than being a "conceptual determinant,"[120] proximity, that is to say the closeness between persons, is a fact: a relationship of vulnerability and response ability. The *event* of proximity, not the concept or "truth" of proximity,[121] is what determines its parameters. It is clear enough that this relationship actually existed between the driver in the front seat and the passenger asleep behind him. Second, rather than smuggling public policy in under the capacious folds of proximity, the Court could have decided that, except in the very limited circumstances recognized by the Canadian Supreme Court in *Hall v. Hebert,* it had no part to play at all. The effect of these two approaches, which are implicit in the majority judgment's own underlying reasoning, would have been to give added weight to the ethical birthright that alone makes sense of the law of torts.

APPLYING ASYMMETRIC RESPONSIBILITY: A CASE STUDY ON THE DUTY TO RESCUE

One strength of an ethical approach is that it explains and legitimates the *a*symmetry inherent in tortious obligation. The law of negligence is therefore worthy of our respect because it recognizes that we emerge, as responsible individuals, from this structure of asymmetry, rather than from a contractual realm of freedom and equivalence: we do not and never have existed "in and for oneself." "Before the neighbour I am summoned and do not just appear; from the first I am answering an assignation."[122] Moreover, it is neither the State nor contract that constitutes us but, rather, this unique and primary responsibility to an other. It is the foundation of our consciousness, our society – and our selves. "Already the stony core of my substance is dislodged. But the responsibility to which I am exposed ... does not apprehend me as an interchangeable thing, for here no one can be substituted for me ... It obliges me as someone unreplaceable and unique, someone chosen."[123] This responsibility is not merely social and expedient but personal and ethical. It is directed not towards the preservation of autonomy but instead towards the recognition of suffering. The combination of these two features provides us with a new way of conceiving of the justification of a system of private actions in tort law.

In this framework the personal nature of the relationship remains crucial, as it does in corrective-justice models. No system of social security could adequately express our personal and unique obligation to care for those around us. The symbolic and detailed meditation about responsibility that the law of negligence has developed is therefore of enormous and enduring importance. But if we focus on the "other," the way in which suffering is alleviated is not as important as our duty to ensure that it is. Insurance, then, appears in a somewhat different and more attractive light. From a self-centred perspective it might seem to be a way of protecting myself from the perils of a legal action. That is, naturally enough, how insurance companies persuade us to buy their products. It is my insurance against the liability I may incur. But from this alternative perspective, insurance is instead a way of protecting others from the perils of my carelessness. It is their insurance against the damage they may suffer through me: and it is my responsibility to provide it for them. Insurance, then, is an important way in which I protect the vulnerable in advance. This argument connects together personal responsibility and the alleviation of suffering, while recognizing the new conditions of a modern world in which the many prosthetics of technology – ever more powerful, ever more dangerous – have allowed us to inflict a great deal more suffering with a great deal less effort.

Above all, if we focus on suffering, the question of whether we have caused it by our behaviour or merely let it happen by our indifference assumes far less significance. At the moment, the law is committed to a model of responsibility that strongly distinguishes actions from omissions.[124] As Deane J noted: "It is an incident of human society that action or inaction by one person may have a direct or indirect effect on another. Unless there be more involved than mere cause and effect, however, the common law remains indifferent. In that regard, the common law has neither recognized fault in the conduct of the feasting Dives nor embraced the embarrassing moral perception that he who has failed to feed the man dying from hunger has truly killed him."[125] No doubt the distinction is difficult to categorically maintain. The law clearly distinguishes between "mere omissions" and an omission in the course of positive conduct. If one is driving a car it is not an omission just because one "fails to" apply the brakes. But the distinction draws our attention to the law's concern. For example, an omission that arises out of a pattern of previous conduct that creates a situation can be understood in terms of our consent to be involved in the particular behaviour in question. A town council is not liable for failing to supervise children's use of vacant government land as an impromptu trail bike track, but it is otherwise if they have intentionally developed the area and encouraged the community to make use of it.[126] In the latter case, their past voluntary action has created an expectation of future action. But an injurious omission that does not take place in the context of a prior commitment cannot be fitted within a legal framework that sees responsibility as fundamentally stemming from free choice.

Law's commitment to the autonomy of the self and to maximizing the sphere of its freedom demands nothing less. To be responsible for an omission is to be responsible for what one *hasn't done*. This principle has been the graveyard road of the "duty to rescue." If I come across a child drowning through no fault or action of my own, why on earth should I find myself foisted with a responsibility to him? "The law casts no duty upon a man to go to the aid of another who is in peril or distress, not caused by him. The call of common humanity may lead him to the rescue. This the law recognizes, for it gives the rescuer its protection when he answers that call. But it does not require that he do so."[127] As Deane J indicated, there must be a preexisting relationship of care before a mere omission will be culpable. An omission is liable only in relation to what Tony Honoré termed "distinct duties."[128] In this way, the notion of consent is preserved as an autonomous act that justifies the imposition of a responsibility. The general principle was stated by Windeyer J in *Hargrave v. Goldman.* "The trend of judicial development of the law of negligence has been, I think, to found a duty of care either in some task undertaken, or in the ownership, occupation, or use of land or chattels."[129] "There is no general duty to help a neighbour whose house is on fire,"[130] unless some prior undertaking or agreement has lead to an expectation of intervention.[131] The question in every case will be, what responsibilities of positive conduct were voluntarily assumed or undertaken by the defendant?[132] Conversely, if there has been no prior relationship and no agreement to take care can be inferred, an omission will not be culpable.[133]

But what if responsibility is not constituted by choice but by the call of the other? If it is the need of the other person coupled with the capacity of the defendant to respond that determines the ambit of the relationship, then the duty to rescue is no longer an anomaly or an exclusion; it is, on the contrary, the very paradigm for the duty of care.

The duty to rescue *is* the duty of care: they are examples of the same fundamental and soul-searching thing. The reason that we owe a duty of care on the roads, for example, is just the same as the reason that we owe a duty to rescue someone in trouble when only we can help. The real practical asymmetry of the relationship, the vulnerability of the one to the actions of the other, and not their purely theoretical equality or their purely hypothetical agreement, draws forth that duty in each case. The closer we are, conceptually speaking, to the paradigm case of that drowning baby or that house on fire, the stronger the call of the duty of care. That is exactly opposite to the view of most orthodox commentators on the duty of care. It seems to me that a failure to recognize the real ethical significance of that asymmetry[134] and to see the underlying truth about the nature of responsibility that the duty to rescue points us towards is the fatal and irreparable flaw of such a view, and I cannot imagine making it plausible to our instincts or our beliefs.

In many cases, as we will see in the next two chapters, this will parallel the reasoning to which the courts have been drawn. Indeed, in the 1980s and 1990s the High Court of Australia significantly moved away from the language of "assumption of responsibility" and towards a distinct emphasis on elements of the defendant's "control" (which is to say, their response-ability) and the plaintiff's "vulnerability" (which is to say, the call or gaze of the other).[135] The Court itself came to recognize that responsibility can be understood not in terms of the autonomous decision of the defendant alone but in terms of the situation in which they find themselves.

From an ethical starting point, the question of how the relationship began is no longer material to the question of whether my intervention was able to make the difference. The device of act/omission is replaced by the question of the importance and closeness of the actual relationship. Responsibility-as-autonomy decrees that I have no obligation to help a neighbour whose house is on fire because *I* have done nothing to establish the relationship. The situation is not "mine." But responsibility-as-ethics declares that proximity is the description of an event, not an intention; asymmetry is its nature and its justification, not its problem. This seems to me a very persuasive point. It is why Levinas argues so insistently that what matters is "proximity and not the truth about proximity."[136] The origin of responsibility is contact (a fact about the world) and not contract (a theory about it).[137] "We do not conceive of relations. We *are* in relation."[138] It is not choice but predicament that generates a responsibility.

A recent case decided by the New South Wales Court of Appeal provides, I think, a salutary example of the difference between these two models of duty. *Lowns v. Wood* involved a medical emergency.[139] An eleven-year-old boy named Patrick had an epileptic seizure. By the time his mother discovered him, his condition was serious. She sent her fourteen-year-old daughter, Joanna, to get Dr Lowns, whose practice was located nearby. But according to the evidence accepted by the court, Joanna could not persuade the doctor to come and render assistance.[140] As a result, the child suffered profound and irreparable brain damage. The question for the court was: did Dr Lowns have a duty of care in this situation? The majority held that he did but conceded that the main barrier to the action was the principle of nonliability for negligent omissions. Dr Lowns was not the family physician. He had never treated Patrick before. Kirby P held (and Cole JA agreed) that a relationship had been established "notwithstanding their lack of previous professional or personal association."[141] But the judge did so principally by reference to the *Medical Practitioners Act*, which imposed a statutory obligation on doctors to come to the aid of "persons ... in need of urgent attention."[142] In other words, Kirby P attempted to make the situation fit the norm of a preexisting consensual relationship constituting an expectation of positive conduct. While granting that Dr Lowns had not himself consented to a particular responsibility with this family, the judge instead held that the very nature of "the noble profession of medicine" as established in New South Wales had imposed that expectation upon him.[143] By becoming a doctor, Dr Lowns had voluntarily undertaken a general responsibility. In the words of Windeyer J, Dr Lowns was responsible because of the nature of the "task undertaken."[144]

It was on just this point that Mahoney JA dissented. He noted that the court was creating a new duty in this case, pointing out that the professional obligations created under the *Medical Practitioners Act* did not necessarily import obligations in tort. There is no duty of care owed by a doctor to a person, argued Justice Mahoney, "if that person is one to whom the doctor has not and never has been in a professional relationship of doctor and patient."[145] Both sides, therefore, agreed that the issue was one of an omission in the absence of any prior relationship. They disagreed as to whether some prior assumption of responsibility could nevertheless be inferred.

Starting from the idea of autonomy, the doctor's lack of agreement to act is decisive. That is why Kirby P and Cole JA attempted to construct an implicit "contract to rescue" from the nature of the profession and the terms of the *Medical Practitioners Act*. Starting from the idea of ethics, the lack of prior contact is hardly relevant. Contact now, at this very moment, *is* responsibility.[146] A duty to rescue, which is to say, a duty of care relating to positive conduct, arises out of the immediacy of a crisis into which both parties – child and doctor alike – are thrown without their consent. What matters is the *fact* of proximity that Joanna, by asking for his help, had established; the extent of the emergency; and the doctor's response ability, which was of course significant. Understood in this way, the majority's reasoning fails not because the duty is too wide but because it is too narrow. Again, my argument is that the court has not followed its logic far enough. Rather than single doctors out as the subject of special obligations, the court would have done better to think of responsibility as an event that might single any one of us out at some moment. Someday, we might all be called on to render hospitality.

The difficulty with this case is that the notion of a duty to rescue was treated by both the majority and the minority as entirely irreconcilable with standard negligence principles. Both sides sought to shoehorn the doctor's predicament into established principles assuming equality and requiring consent to the burdens of responsibility. But Levinas points us to an alternative theory in which the duty to rescue is central to the duty of care by which we all find ourselves from time to time burdened. Responsibility is always a surprise, never entirely chosen, and never – by its very nature – a symmetrical exchange. That Dr Lowns did not want this responsibility, did not choose it or expect it, was perhaps his bad luck. But that is the way of responsibility. Its always singular demands often arrive unexpectedly; arriving unexpectedly or with unexpected dimensions or aspects, they cannot therefore be completely consented to; and not being consented to, they may sometimes prove burdensome. Responsibility, in short, is never entirely predictable and never entirely convenient. I venture to say that we would not feel or be truly responsible if it was. Yes, responsibility is a kind of intrusion on our solipsism: surely that's the whole point. And the duty to rescue is not alone in possessing these features; it shares them will all aspects of the duty to care, though in stark and clarified form.

Justice Mahoney insisted that "moral obligations are not legal obligations."[147] But of course some are. Law inevitably bears the trace or scar[148] of ethics. The question is, why or why not? In confronting this question, Justice Mahoney indicates the difficulty of establishing the parameters of a duty to rescue. These difficulties would, no doubt, be even greater if one were to concede that the duty arose not out of the profession of medicine or out of the requirements of legislation but out of the nature of humanity. What if the doctor were not experienced in the particular specialty involved? What if he or she were too busy with their own practice? What if they judged that they were not needed? What if the rescue would have placed their own lives at risk?[149]

These are important matters of limitation, but the law is capable of accomodating them. In the first place, the duty of care arises from one's response ability. Though the duty may fall to any one of us, its extent will depend on our capacity.[150] Responsibility encumbers me commensurate only with my ability and my resources.[151] Perhaps I can do no more than lend someone a mobile phone or call an ambulance. Perhaps if someone is drowning, I can do no more than raise the alarm. But if I can do more, I must. There is no symmetry in responsibility. On the contrary, responsibility derives from the asymmetrical nature of the relationship – power and capacity, on the one hand, and vulnerability or dependence, on the other. Colin Davis remarks that "the decoupling of responsibility from reciprocity has been described as the decisive act that distinguishes Levinas' ethical theory from all others."[152] So the special situation of a doctor arises not from statute but from the fact that he or she can make a difference. From those who have more to give, more will be asked.

Second, the establishment of an obligation of responsibility does not yet determine whether the duty has been breached. We must still determine the nature of a reasonable response in all the circumstances. But this will in turn depend on our own expertise and the other demands upon us. This is what Levinas means when he indicates that justice still requires "comparison, coexistence, assembling, order."[153] We must balance our responsibility to the other against our responsibility to the third party who is also a neighbour.[154] And, of course, our own security is not irrelevant. "The ego can, in the name of this unlimited responsibility, be called upon to concern itself also with itself."[155] Undoubtedly, these are difficult questions to balance. Yet this is not surprising. In its stuttering way, the law has always determined the unpredictable and complex factual questions of reasonableness by reference to just such circumstantial specifics.

5

Proximity, *Proximité*

Proximity, Proximité, there's nothing like Proximity,
It's broken every human law, it breaks the law of gravity.
Its powers of levitation would make a fakir stare,
And when you reach the scene of tort – Proximity's not there!
You may seek it in the basement, you may look up in the air –
But I tell you once and once again, Proximity's not there!

With apologies to T.S. Eliot.[1]

PROXIMITY AS AN APPROACH

Two things should guide our reading of the fiction of Jorge Luis Borges.[2] First, his style. Borges is alcoholic. The Arabic *al-kuhl*, first of all, refers to a process of distillation. It is Borges' relentless purification towards an essence that produces such a giddy effect upon his readership. In other words, he writes in parables that intoxicate. Second, his themes. Borges' stories concern the gulf between appearance and reality; a gulf that is infinitesimal in the twin sense of being both indescribably small and impossibly distant. His stories are full of masks and mazes and mirrors,[3] of narratives about narratives and tales retold.[4] We brush against his worlds, but we cannot ever completely come to terms with them. As is the nature of good writing, the structure is the message: it conveys something of the absolute unknowability of other people, even of our ourselves,[5] and at the same time our sense of a connection to them that cannot be ignored. The mystery that enshrouds others – their confoundedness – deserves to be cherished for its own sake. In this, Borges illustrates Levinas' argument. Responsibility comes from a closeness to something that cannot be reduced to knowledge and that, on the contrary, describes a gulf to be preserved. In Borges we are faced with differences from our own worlds that are sometimes imperceptible and sometimes seem almost complete. But he never explains away that difference so as to reduce it to familiarity. On the contrary, he enriches it, transforming it into a value for us. Difference is not reduced to sameness but rather transformed into non-indifference.

Borges' "The Approach to Al-Mu'tasim" is exemplary in both respects.[6] It concerns a novel whose merest outline is described by an author who claims to have read only the second edition (the first and "greatly superior" having supposedly been lost). In that spirit, one might further distill the plot thus: Our hero (or perhaps I should say the hero of our narrator of our author) finds himself involved in a bloody riot. Someone dies and he feels himself responsible. Now on the run and after a series of adventures, he ultimately lands "among people of the vilest sort." But there he experiences an epiphany: he detects "a moment of tenderness, of exaltation, of silence, in one of the abominable men." He surmises that he has encountered some pale reflection of an originary goodness whose well-spring he begins to seek out. "Thus we begin to see the book's general scheme: The insatiable search for a soul by means of the delicate glimmerings or reflections this soul has left in others – at first, the faint trace of a smile or a word; toward the last, the varied and growing splendours of intelligence, imagination, and goodness."[7] The story ends just as the hero is at last about to meet this Al-Mu'tasim, for whom he has been searching all these years. We are left, naturally enough, with a mystery. The novel, suggests Borges' anonymous glossator, "may signal the identity of the seeker and the sought. [It] may also signal that the sought has already influenced the seeker."[8] Or perhaps, he finally concludes, Al-Mu'tasim is the same Hindu whose possible murder, all those years ago, precipitated our hero's flight.

We do not know the name of the main character. But we do know his occupation. Rather like the person to whom Christ explained the parable of the Good Samaritan, perhaps even like Kafka's "man from the country,"[9] he is a student of law. From these disparate, though revealing, characters and from my own, not unusual, experiences as a teacher, I suggest that the law student is a very particular character type: literal, practical, perhaps even a "blasphemous … unbeliever," but at the same time sincerely idealistic. There is no paradox in this. Quite often it seems to me that the law student is on a quest for justice, but it must be a justice capable of being rendered in the everyday, governed by discernible forces, and distilled into the language of rules. The law student is not interested in abstraction or mysticism: she wants to give the world its code for living. She typically believes in rules and the power of rules and wants to learn them. Too often it is our duty as law teachers to disabuse our students of their over-confident homologies: to show them the manipulative power of rules and the inevitable indeterminacy of their operation. In a way, the first order of business in a law school is a crash course in disillusionment. Too rarely do we make any effort to instill in our students an alternative prescription or indeed to suggest any way other than by rules that justice might effect the law. Legal education suffers in this respect from a fatal flaw: it is vigorously critical of legal forms and analyses, but it frequently lacks any theoretical framework that would help our students work towards a better system or a better way of explaining it. In short, pedagogy emphasizes law "as it is," to the detriment of the broader or normative concerns that actually attracted many of our students to the discipline in the first place.

We form in our students an abscess that we do not dare to treat. In all this, then, the law student is a fascinating character not just for her practicality and her optimism but because she might appear to us as already marked out for disappointment. For their part, many law students already know their destiny: they have another model before them, and it gathers force and corporeality as their optimism fades. The contrast is made clear for us in Borges' story, for the questing student devotes his life to an endless challenge, while the narrator is nothing but a "Bombay attorney." From law student to lawyer is a foreshadowed corruption. The fatal flaw of legal education drives our students towards a destiny they (and we) may often dread but from which they have been given no means of extracting themselves. The law student is not born a cynic, but she graduates.

Borges' student solves the problem of ethics by giving up the study of law altogether and embarking instead on a quest. Those of my readers who have followed the argument so far will detect here a strong resonance between this quest and that described by Levinas. The soul is the other in us; we have no direct access to it but perceive it only through mirrors and reflections. It is the product of an endless search. To approach Al Mu'tasim, the distilled source of goodness that we perceive only in its reflection around us, is precisely to approach ourselves and to do so by living in a perpetual state of exile from our power and autonomy.[10] Borges is saying that the soul *is* this otherness in us, this restlessness. The point is made still more strongly when Borges remarks that the name Al Mu'tasim might be translated as "He who goes in quest of aid."[11] So the soul is both the capacity to help and the capacity to seek. It is a relentless pilgrimage that is never satisfied; it gives itself to the giver.

But Borges is also saying that all our relations with others are inevitably experienced indirectly and imperfectly. Another person – another story – is not to be consumed like food or information. It cannot be absorbed and converted to our own purposes, which Levinas termed mere "enjoyment."[12] As Borges tells the story, we never meet Al Mu'tasim; just as, in terms of its form, we have no access to the first edition of the novel in question (or for that matter to the second edition). What you are reading now is a summary of a summary of a story. We experience only the trace of these things. The title's use of the phrase "approach to" is significant. We approach *to* others, but we never reach them. Our access to others is asymptotic. The infinitesimal gulf that divides us – the indigestible otherness that sticks in our gullet – is nothing other than our soul. The brilliance of Borges lies not just in his ability to express these ideas, but in the development of a form that mirrors them.

The idea of approaching another without appropriating or defining them was of critical importance to Levinas. He referred to it variously as *l'approche* and, of course, as *la proximité*,[13] and he speaks of "the neighbour" as *le prochain*, one who is nearby, or proximate. "Perhaps because of current moral maxims in which the word *neighbour* occurs, we have ceased to be surprised by all that is involved in proximity and approach."[14] Proximity for Levinas must be understood in terms that I have previously sought to explain by reference to a caress, which does not grasp or seize. "It searches, it forages," but it does not attempt to control or pin down.[15] It is a contact, an experience of the senses, that does not take hold of either person or thing.[16] Levinas' work is marked by his insistence on proximity as something nonconceptual and nonintentional and by his connecting the neighbour, *le prochain*, with this kind of approach, *l'approche*.[17]

Proximity in Levinasian ethics and in negligence law are the indispensable terms of art of their respective genres. The word is freighted with a new set of implications in the work of Levinas, beginning with "La Proximité" in 1971 and further amplified in *Autrefois qu'être* in 1978, translated as *Otherwise than Being* in 1981. Likewise, in the Australian context that will form the detailed subject of the case study that comprises this chapter and the next, proximity is freighted with a new set of legal implications in *Caltex Oil (Australia) Pty. Ltd. v. The Dredge "Willemstad"*[18] in 1976 and further amplified in *Jaensch v. Coffey* in 1984.[19] Both disciplines seek through this word to capture a new ethics of relationship and responsibility that is not reducible to a code. Joseph Libertson's monumental book on the philosophy of proximity[20] explains it as a recognition of our relationship with others that does not reduce them to a term in our equation, which is sensitive to vulnerability, and which acknowledges our own dependence on others.[21] Libertson argues that neither communion with others (a social origin for responsibility, such as we might find in distributive justice) nor our separation from others (an individualistic origin for responsibility, such as we might find in corrective justice) best defines or delineates our true relationship with others. As we have already seen, the defence of proximity involves a critique of these alternative modes of understanding responsibility.

To approach *to* someone, as we have already seen in Borges, is thus not to re-present them, but, on the contrary, to preserve something of their unique and nonrepresentable alterity. On the one hand, proximity stands for this intimate but unassailable distance and the ethical obligations it places upon us: "a rapport produced by a lack of relation."[22] On the other hand, relationships of proximity constitute *us*: they do not "collide with freedom, but invest it."[23] The approach of another awakens us from the deep sleep of introspection: it gives us an intensity and a feeling of existence, and, by the very fact of becoming aware that we are not alone and find ourselves implicated in this non-indifference, we are aroused to consciousness.[24]

This is what Levinas means by proximity: a presence nearby that excites the skin – like a blush. It creates an obligation of non-indifference but not of incorporation. By "calling us in question" – by singling us out as responsible for others – it makes us acutely aware of ourselves. At the same time, since Levinas believes not that proximity is a social relationship but that it is a sensation, an experience, he does not believe that we are all equally proximate in the eyes of man. This important point, which is not always appreciated, is already apparent from the very first page of *Otherwise than Being*, dedicated, after all, "to the memory of *those who were closest* among the six million assassinated by the National Socialists,"[25] and for whom Levinas, it is abundantly clear, felt a unique and unsubstitutable responsibility. This psychological reality was the node of his life.[26] It is true that Levinas speaks of responsibility in virtually unbounded terms and as something beyond our choice and imposed upon us. Responsibility is "unexceptionable ... preceding every free consent, every pact, every contract."[27] Since it is not our ego that chooses it, we may even feel hostage to it and persecuted by it.[28] Neither, as we have seen in previous chapters, is responsibility relative to consent or intent. Rather, it is relative to a circumstance of vulnerability that may not be of our own making. In triumphal vein he declares that we are "chosen without assuming the choice!"[29]

Yet it is equally true that this circumstantial and terrifying responsibility arises from the particularity of a relationship. He speaks of the "responsibility *for* my neighbour ... *for* the stranger or sojourner."[30] Not then, a responsibility to the whole world but to those whom we experience as a face or a touch. The very sensate and violent metaphors that Levinas uses to convey the nature of our responsibility to others – face-to-face, exposure, nakedness, and bleeding wounds – clarifies the point that responsibility comes from our proximity to them.[31]

Proximity, unlike Christian love or Marxist brotherhood, is a relative closeness, not a universal kinship. Levinas does not imagine that we are all neighbours all the time. Isn't that what lies behind the word "neighbour" itself, a word at once distinctly Levinasian and decisively legal? It marks the boundary within which we find ourselves responsible. Or, to put it perhaps more precisely, proximity is in fact the origin of responsibility: it is the experience that leads us to catch sight of it. That is its role in ethics and in law. Proximity does not limit responsibility: it augurs and inaugurates it. It inspires it.

The law of negligence for its part has struggled to answer the question of boundaries: when and to whom are we responsible? This is what has frequently been termed "the duty question." And here the complex history and discourse of the Australian common law provides us with a case study of quite unparalleled richness. I turn to the specifics of this case study now, before ultimately expanding the argument once again in the last chapter. The argument will be, particularly to those unfamiliar with the basic outlines of the law of negligence, unavoidably detailed and sometimes technical. Proximity provided the principal way in which the High Court of Australia, particularly during the 1980s and 1990s, sought to develop a new answer and a radical new language concerning the duty question. I will argue in this chapter that the Court in so doing gestures towards the ethical framework that Levinas makes explicit. Understood in this way, proximity evokes for us the ethical justification of law. As opposed to some of the Court's own language, however, in which proximity is understood as a *limit* on responsibility, I will argue that proximity is what explains and justifies responsibility. It also indicates the direction that the Court ought to go in determining its nature and boundaries. What I want finally to show is that the Court's work in this area indeed came close to providing an interpretation of proximity akin to that of Levinas.

Unfortunately my case study is the history of a lost opportunity. Proximity was a celebrated battleground in the Australian courts for fifteen years, but finally it was as good as abandoned by their Honours. Because the court failed to understand the term as a normative justification and because, instead, its value was assessed in terms of whether it could be treated as a determinate "rule," it was eventually dismissed as being insufficiently legally precise. The result has been, over the past few years, a turning away from proximity in two ways: substantively, by confining responsibility more closely to situations of consent and choice; and methodologically, by insisting on the need for legal judgment to provide rules capable of an entirely certain future application. Both in Levinas and in the law, these two dimensions of the proximity debate are connected. Proximity stands for both an expansion of the ambit of responsibility and an expansion in our understanding of the nature of judgment. If the court had understood proximity in Levinasian terms – as a starting point and justification for our duties to others, on the one hand, and as an ethical or self-reflective moment that *confronts* our rules on the other – then the unique discursive contribution of proximity to the duty of care and to the common law might have been better appreciated. Proximity is not just a question of semantics. It tells the story of a battle about why and how much we care for our neighbours, the others.

PROXIMITY AND POLICY

Proximity is distinct from either of the two limits upon responsibility to which the law of negligence has typically made reference in order to determine those persons to whom we owe a duty of care, namely policy considerations and reasonable foreseeability. Levinas would be rightly critical of these concepts, in that they remove our attention from care of the other, and direct our attention instead to the twin modes of totality. Let us look at policy and foreseeability in turn, and see how proximity differs from them.

The concept of policy considerations limits responsibility by reference to *we*, the sociopathic grammar. It imports the social outcome of legal judgments as a relevant constraining factor. For Levinas, as we have seen, this emphasis undermines the intrinsic constitutive function that responsibility serves in *relation* to society. It is no secondary grammar.

The first point to make about the relationship of proximity and policy is that they are concerned with quite distinct relationships. Proximity orients responsibility by reference to *you*; policy by reference to *us*, in terms of society's interests as a whole. There are two parties to the former equation; the third party (indeed lots and lots of them) enters in the latter.[32] As elementary – meaning both facile and fundamental – as this distinction might seem, the court has not always been sensitive to it. The conflation dates even from Deane J's first discussion of proximity in *Jaensch v. Coffey*. In attempting to distinguish proximity from reasonable foreseeability, Deane J proceeded immediately to conflate it with policy. "The essential function of such requirements or limitations is to confine the existence of a duty to take reasonable care to avoid reasonably foreseeable injury to the circumstances or classes of case in which it is the policy of the law to admit it. Such overriding requirements or limitations shape the frontiers of the common law of negligence."[33] Perilously, then, Deane J presents proximity as a policy or limitation upon a naturalized class of "reasonably foreseeable injuries." Once that approach is taken, there is no limit to the kind of policies that might be incorporated under the guise of proximity. Proximity becomes simply a limiting device and an aspect of social policy. This is an unpardonable error. Proximity, properly understood, is not a limit on a relationship that otherwise exists. It is, on the contrary, the very element that creates the relationship in the first place. In this sense, proximity represents the core element of negligence that recognizes a connection between the parties and not simply a way of carrying out "the policy of the law." And as we have seen, proximity involves a one-to-one relationship, while policy imports a one-to-many relationship. The approach to be taken in their analysis is therefore – and ought to remain – quite distinct.

Indeed the fire of criticism that engulfed the High Court's use of proximity in the early 1990s was inflamed by the Court's own carelessness in just this regard. So enamoured did the High Court become of the idea of proximity as the "touchstone for determining the existence and content of any common law duty of care"[34] that policy itself became entirely subsumed within it. As Levinas shows us, this is a profound mistake that undermines the unique and personal (world-making), rather than the social relationship (world-maintaining), that proximity describes. In *Gala v. Preston*, as I remarked in the previous chapter, the court unconvincingly combines the two. The majority goes so far as to describe proximity as "includ[ing] policy considerations."[35]

The danger is, as Brennan J and others were quick to point out, that proximity used in this way provides no basis of reasoning capable of guiding future courts and future citizens. The word becomes simply the description attached to the outcome of the court's deliberations. "Better to identify the consideration that negates the duty of care than simply to assert an absence of proximity."[36]

Policy considerations are by their very nature *extra*-legal values that serve to exclude or control a personal relationship between the parties otherwise established. As exceptions, they must be explained and justified specifically and not concealed under general conclusions. But this is not to say that proximity qua proximity is similarly contentless. So it was that in *Pyrenees*[37], Kirby J, having dramatically declared that "it is tolerably clear that proximity's reign ... has come to an end,"[38] proceeded immediately to advocate a three-fold test[39] including, as separate matters, reasonable foreseeability, policy issues, *and* proximity. Far from being extra-legal or social, proximity is the foundational principle of closeness to whose fate responsibility must in some form be tied. This does not solve the problem of determination – of how close is close enough. In this chapter I will endeavour to show that the problem is inevitable and intractable and that Levinas' idea of proximity does allow us to focus on the right relationships and in the right ways. The disarticulation of proximity and policy is the first step towards such a rehabilitation.

The second point to make about the relationship of proximity and policy is that, because of its constitutive role, the responsibility that proximity arouses ought not to be too hastily undermined by policy considerations. We have already seen this argument in the discussion of the relationship of illegality to liability in tort. A similar argument is relevant to other areas in which proximate relationships have been nevertheless ignored by the courts. One such area concerns the immunity of legal advocates (mainly barristers) from actions in negligence.[40] The immunity is a dramatic derogation from the common law duty of care. Although it has long been held inapplicable in Canada[41] and although it was recently overturned in the House of Lords,[42] the principle continues in good standing in Australia. The leading case of *Giannarelli v. Wraith*, only recently affirmed as good law, concerned a conviction for perjury that had relied upon evidence given before a royal commission that had previously investigated the Painters' and Dockers' Union.[43] The evidence was inadmissible, but the defendants' counsel failed to object at trial, and they were convicted. When they were finally released, they sued their barristers for negligence. The High

Court held that "considerations of public policy" rendered the lawyers immune from suit.

There is, as Levinas says, an "an ethical limit to this ethically necessary political existence."[44] The relationship between a lawyer and his or her client is perhaps archetypical of proximity, but the strength of Levinas' approach is to emphasize, on the one hand, how common such relationships are and, on the other, how much we owe to them for everything we take for granted: communication, the State, justice – "even the little there is, even the simple 'after you, sir.'"[45] As Levinas warns, the State "issued from" the neighbour and is always "on the verge of integrating him into a we, which congeals both me and the neighbour."[46] Responsibility "is not the limit case of solidarity, but the condition for all solidarity."[47] This is why we must be most wary of sacrificing law's foundations on the altar of its institutions and administration.

It is not just that *Giannarelli v. Wraith* appears to secure a benefit for legal counsel to which other professionals, faced with equally difficult conflicts and decisions every day of their lives, are not entitled.[48] It is rather that the Court would appear to have decided that the trusting relationship expected in social life, does not always extend to the justice system itself. To reach this conclusion, the High Court treated a duty of care as an outcome of the administration of justice but decided that broader policies ought to be given precedence. In this they have failed to take the philosophy of the neighbour seriously enough. Proximity and the duty of care are not administrative conveniences or even just useful social policies. They are foundational to the possibility of justice, which the courts no doubt "administer" but did not invent. To refuse to recognize their application within the "system of justice" itself is to profoundly undermine that system under the guise of protecting it. Proximity is not the child of our legal structures but their parent. As community outrage over the High Court's affirmation of barristers' immunity in *D'Orta-Ekenaike* continues to grow, we see a foolhardy spectacle: the Court sacrificing its ethics – and therefore its respect – in order to preserve its politics.

PROXIMITY AND FORESEEABILITY

The legal doctrine of "reasonable foreseeability," on the other hand, limits responsibility by reference to *I*, the psychopathic grammar. It asks the question, what persons could I foresee as being affected by my actions. In the classic words of Lord Atkin, the focus in establishing whether I have breached my duty of care to another person is on whether I "ought reasonably to have them in contemplation as being so affected."[49] But in this section I want to argue that responsibility is not about what I might foresee at all. Culpability might be – that is the question of fault, which is to say, whether the responsible person would and ought to have behaved differently in all the circumstances. This is what, in negligence law, is called "the breach issue." Did the person live up to our reasonable expectations of their responsibility? Are we, in short, to blame them for their actions? In this analysis, what the defendant could foresee as the outcome of their behaviour is entirely relevant. But whether they had such a responsibility is a prior question, governed not by concept but by experience. For Levinas, responsibility is determined by a relational contiguity and not our perception of it. This is the consequence of his insistence on responsibility not as a choice but as a predicament: I do not *take* responsibility; I am encumbered by it.[50]

The emphasis on reasonable foreseeability derives from an insistence on individualism and theories of autonomy. It is just this enshrinement of free human agency[51] that Levinas insists responsibility is most definitely not about. Stephen Perry, in a recent and very helpful review of the literature, argues that "the key moral concept that underpins ... responsibility is, as Holmes suggested, avoidability."[52] From this he concludes that reasonable foreseeability is central to the notion of responsibility, since "one cannot avoid what one cannot foresee."[53] This approach conflates the fundamental distinction between duty and breach issues. Breach determines whether we have behaved reasonably, and it makes perfect sense to think about what could be foreseen and what could be avoided by the reasonable person. But as to the question *to whom* we are responsible, it is not our choice or our judgment that is yet in issue.

The distinction is perhaps slight and made still slighter by the very broad interpretation that foreseeability has received in the common law. The law has tended to hold legally foreseeable a whole range of events that are, in practice, probably not. Given enough time and imagination, most anything is foresee-*able*.[54] Theoretically, however, the distinction is important because our neighbours are not defined by our perceptions of them. And in recent cases the question has become of considerable significance, because the courts, in determining the ambit of duty, are fundamentally making judgments about the relative recognition to be given to the defendant's autonomy, on the one hand, and the plaintiff's vulnerability, on the other.[55] As between the two, Levinas argues that responsibility is a function of the latter, not the former.

Indeed, the essential distinction between foreseeability and responsibility emerges even in the celebrated and much-parsed passage of *Donoghue v. Stevenson*. Lord Atkin there asks, "Who is my neighbour?" He then remarks that "You must take reasonable care to avoid acts or omissions which you can reasonably foresee would be likely to injure your neighbour." This is, in fact, the only point in the whole judgment at which Lord Atkin expressly refers to reasonable foreseeability. If it is intended as a definition of neighbourhood, it is transparently and woefully circular. This is precisely Justice Deane's analysis of the text in *Jaensch v. Coffey*.[56] The only feasible explanation is that in this sentence Lord Atkin is foreshadowing the circumstances in which a duty of care will be breached, and not what gives rise to the duty at all.[57] As a matter of semantic interpretation, the point is unarguable. Not having yet answered it, Lord Atkin is forced immediately to repeat the question, "Who, then, in law is my neighbour?" – that is, who are the class of persons for whom I must take reasonable care? He then answers as follows: "The answer seems to be – persons who are so closely and directly affected by my act that I ought reasonably to have them in contemplation as being so affected when I am directing my mind to the acts or omissions which are called in question."[58]

Again it is evident that the second half of the sentence is a consequential and not a limiting clause. Our neighbours are those who are "closely and directly affected" by us "*so ... that*" we ought reasonably to bear them in mind as we go about our business. The clause once more foreshadows the issue of breach, rather than further defining the criteria of duty. Only later does Lord Atkin attempt to explain what might constitute "closely and directly." He does so by reference to proximity. "I think that this sufficiently states the truth if proximity be not confined to mere physical proximity, but be used, as I think it was intended, to extend to such close and direct relations that the act complained of directly affects a person whom the person alleged to be bound to take care would know would be directly affected by his careless act."[59] Here at last Lord Atkin would appear to link proximity to some species of knowledge. But at the same time, it must be conceded that it is difficult to make even grammatical sense of the sentence. It is testament to the confusion that the whole idea of neighbourhood has engendered that in this, its very baptismal font, Lord Atkin, so often the stylist of the House, has recourse once more to mere circularity:

proximity extends to such close and direct relations as are suitably direct. To this he adds the proviso that the responsibility arises only if the defendant "would know" of the person so affected. Perhaps this might fairly be construed as a requirement of personal knowledge. If this be the charter of reasonable foreseeability, it is a fairly attenuated one, and it makes its delayed appearance as the supplement of proximity and not, as most scholars would have it, vice versa.

Neither does an emphasis on consciousness or knowledge solve the problem of delineation. Even within this final formulation of Lord Atkin's, our responsibility to others is clearly governed not by what we actually know or foresee but, rather, by what we ought to know.[60] Since this is determined ultimately by the court, this is simply another way of begging the question. In a society in which law helps to constitute patterns of behaviour, it is surely reasonable for us to foresee all those to whom we owe a duty, and it is against this rock that Lord Atkin continually stumbles. It is a rock that, in a later critique of the concept of proximity, Robert Goff LJ ignores. In a much-cited critique, he argues that "once proximity is no longer treated as expressing a relationship founded simply on foreseeability of damage, it ceases to have an ascertainable meaning."[61] But since the test is not "simply" foreseeability but, rather, "reasonable" foreseeability, it contains, as it must, the same element of subjective judgment as that of proximity, the same inescapable moment of indeterminacy.

For this reason, if reasonable foreseeability suddenly became the exclusive requirement of duty, it would prove every bit as troublesome as the other tests and practices that have risen to supplement it. Ironically, because the courts have invested other concepts, in particular proximity, with the element of discretion and judgment, reasonable foreseeability has not had to do much work. The difficulty arises from the very idea of attempting to determine abstractly to whom we are responsible, rather than in any linguistic formulation whatsoever. The use of the word "reasonable" at once smuggles in the very exercise of judgment it purports to objectify.

In practice, the notion of reasonable foreseeability, particularly "at the duty stage," has barely limited the idea of responsibility at all. It is this reason, and not its inherent clarity, that accounts for its supposed legal viability. The concept has been rendered certain simply by being rendered anodyne. Dixon CJ remarked that for something to be foreseeable was a long way short of being likely. "The words 'reasonable foreseeable' seem to be much more against the contention you are making than words such as 'reasonable' and 'probably' which introduce likelihood; foreseeability does not include any idea of likelihood at all. I cannot understand why any event which does happen is not foreseeable by a person of sufficient imagination and intelligence."[62]

It is said that the common law imposes a duty only upon those persons who we can foresee will be affected by our actions. But a closer examination reveals that this is very rarely a relevant consideration. On the one hand, one might argue that in cases of "ordinary physical injury or damage caused by the direct impact of a positive act" the test of reasonable foreseeability is "commonly an adequate indication" of the existence of such a relationship.[63] This is only because the responsibility owed, for example, by a driver to his passengers or other road users is self-evident, and not because it is fundamentally a question of what is foreseeable. On the other hand, the very expansiveness of the legal definition of "foreseeability," as we have seen, has meant that the courts have had to find other ways of delimiting when and whether a duty of care is owed. To give but one significant example, the proprietors of a business can certainly foresee and may even desire that their competitive actions will harm a rival: but that hardly imposes upon them a duty of care not to do so. As Deane J notes, "unless there be some particular relationship, personal or proprietary right or other added element, the common law imposes no liability."[64] Either way, in the vast run of cases, reasonable foreseeability will prove surplus to the reasoning as to whether a duty of care was owed. Perhaps nothing better demonstrates the actual irrelevance of the concept of foreseeability to our understanding of responsibility than the interpretative direction the courts have taken. Because other linguistic formulations – most notably that of proximity and most influentially in the Australian context – have been called on to do the inescapable work of judgment, foreseeability has been shorn of both content and contention.

Justice Deane concludes that "Lord Atkin's notions of reasonable foreseeability and proximity were, however, distinct."[65] I would go further. Reasonable foreseeability is best understood as a test of breach and not a test of duty at all. The judgment of duty was expressed in *Donoghue* in terms of neighbourhood, closeness, directness, and proximity. And as Levinas explains, this proximity cannot be placed within the boundaries of a formula. "Proximity is not an intentionality,"[66] which is to say, it is not a question of choice or prior knowledge. It is a question rather of contact and experience. Where there has been an actual contact – "this face and this skin"[67] – the reality of proximity

will not be in issue with or without the concept of reasonable foreseeability. Where there has not – if, for example, the harm to the plaintiff
was only economic or psychological – then it is commonplace that the
so-called test of reasonable foreseeability does not provide a satisfactory answer. As an index of responsibility, it turns out to be a sprinkler
system that cuts out the moment the fire gets hot.[68]

Instead, we need to focus on the nature of the relationship between
the parties, the power and the passivity of their dynamic, and not the
knowledge that one "reasonably" "ought to" possess of the other. The
question will be resolved only by a greater concentration on the actual
and lived connection between the two parties, and not by a greater
abstraction. The inability of neighbourhood to be understood at the
level of rules and the necessary particularity of its analysis is an insis-
tent aspect of Levinas' explanation of proximity. His approach has
continually been borne out by the struggle of the courts.

So far I have argued, somewhat against the tide of current judicial
opinion, that proximity, or some like word importing judgment, particularity, and connection, is in fact the necessary determinant of the
"duty issue." Reasonable foreseeability for its part is, by and large, a
red herring, unnecessary for the most part and inadequate for the rest.
Very little would be lost by removing the whole idea to the question
of breach. There are, however, a few cases in which such an approach
might be thought to make a difference. *Palsgraf v. Long Island RR Co*
is the *locus classicus*.[69] Mrs Palsgraf was waiting on a train platform
when a man ran to catch a train as it left the station. Two guards,
trying to help, dislodged a parcel he was carrying. Unbeknownst to
them, it contained fireworks, the explosion of which dislodged "some
scales at the other end of the platform, many feet away."[70] They hit
and injured Mrs Palsgraf. Chief Justice Cardozo's remarkable judgment
argues that while the guards may have committed a wrong, they cannot
be responsible for what happened to the plaintiff "standing far away."
"Negligence, like risk, is thus a term of relation. Negligence in the
abstract, apart from things related, is surely not a tort."[71] The question
for Cardozo, therefore, was not whether the guards were careless (perhaps they were) or whether this carelessly caused the injury (no doubt
it did) but, rather, whether there was any relationship of duty between
the defendant and the plaintiff.

The case is typically understood as resting on the necessity of
"reasonable foreseeability" in founding a relationship between the parties. Much in this judgment supports such an approach. It is "the eye

of ordinary vigilance" – that is, the defendant's eye – that determines the extent of his responsibility. Put at its strongest, Cardozo CJ argues, "the risk reasonably to be perceived defines the duty to be obeyed, and risk imports relation; it is risk to another or to others within the range of apprehension."[72] Fundamentally, then, Cardozo CJ concludes that the defendants could not have expected to have caused any harm to Mrs Palsgraf by their actions and were therefore not responsible to her. But there are difficulties with the analysis here on which I wish to elaborate, in order to demonstrate that the distinct test of reasonable foreseeability is neither a solution to any duty questions nor even a necessary component of them.

If the question is simply whether Mrs Palsgraf was "within the range of reasonable apprehension" as a person to whom the defendant owed a duty, the answer is surely not so straightforward. Under basic negligence principles, one does not need to foresee the plaintiff specifically or yet the precise (and no doubt wildly improbable) manner in which harm befell her.[73] Everything will depend therefore on what "class of persons" Mrs Palsgraf is said to belong to, and, again, it is inherent within the legal process that no formulation can determine in advance how wide or narrowly the class is drawn. Here is the inescapable moment of judgment and discretion described elsewhere by Professor Stone as a "category of illusory reference,"[74] by Professor Derrida as "the ordeal of the undecidable,"[75] and by Justice Windeyer as a "comfortable latitudinarian doctrine" that "leaves the criterion for classification of kinds ... undefined."[76] Surely it was foreseeable that the guards owed a responsibility to all persons on the platform of their train station? Surely they ought to have foreseen that such a person might have been "directly affected" such that "I ought reasonably to have them in contemplation as being so affected?" Instead, Cardozo CJ chooses to describe the plaintiff not just as a customer or as a passenger but as one "standing far away." This is a choice of characterization that is not of course determined by the test of reasonable foreseeability at all. It reflects instead a prior judgment that the two were not, in fact, closely enough related to each other. It is not the eye of vigilance but the experience of relatedness that matters.

When we examine Cardozo's justification for this conclusion, it becomes clear that other considerations were material. Foremost among them was the kind of damage suffered by Palsgraf. This point is constantly made throughout the judgment, nowhere more clearly than in the following passage: "In this case the rights that are said to have been violated, the interests said to have been invaded, are not even of the same order. The man was not injured in his person nor even put in danger ... If there was a wrong to him at all, which may very well be doubted, it was a wrong to a property interest only, the safety of his package. Out of this wrong to property, which threatened injury to nothing else, there has passed, we are told, to the plaintiff ... the right to bodily security."[77] At base the judgment therefore concludes not that this particular person could not have been foreseen to have been affected by the defendants' action but rather that this particular *damage* could not have been foreseen.[78] The conflation of the two issues was perhaps understandable given the state of the law at the time.[79] But long after the decision in *Palsgraf*, the Privy Council (and through it the Australian common law) specifically addressed and distinguished this very issue under the rubric of the doctrine of remoteness. A duty of care to another does not extend to liability for damage of a kind that is not foreseeable.[80] No doubt remoteness is an area of negligence law no more certain than any other.[81] At the same time, Cardozo's concerns are more accurately described within the ambit of the contemporary discourse in terms of the proximity or otherwise of the parties, on the one hand, and the remoteness of damage, on the other, than by conflating the two in terms of the supposed unforeseeability of the plaintiff.

Even in this seminal case, the test of duty was not really one of reasonable foreseeability. This would hardly matter except that posing the question in those terms distorts the real issue in two ways. First, it poses a question that is completely artificial. To ask what a reasonable person would have foreseen as the class of persons affected by their actions at the moment when they are, for example, rushing to pull someone on to a moving train, is disingenuous nonsense. Indeed, as we have seen, the courts have in fact responded to this fiction by · expanding the meaning of "foreseeable" beyond the bounds of realism. Reasonableness in terms of conduct (breach) continues to be judged by the courts by asking what "a reasonable man [*sic*], guided upon those considerations which ordinarily regulate the conduct of human affairs, would do."[82] But reasonableness in terms of foreseeability (duty) no longer has any reference to what Cardozo called the "ordinary eye of vigilance." The question is no longer, if it ever was, what the ordinary person might actually foresee "when directing their minds to the acts or omissions which are called in question," but simply whether the class of persons to whom the plaintiff belonged was "far-fetched or fanciful."[83] The conclusion must be that we actually do owe a duty to many persons whom we will not in fact foresee and cannot in fact be reasonably expected to foresee. The courts have clearly recognized as much. Such a conclusion suggests that reasonable foreseeability is not, after all, relevant to the determination of responsibility and that responsibility is a broader (rather than a narrower) category.

For although Levinas concedes that justice exists as a limit, an order, and "a question of consciousness,"[84] he nevertheless insists that the experience of proximity precedes the concepts that come to govern it. I do not *foresee* responsibility. On the contrary, it calls to me with an "immediacy," a "sensibility," and a "vulnerability."[85] Responsibility comes to me and not the other way around. All this means is that proximity, the core of duty, cannot ever be reduced to a precise concept, because it is prior to consciousness.[86] And for that reason we experience it not in terms of anticipation but as a surprise. Levinas argues that "consciousness is always late for the rendezvous with the neighbour."[87] We already find ourselves in a relationship before we can ever think about it. The value of this analysis is not that it solves the complex judgments of what counts as close enough or direct enough – it cannot – but that it captures so precisely the experience of responsibility that negligence addresses. Negligence is precisely about the unexpected, the careless, or the thoughtless. It is a judgment passed on our responses when "respons-ability" suddenly approaches *to* us: at a busy intersection, on a quiet road, on a train platform. In that moment, we find that we are already responsible for the welfare of another.

The second way in which the language of reasonable foreseeability distorts our understanding of what it is to have a duty to another is that it misleadingly seems to privilege the perception of the defendant. Perhaps the clearest example of why this can become a problem is the somewhat notorious decision of *Chester v. Waverley Municipal Council*.[88] This is no less than the "leading application of the 'unforeseeable plaintiff' doctrine in Anglo-Australian law."[89] A little boy drowned in a trench that had not been properly fenced off by the council. His mother witnessed the search and recovery of his body and suffered psychological trauma as a result. But the High Court (Chief Justice Latham's judgment, in particular, was a model of callous misanthropic disregard) ruled that the council owed a duty of care to the child but not to the mother. "A reasonable person," he concluded, "would not foresee that the negligence of the defendants towards the child would 'so affect' a mother ... It is ... not a common experience of mankind that the spectacle, even of the sudden and distressing death of a child, produces any consequence of more than a temporary nature."[90]

Even conceding that "grief and sorrow" themselves do not sound in damages,[91] the remark is, to present eyes, scarcely to be credited. Deane J, overruling the decision in *Jaensch,* implies that times and knowledge have changed. "The judgments of the majority in *Chester's* case have not worn well with time. It is simply out of accord with medical knowledge and human experience to deny that it is reasonably foreseeable."[92] Yet it hardly seems plausible that society has altered so much in the course of the past sixty years that the statement was true in the 1930s but false now. Evatt J's dissent in *Chester* itself, which has secured the respect of commentators and judges ever since, would suggest otherwise.

The dissent is highly unusual in the way in which the evidence is presented. Evatt speaks of the experience and pain of mothers, and he draws heavily on works of literature to sustain his argument. These analogues not only demonstrate that the breakdown of a mother on the death of her son is culturally familiar. They help the reader feel the gravity of the tragedy that befell her and the injurious anxiety that overwhelmed her. So, too, does Evatt's vivid and specific description of the events of that terrible afternoon. Rich J speaks of "a mother's shock on the *production* of the dead body of her child."[93] Evatt J focuses instead on her growing anxiety over time – "from the moment when the plaintiff discovered that her child was missing she searched for him without intermission."[94] And he uses telling details to convince us: "the plaintiff was at once beset with fear at the sinister significance of the trench, especially when one of the searchers was unable to plumb the depth of its water."[95] Having positioned us imaginatively in the very heart and mind of Mrs Chester, Evatt *then* asks whether the council should have foreseen the plaintiff's response. By the groundwork he has laid, the reader is drawn to conclude that "only the most indurate heart"[96] could have imagined otherwise.

The majority, for its part, approach the question by starting from the misdeeds of the council in failing to fence or fill the trench. In that light, the mother's response to the death of a child seems a distant consequence. So Rich J: "her subsequent shock is not reasonably within the contemplation of the defendant *as a consequence of the condition of the road.*"[97] The Court's reasoning, though ultimately no more convincing as a statement of what might be predicted as an outcome of the council's behaviour, becomes more comprehensible once we appreciate that it is the council's experience that forms their starting point.

It is a question of perspective. What you can see depends on where you stand. Latham cj concluded that "a reasonable person would not foresee that the negligence of the defendants towards the child would 'so affect' a mother." But what he means is that a reasonable person in the position of the defendant council would not so foresee. Evatt begins by thinking about what a reasonable person in the position of the plaintiff would foresee. His answer, perhaps not so very surprisingly, is rather different. In the final analysis, Evatt's response is correct because the council themselves ought to have imagined things from the point of view of the plaintiff – they ought to have foreseen how a mother might react. But the test of reasonable foreseeability in the context of duty clearly gets the analysis off on the wrong foot. The law as it stands requires of the defendant an empathy that the terminology actively discourages.

When I teach this and related cases to my students, they frequently insist to me that it is not reasonable to expect a council or its workers to foresee, at the very moment of their negligence, which is to say their inattention, the death of a child and the reaction of his mother. The exercise seems to them not just hypothetical but contrived. To justify the courts' approach I have to explain to them that the test is a way of circumscribing, in very general terms, the community of persons for whose harm one might be responsible. The hypothetical question is simply a way of testing, after the event, our intuitions as to the scope of our responsibility. It does not refer to any actual expectation of foresight, reasonable or otherwise. The test that speaks of reasonable foreseeability is not about reasonable foreseeability at all.

This is not to call for a return to the dissenting judgment of Andrews J in *Palsgraf*. He reasoned that "everyone owes to the world at large a duty of refraining from those acts which unreasonably threaten the safety of others ... It is ... a wrong to the public at large."[98] On the contrary, it is well established that, in the words of Lord Wright in another nervous shock case, "if the appellant has a cause of action, it is because of a wrong to herself. She cannot build on a wrong to someone else."[99] Negligence concerns responsibility between individuals: between the train guards and Palsgraf or the Council and Chester, and not just as a result of their carelessness "in the air."[100] But I have argued that the very essence of that responsibility is the actual relationship of the parties to each other. As a paradigm, reasonable foreseeability privileges the perceptions of one of them over the experience of both of them. Neither does it describe how we feel or behave in those moments when responsibility approaches to us. Neither is it legally necessary or sufficient for the determination of duty. In all these ways, proximity – not foreseeability – turns out to be the central element of the duty of care. It is to a short history of this term that I now turn.

THE EARLY HISTORY OF PROXIMITY: RESPONSIBILITY AS A SHOCK

Proximity is Levinas' word, and that of the High Court of Australia over part of its influential and controversial history, to describe the origin of responsibility as it arises outside of us, "without this obligation having begun in me." It arises not from my choices or foresight, nor from our policies, but from your vulnerability. It is clear enough that its nature is distinct from the other approaches to which the duty of care has been subject. What is not clear is how, once identified, it could ever serve as a "criterion for liability."[101] For this reason, the cases that originally followed *Donoghue v. Stevenson* treated proximity as if it were simply a physical connection. But gradually a wider range of cases, involving relationships distant in time and place, began to come before the Court. The first inkling of the role that proximity might play in this expansion emerged in *Caltex Oil v. The Dredge "Willemstad."*[102] The case concerned liability for an economic loss suffered by Caltex without injury to any of their equipment or property whatsoever (a pipeline they were merely leasing was damaged). Traditionally, "pure economic loss" had not been compensable in negligence.[103] The High Court here recognized that one could be "closely and directed affected" by another without actually touching them.[104] Amid a great diversity of approaches (the Privy Council chose to ignore the decision because "their Lordships have not been able to extract … any single *ratio decidendi*"),[105] Stephen J sowed the seeds for the future line of cases by specifically expanding the idea of proximity beyond a physical propinquity.[106] "The need is for some control mechanism based upon notions of proximity between tortious act and resultant detriment to take the place of the nexus provided by the suggested exclusory rule which I have rejected … [I]t may be that no more specific proposition can be formulated than a need for insistence upon sufficient proximity between tortious act and compensable detriment. The articulation, through the cases, of circumstances which denote sufficient proximity will provide a body of precedent productive of the necessary certainty."[107] In this, his honour was perhaps a tad sanguine. Nevertheless, Stephen J's judgment is significant in bringing together the two elements around which the whole debate on proximity was to develop in future years. First, the notion of proximity as a general principle of linkage incapable of more definite formulation. Second, the "gradual accumulation" of "a body of precedent" in specific areas as a means of stabilizing the law. In this way, "piecemeal conclusions arrived at in precedent cases" would serve to determine, over time, "some general area of demarcation between what is and is not a sufficient degree of proximity."[108]

The theme of proximity was greatly developed in a series of cases decided in 1984–85, beginning with *Jaensch v. Coffey*. It is significant that the case concerned that other vexed area of nonphysical harm: so-called nervous shock, that is, psychological injury unaccompanied by any physical harm to the plaintiff. Perhaps no case better demonstrates the difficulties, potential, and meanings of the word proximity than this first one. A police officer had been seriously injured by a negligent driver, and his wife suffered psychiatric illness as a result. She had not witnessed the accident but had gone to visit him in hospital "with all these tubes coming out of him."[109] Over the years, a disparate range of factors had been found to be relevant to determining whether a person who suffers serious psychological trauma in reaction to an injury to someone else (like the mother in *Chester*, who was affected by the death of her son) can sue for the nervous shock thus caused. These factors included who was injured, how the plaintiff experienced the shock, and when and where. Neither could those different aspects be readily incorporated within the general framework of negligence. They seemed, rather, to be an arbitrary series of limitations designed simply to prevent the expansion of liability that the application of a simple test of reasonable foreseeability threatened.

In *Jaensch*, the court's focus on the twin limitations of reasonable foreseeability and policy is striking. Brennan J attempted to explain the different limiting criteria as elements going to establish reasonable foreseeability. Yet it hardly seems credible to argue that "mere bystanders" with no prior relationship to the injured person cannot sue for nervous shock, just because they are in some sense unforeseeable plaintiffs. In the very broad sense that we have seen the courts apply in other contexts, it is entirely foreseeable that any person who witnesses a serious accident might be shocked and traumatized by it. This was indeed Latham CJ's principal concern in *Chester*. The duty could hardly be "confined to mothers," he argued; but if not, there seemed no reason that it should not extend "to all other persons, whether they are relatives or not."[110]

Dawson and Murphy JJ, for their parts, contrast this supposed legalism with the dictates of policy. Dawson concludes that "there appear to be strictures upon liability for the infliction of nervous shock that are not readily explicable in terms of foreseeability and that may be seen to be the result of the application of policy considerations."[111] This is to say that there are limits to claims of nervous shock beyond mere reasonable foreseeability. But the mantra of policy considerations does not determine the grounds on which such limits should be imposed unless the policy in question is simply to limit the scope of liability come what may, in which case any old criteria would do.

It is here that Deane J's seminal analysis turns out to be of real assistance. Notwithstanding his own conclusion that proximity is itself an "external [policy] limitation upon the ordinary test of reasonable foreseeability,"[112] there are glimmers throughout the judgment that proximity is best understood as a distinct approach. It is not just a way of limiting otherwise legal claims but a way of describing the normative grounds of responsibility that underlie those claims.

Deane J's approach was relational. He argued that there are a number of features that might go to establish a special connection or closeness between the physical injury suffered through the defendant's negligence and the psychiatric injury suffered in consequence of it. These include the "close, constructive and loving relationship"[113] between the two; how immediately the physical injury was observed or experienced that led to "nervous shock"; and the manner in which the news of the injury was learnt by the plaintiff. These distinctions were really ways in which Deane J attempted to reconcile a long, complex, and somewhat incoherent line of cases stretching from *Coultas* to *McLoughlin v. O'Brien*.[114] But the central point of his analysis is that these elements are not part of the doctrine of reasonable foreseeability but, on the contrary, quite separate from it. Neither does he understand them as rules that can simply be applied in an all-or-nothing fashion in every case. Again to the contrary, Deane J presents them as aspects of an overriding principle called proximity without which "the relationship will not be adjudged 'so' close 'as' to give rise to a duty of care."[115] The distinction between principle and rule that lies behind Deane's discussion and that has been drawn out in some of the academic commentary on the case is based on Ronald Dworkin's influential formulation.[116] It allows Deane J to treat the features of previous cases not as stand-alone criteria but as elements that go towards making up something more fundamental – "the requisite proximity of relationship."[117]

In the first place, then, the adoption of proximity was not just a way of characterizing the preexisting rules applicable in cases of nervous shock. It was a way of justifying them. The point is that our proximity to others – the shared neighbourhood of our relationship – is not just one factor among others that governs legal liability. It is the reason that the law recognizes responsibility at all. The concepts and rules used by the courts are manifestations of an underlying norm. So too for Levinas, proximity expresses "the relationship with the neighbour in the moral sense of the term."[118]

Regrettably, having begun with this insight, Deane J consistently speaks of proximity as an "operative limitation or control upon the ordinary test of reasonable foreseeability,"[119] while in later cases proximity is sometimes treated as a mere cipher for social policy. Both approaches treat proximity as a supplement for the sake of convenience. This profoundly misunderstands its role. By *Sutherland Shire Council v. Heyman*,[120] decided the following year, Deane had to some extent recognized his mistake and reversed the logical priority of the terms. There, reasonable foreseeability is described as merely an "indication" "that the requirement of proximity is satisfied."[121] So by *Heyman*'s case proximity had become the basal criterion for responsibility. Most clearly, he there clarified the importance of proximity "as the unifying rationale of particular propositions of law which might otherwise appear to be disparate."[122] The majority judgment in *Burnie Port Authority* similarly insists that "without it, the tort of negligence would ... rest on questionable foundations since the validity of such reasoning essentially depends upon the assumption of underlying unity or consistency."[123] But Levinas would clarify the role of proximity still further, I think. Proximity is not just "the general *conceptual* determinant and the unifying *theme*"[124] of negligence. It describes the corporeal experience of relatedness that inspires and provokes responsibility at all. This is what it means to recognize as basal "proximity and not the truth about proximity."[125]

Second, the adoption of proximity in *Jaensch* was not just a way of characterizing the preexisting rules applicable to cases of nervous shock. It was also a way of liberating them from what he later described as "the strait-jacket of some formularised criterion of liability."[126] As Levinas insists, proximity, being experienced first, must exceed our prior categories of it. (You may recall that for Levinas proximity is the event that takes place prior to our having any conceptual categories in which to confine it.) Proximity must come as a surprise. It is implicit in such an approach that the absence of one of these elements may not by itself prove fatal to the establishment of a "sufficient degree of proximity" if the relationship can be shown to be close enough in other ways. In other words, proximity is a currency of closeness that may be assembled through various permutations of coins. In future cases, this was to prove both the strength of the approach and its inherent weakness. Proximity, or closeness, must be established in very different ways in different kinds of cases.[127]

What, then, will constitute kinds of relationships that will prove close enough? Here too my argument will be that the "father of proximity" does not take proximity seriously enough. The matter comes to a head in his consideration of the "mere bystander." The question is, can someone who "merely" observes the negligent injury of another, no prior relationship existing between them, sue for the psychiatric illness they suffer as a result? Deane J thinks not, but his reasoning is curious. On the one hand, "a person who has suffered reasonably foreseeable psychiatric injury as the result of contemporaneous observation at the scene of the accident is within the area in which the common law accepts that the requirement of proximity is satisfied regardless of his particular relationship with the injured person."[128] On the other hand, this conclusion "should not be seen as indicating that the relationship between the plaintiff and the injured person will be unimportant on the prior question of reasonable foreseeability of injury in that form."[129] The reasoning, then, is parallel to Brennan J's own, with the added perplexity that Deane J thus wishes us to believe that the bystander does not fall within a reasonably foreseeable class of persons *even though* they are proximate. It is hard to imagine how this could be. It is even harder given the "undemanding test" of reasonable foreseeability, as I have already noted.[130] It is harder still given that Deane J himself had earlier described proximity as a limitation on the "ordinary test of reasonable foreseeability."[131] And finally, as I have previously noted, it is a language that does no justice to the actual circumstances of plaintiffs and defendants.

Deane's solution is to emphasize that the "prior question" is determined as "a matter of law." One might think that he means to distinguish it from a matter of fact to be determined by the trier of fact. But of course proximity is also a matter of law in this respect.[132] It begins to look like a "matter of law" is to be distinguished not from fact but from logic. In other words, Deane J concedes here that the use of reasonable foreseeability in order to exclude the bystander can only be justified as a legal fiction. But by this we mean that it is a way of preserving the mere form of a coherent argument in circumstances in which there is no coherent substance.[133] Yet it is precisely Deane's argument, and that of the High Court in later cases, that the legitimacy of tort law "depends upon [an] underlying unity or consistency,"[134] rather than on its mere appearance. Legitimacy can hardly be inferred by a process of deeming.

Deane J struggles to distinguish the "mere" bystander from someone who suffers nervous shock as a result of their efforts to help, rescue, or comfort the victims of an accident. The law has long recognized the responsibility of the defendant for the injury, physical or psychiatric, suffered by their rescuers or the rescuers of their victims.[135] As Cardozo J put it, "Danger invites rescue. The cry of distress is the summons to relief. The law does not ignore these reactions of the mind in tracing conduct to its consequences. It recognises them as normal. It places their effects within the range of the natural and probable. The wrong that imperils life is a wrong to the imperilled victim; it is a wrong also to his rescuer."[136] There seems to me, purely as a question of its foreseeability, no difference between the psychiatric harm suffered by a rescuer and that suffered by a bystander. It is true that in a situation of disaster the involvement of rescuers may be both lengthy and harrowing. The trauma and stress that they suffer is well documented. On the other hand, there is something to be said for the view that those for whom rescue is a profession might be less likely to suffer trauma than a bystander with no experience or preparation to fall back on. Yet the law admits of no such distinction.[137] Even were one to conclude that the greater the active involvement, the greater the probability of harm, foreseeability has never been analyzed in terms of degrees. It is simply a threshold test, a yes/no question – a rule – and it could hardly be said that a bystander could not be reasonably foreseen to suffer mental illness. Ironically, the very structure of nervous shock would sustain such a conclusion. Shock, says Brennan J, means precisely a "*sudden* sensory perception ... so distressing that [it] ... affronts or insults the plaintiff's mind and causes a recognizable psychiatric illness."[138] Such a moment of horror could just as foreseeably befall a bystander to a tragic accident as a rescuer.

There is, however, a discourse that is both substantive and analyzed in terms of degrees. It is not about reasonable foreseeability. It is about proximity. In *Sutherland Shire Council v. Heyman*,[139] decided shortly after, Justice Deane was forced to defend it from criticism. He rightly conceded that it cannot "provide an automatic or rigid formula for determining liability."[140] "[Proximity] involves the notion of nearness or closeness and embraces physical proximity ... [,] circumstantial proximity such as an overriding relationship of employer and employee or of a professional man and his client [,] and what may (perhaps loosely) be referred to as causal proximity."[141] Alas, in attempting to provide the Courts with rules to quell their anxiety, Deane J offers an enumeration and not an explanation. The growing chorus of criticism to which proximity has been subject was due in no small part to the circularity of Deane's discussion.[142] But it is possible to pursue our thinking as to the circumstances that give rise to proximity a little further, and without recourse to the language of reasonable foreseeability on which Deane falls back.

The true distinction is this: in each case of proximity, plaintiffs find themselves vulnerable to the defendant in a manner that is outside their control and to a degree that sets them apart from the world at large. In the first place, their proximity derives from the experience of relationship between the parties and not from the intentions or mind of the defendant. But at the same time, the person who is responsible is called in question – called to account – by the suffering of the other. They have been rendered unique; they can field no substitutes in the fulfillment of their unchosen duty.[143] As Levinas likewise makes clear, proximity can be understood as a way of describing a situation of distinct vulnerability: it *singles out plaintiffs*.

We are proximate to those who are distinctly vulnerable to us, regardless of what we know. And those who are hostages to our fortune return the favour, making us hostage to our responsibility for them in turn. We do not choose to be responsible; on the contrary, their vulnerability identifies us.

Let us return to Michael Jaensch, who carelessly drove into Allan Coffey's motorcycle. Vicki Coffey's trauma was not just a function of seeing the accident, as might happen to anyone. On the contrary, she was placed in a circumstance where she was particularly, one might even say uniquely, vulnerable to harm by virtue of her relationship with Allan, "close, constructive and loving." She was not in the same category as a bystander, because she was in danger before the accident. Her relationship already exposed her to it. Her vulnerability involved a capacity to be harmed that she could not avoid. None could deny that love puts us at risk. It draws us close. And while this intensifies joy, it intensifies pain as well. We are no longer in control of our happiness. This loss of control places us in proximity to those we love and in proximity to those who might harm them, too. All the language of Levinas insists on this. Proximity arises through "an exposure to the other," "an exposure to traumas," "vulnerability."[144] Exposed by her relationship, unable to avoid the gathering trauma, she had no choice but to rely on others. A bystander can close their eyes. A bystander can walk away. Vicki Coffey could not. Her love imperilled her. In that regard, then, she was subject to a distinct vulnerability not of her making, and that set her apart from the rest of the world. That proximity was the description of a state of affairs, an experience, that did not depend on Michael Jaensch's ability or otherwise to reasonably foresee it.

What of the rescuer? They too are distinguished from the bystander not by their foreseeability but by their proximity. It is immaterial whether the rescuer is a professional or motivated instead by some instinctive response to need. They, too, are drawn close to the accident, answering a call that comes from outside them and acts upon them. "The cry of distress is the summons to relief," as Cardozo put it. But it is not that such an instinct is "natural and probable."[145] It may, on the contrary, be rare and exceptional. The likelihood of rescue is surely beside the point. As Cardozo remarks, "The wrong that imperils life is a wrong to the imperilled victim. It is a wrong also to his rescuer ... The wrongdoer may not have foreseen the coming of a deliverer. He is accountable as if he had."[146] The reason is surely clear. It is the very circumstance of a rescue, and not its foreseeability, that establishes a bond of responsibility between the two. Rescuers are like loved ones. They find themselves endangered by an exposure and a vulnerability over which they have no control. They cannot walk away. It is this incapacity that sets them apart from the rest of the world and creates within them an intrinsic and distinct vulnerability. Not choice but the lack of it defines and limits proximity.

The explanatory model I have proposed finds most difficulty in dealing with the court's rejection of liability for those "involved in the nursing or care of a close relative." The High Court, in keeping with the English common law in *McLouglin v. O'Brien*, distinguishes shock experienced at the scene of the accident or shortly thereafter ("the aftermath") from psychiatric injury resulting from subsequent contact (for example, by "carers"). Certainly there is an extra distance here, but it is difficult to see why this should be a blanket bar to recovery if the love that originally constituted the plaintiff's vulnerability is still at work. In legal terms the explanation is simply that psychiatric injury suffered over time does not derive from a shock and is therefore *damnum absque injuria* (a loss without a remedy).[147] Yet as Kirby P observes, the word "shock" appears to enshrine an "outmoded scientific view about the nature of" psychiatric illness, i.e., that in the nineteenth century it was thought to derive from a physical disturbance to the brain.[148] It is hard to believe that such an improbable "subservience to nineteenth century science" can long be maintained.[149] If so, then surely there is no statute of limitations on acts of love or instinct, the compulsions I defended above? I am tempted, therefore, to suggest that nervous shock may yet expand in precisely this direction.

Yet proximity provides a clearer way of addressing the problem. The longer the time between the accident and the mental distress it occasions, the less distinct and unavoidable is the plaintiff's vulnerability to harm. This is not to say that a nurse or carer can avoid emotional commitment and emotional pain, but there are ways of managing these experiences that do not lead to psychiatric illness. In other words, if we understand proximity as based on a lack of choice in the plaintiff that constitutes a singular vulnerability to the defendant's actions, then the more distanced and gradual the problem, the more we must conclude that the vulnerable person was not simply – and at some point, no longer – "hostage" (as Levinas puts it) to the defendant's power. The ties that knotted together plaintiff and defendant and that were the cause of the plaintiff's injury are now considerably loosened. More is a function of the choices, behaviour, and particular background of the plaintiff; less is due to the irresistible force of the defendant.

One might therefore understand the requirement of "shock"[150] not as the aetiology of a kind of injury (an approach that Kirby rightly criticizes) but, rather, as the phenomenology of a kind of relationship. A shock suggests the immediacy of an injury that impacts on a person unavoidably; just as if they had been hit by the car themselves. We cannot avoid a shock; we cannot see it coming or step aside from it or guard against it or protect ourselves from it – or foresee it – no matter what kind of person we are, precisely because it comes to us, as Levinas so rightly insisted, before the ability of the reasoning mind to control it, "before any understanding … and before consciousness."[151] Proximity, in short, always comes not as an exercise of choice or reason but as a shock, to plaintiff and defendant alike. What seemed to be the most arbitrary and archaic limit on recovery turns out, properly understood, to point to the very meaning of proximity in this context.

Of course, outside the area of psychological injury, the parameters of a relationship established by shock will inevitably change. But the idea will not: to be shocked is to be deprived of choice, to be exposed to a wound, to be inescapably vulnerable.

THE LATER HISTORY OF PROXIMITY: RESPONSIBILITY AS VULNERABILITY

Proximity is not just a synonym for closeness. It identifies a certain kind that matters for the purpose of thinking about responsibility. It specifies that kind in terms of a vulnerability that singles a person out without their choice and that therefore singles out the one who has a special response ability with respect to them. It determines that relationship not in terms of the intention, foresight, or choice, which is to say the mental state, of the one' encumbered by a duty but, rather, in terms of the inescapably shocking experience of relationship they share. Proximity therefore binds together the why, who, and how of the duty of care: it points to a normative foundation, a language of analysis, and a mode of proof. All this is abundantly clear in Levinas' work, particularly in *Otherwise than Being*. Proximity is there elaborated in just these terms, and its importance furthermore defended as a human necessity.

These elements can be detected even in the earliest cases of proximity's renaissance. The High Court failed in following through on these insights. Once again the difficulty stemmed from not taking proximity seriously enough. As I have already indicated, the confusion of proximity and policy, on the one hand, and the description of proximity as a limit on foreseeability, on the other, manifested this failure. So too did the Court's incapacity to mount any argument as to what elements might indicate the presence or otherwise of proximity. Without more, Michael McHugh was surely right to remark, adopting the celebrated phrase of Professor Julius Stone, that proximity "is a category of indeterminate reference *par excellence*."[152] It was not, argued Brennan, a rule, since proximity could not be limited to any specific "issue of fact on which a legal consequence depends ... A rule without specific content confers a discretion."[153]

The Court too often simply asserted the presence or absence of proximity, as their critics contended. Dawson J remarked in *Gala v. Preston* that "merely to describe it as a matter of proximity is to mask the problem."[154] Brennan CJ was particularly critical of "proximity in the broader sense." By importing but never defining the diverse notions

of public policy that were said to "underlie and enlighten proximity,"[155] the Court had effectively created a "juristic black hole into
which particular criteria and rules would collapse and from which no
illumination of principle would emerge."[156] My point has been to argue
that the equation of proximity and policy has been a mistake not just
from the point of view of the court's emerging doctrine but from the
point of view of an ethical philosophy.

Attempts to clarify the content of proximity focused, initially at
least, on the related ideas of "assumption of responsibility" and "reliance." These terms had in common the idea that proximity derived
from some kind of agreement between the parties, some mutual understanding or consciousness. Like reasonable foreseeability, then, they
relate responsibility to the existence of a particular mental state by
one party or the other. And we can also see how indebted this theory
of responsibility is to ideas of consent, contract, and individual autonomy. Responsibility is understood as a kind of choice made and acted
upon by the parties: I consciously take on something and/or you consciously rely on it.[157] Proximity is here understood as being governed
on both sides by perception and intention. This was particularly the
case in relation to liability for omissions. So in *Sutherland Shire Council v. Heyman*, a homeowner sued the local council for its failure to
properly inspect a house in the course of its construction. As a result,
a latent defect remained undetected in the home, with disastrous
results some years (and some owners) later. The key factors for both
Mason and Deane JJ were that the council had not represented themselves as having thus inspected, nor had the purchaser in any way
relied upon any supposed representation. There had therefore been no
"assumption of a particular obligation to take such action or of a
particular relationship in which such an obligation is implicit."[158]
Absent any voluntary commitment to a course of conduct by the defendant, there could be no proximity. Proximity, then, involves the taking
on of a responsibility.

But it soon became apparent that the concept could not adequately
accommodate the court's instincts as to the extent of proximate relations. In *Shaddock v. Parramatta City Council*,[159] the Court emphasized
that responsibility for a negligent misstatement hinges upon whether
one has "assume[d] a responsibility to give advice or information to
others on serious matters."[160] But at the same time Stephen J was forced
to admit that a council might be liable even in circumstances in which
they had expressly refused to accept responsibility for the information

they provided. In *Shaddock*'s case, the information sought by the plaintiff pertained to the council's own policies and intentions. "Were a council expressly to qualify its answers," said Stephen J, "stating that they might be subject to errors for which it accepted no responsibility, the present practice would be rendered largely worthless."[161] Clearly, then, in certain situations reliance will trump consent.

Neither, however, did the plaintiff's actual reliance necessarily prove definitive. In *Sutherland Shire Council*, Mason J introduced the concept of "general reliance" to cover those core functions of a council or authority that the public generally and reasonably expects will be exercised with care.[162] His examples were of fire-fighting or of air traffic control.[163] The argument was further developed by McHugh J in the NSW Court of Appeal.[164] In such cases, according to their Honours, the council might not actively or willingly "assume" a particular responsibility. The obligation is foisted upon them. Neither will the plaintiff need to show that they in fact relied on the council to do its job. The plaintiff may indeed be unaware of it. The relationship is somehow already proximate regardless of the conscious understanding of either party to it. "General reliance" in fact implies a proximity that simply inheres in the relationship of the parties quite apart from their perceptions of it – a point that I have been insisting is essential to the very idea of responsibility but that does not emerge clearly from the High Court's orthodox efforts to fit proximity into the existing doctrinal justifications.

This reasoning was vigorously criticized in *Pyrenees Shire Council v. Day*. A majority of the Court (Toohey and McHugh JJ dissenting) rejected its application. In language supported by the Court, Gummow J described general reliance as a "legal fiction." There would be appear to be no evidence to support Mason's contention that some governmental functions are "generally relied upon," nor any way of garnering it, nor any way of distinguishing between those functions that the public relies upon and those it does not. Gummow J concluded that liability must be related not to social surmise but to "basal principle."[165] There is something to be said for this. As we will shortly see, the intuition behind general reliance recognizes relationships of responsibility in circumstances in which neither the defendant has agreed to it nor the plaintiff has knowledge of it. "General reliance" is an attempt to capture the fact of a relationship of dependence regardless of intention. It does relate therefore to the basal principle of proximity. The problem in Mason J's formulation lies in his attempt to explain this principle in terms of reliance and consent. "General reliance" is a misnomer, because it is not privity but proximity that grounds a responsibility "before all assumption, all commitment consented to or refused."[166]

That proximity cannot be reduced to mental states and conscious expectations – that it is not a species of reliance and is sometimes quite the opposite – became even clearer in *Hawkins v. Clayton* and finally in *Hill v. Van Erp.*[167] In *Hawkins*, a solicitor negligently failed to contact the executor of an estate for a period of some years following the testatrix's death, causing the estate to fall into disrepair. Mason CJ and Dawson J, in dissent, provide the clearest demonstration of the consequences of adopting the familiar language of responsibility-as-consent. The solicitor had not assumed any responsibility for the welfare of the executor, nor had he "assumed the custodianship of the testatrix's testamentary intentions."[168] Nor, of course, had the executor, who remained ignorant of the will, in any sense actually relied on the care or skill of the solicitor. The solicitor's only contact was with the testatrix herself. If proximity is limited to a relationship that is understood in a certain way, then there is no proximity here, since neither party to the action was consciously or intentionally connected to the other.

On the contrary, Deane and Gaudron JJ's real concern lay in the exclusive control vested in the solicitor that enabled him to prevent all access to knowledge about the will. Gaudron J sees the "exclusivity of possession of information" as central here, just as it was in *Shaddock.*[169] The situation of unique power held by the solicitor prevented the defendant from refusing to assume responsibility. This was not because the plaintiff relied on the defendant to act with due care. It was because the solicitor had the power to keep the putative executor in ignorance of the will and therefore precisely to prevent him relying on it. Deane J speaks of proximity as emerging from "reliance (or dependence)."[170] But the two are entirely different. The plaintiff had been kept in the dark. He never formed the intention to rely on the defendant, because he was never given the opportunity. This was the nature of his dependence. It stemmed from an *absence* of reliance.

Justice Gaudron was right, therefore, to conclude that reliance and assumption of responsibility are not the only criteria by which to establish proximity.[171] Indeed, as we have just seen, the language is positively misleading about the dynamic that proximity seeks to protect. *Hill v. Van Erp* further established the point. Is a solicitor liable to a beneficiary who failed to gain an intended gift due to the solicitor's negligence in drawing it up? Again, Gaudron J (and Gummow J too) conceded that assumption of responsibility and reliance did not arise "where, as here and as in *Hawkins v. Clayton*, the plaintiff is not even aware that his or her position may be affected."[172] Although Dawson J attempts to argue that "there is both an assumption of responsibility of a kind and reliance of a kind," he is immediately forced to concede that this is only because proximity ought to be recognized *"even though* neither is in a form which would suffice in cases where those elements are crucial to a relationship of proximity."[173] In other words, the real criteria here remain unexplored.

Admittedly reliance may be relevant in some cases, but for rather different reasons. This was made quite clear in *San Sebastian v. The Minister*,[174] which concerned a negligent misstatement allegedly made by state planning bodies regarding the redevelopment of Woolloomoolloo. The majority conceded that it is only in relation to negligent words that the element of reliance is required.[175] Furthermore, it is apparent both from the majority judgment and from that of Brennan J that its importance arises not because it constitutes the duty of care but rather because it proves causation. As Brennan explained, "A causal relationship between a representation (a term which I shall use to embrace any verbal statement made by one person to another) and economic loss does not exist because of the operation of the laws of nature. It exists because the representation induces the representee to do something which causes the loss … in other words, he acts or refrains from acting in that manner in reliance on the truth of the representation."[176] Without actual reliance, the negligent words will not have caused the plaintiff to act in a way that harmed them.[177]

McHugh J pointedly asked in dissent in *Hill v. Van Erp*, "but absent an assumption of responsibility for the beneficiary's interest or a promise or representation to the beneficiary, why should the solicitor owe a duty of care?"[178] This was a question that the courts had not yet answered. Their failure to do so, coupled with the rejection of reliance and assumption as appropriate explanations in their own right, led to a dramatic change of direction. Scarcely a year after the retirement of Mason CJ and Deane J during 1995, first in *Hill v. Van Erp*[179] and then later in *Pyrenees Shire Council v. Day* (1998)[180] a majority of the High Court confessed to apostasy and abandoned proximity.

PROXIMITY LOST …

It remains unclear precisely what might replace proximity as the analytic basis for the Court's approach to the duty of care. It is not the purpose of this book to explore the implications of their reversion, although it seems to me that in recent years, as others have argued, the decline of proximity has been matched by a narrower conception of our responsibility to others and, at the same time, a narrower conception of the role of judicial reasoning in response to the unique cases before it.[181] The trend is by no means univocal, and we will see that in cases such as *Perre v. Apand* the High Court appears to continue to draw upon the philosophical insights that proximity occasioned, while studiously eschewing the tainted term itself. But still other cases, such as *Romeo v. Northern Territory* and *Modbury Triangle*, which I discuss in the next chapter, display the revival of a constraining spirit in which the protection of individual autonomy trumps any recognition of the suffering other. The loss of proximity has been accompanied, then, by the loss of an expansive movement in the Court, of an imaginative empathy directed towards actual experiences of vulnerability, and of an idea of justice located in singularity and critical reflection. Instead, the Court in recent years appears increasingly to equate responsibility once more with choice and self-reliance, and justice with rules of general application.

At the very least one might say that the "judicial menus"[182] have turned into an eclectic smorgasbord of approaches. One approach has been to speak in terms of an "incremental approach" such as had always been favoured by Brennan J. On this approach the attempt to apply a universal determinant of duty would be abandoned and instead the courts would look to "appropriate limitations in particular propositions of law, applicable to differing classes of case."[183] Likewise Dawson J in *Hill*: "Reasoning by analogy from decided cases by the processes of induction and deduction, informed by rather than divorced from policy considerations, is not, in my view, dependent for its validity on those cases sharing an underlying conceptual consistency. It is really only dependent upon the fact that something more than reasonable foreseeability is required to establish a duty of care and that what is sufficient or necessary in one case is a guide to what is sufficient or necessary in another."[184] The position is perhaps most forcefully expressed in McHugh J's judgment in *Perre v. Apand*:[185] "We have the established categories, a considerable body of case law and the useful concept of reasonable foreseeability. If a case falls outside an established category ... we have only to ask whether the reasons that called for or denied a duty in other (usually similar) cases require the imposition of a duty in the instant case ... In my view, given the needs of practitioners and trial judges, the most helpful approach to the duty problem is first to ascertain whether the case comes within an established category ... The law should be developed incrementally by reference to the reasons why the material facts in analogous cases did or did not found a duty."[186]

As Gaudron J has noted, "the proposition that the law should develop incrementally and by analogy" likewise lacks "the specificity of a precise proposition of law."[187] The very idea of a test formulated in terms of the incremental development by analogy with established categories begs the question as to what makes a case *so* close as to justify analogous treatment. Every case is like every other case; and every case is different. This is the problem within any system of reasoning by analogy to which Professor Julius Stone drew our attention in his influential discussion of *Donoghue v. Stevenson* itself. The classical doctrine of precedent speaks of "material facts" that form the basis of the decision of a case.[188] A case will be analogous when its material facts are the same. But of course there is nothing to determine either what makes a fact material or yet what level of generality to apply to such facts.

This was so important to Stone that he just about shouted it: "THE SYSTEM OF PRECEDENT ITSELF IS BASED ON A LEGAL CATEGORY OF INDETERMINATE OR CONCEALED MULTIPLE REFERENCE, NAMELY 'THE RATIO DECIDENDI OF A CASE.'"[189] It would appear that the High Court – mostly students or disciples of Professor Stone, I might add – have failed to read the large print. The category of determinate reference par excellence is none other than the incremental approach. Brennan J insisted that, unlike proximity, the incremental approach permits the application of "particular propositions of law, applicable to different classes of case."[190] It is true that proximity requires greater specificity if it is to assist in the determination of cases. But no amount of particularity will help us decide if a case belongs within a certain class or not. That requires a normative judgment that proximity, for all its failings, provides.

The judges have no doubt been aware of the fundamental inadequacy that lurks within incrementalism. An alternative approach has therefore been to speak in terms of policy. Thus, as we have already seen, Dawson J speaks of analogy as "informed by rather than divorced from policy considerations."[191] So, too, McHugh J writes of an incrementalism controlled not by "the material facts in analogous cases" *simpliciter* but, rather, "by reference to the reasons why the material facts in analogous cases did or did not found a duty."[192] The adoption of a policy approach can be seen most clearly in recent cases concerning liability for pure economic loss. In *Hill v. Van Erp* Dawson J allowed that "the considerations which ordinarily prompt concern about imposing liability for such loss are absent."[193] Similar arguments were put by Toohey and Gummow JJ. Once more, *Perre v. Apand* took a similar approach. There, the judges unanimously emphasized the "policy considerations" that, according to the Chief Justice, "restrain ... acceptance of such a duty of care in particular cases or categories of case."[194] Policy is therefore understood negatively to limit the expansion of duty in "a comparatively new and developing area of the law of negligence."[195]

The nature of these arguments points to an absence and a quest. This is to say no more than Lord Atkin, who so prophetically insisted that there "*must* be ... a general conception of relations giving rise to a duty of care, of which the particular cases found in the books are but instances."[196] Must be, because otherwise there would be no justification for the law's demand for responsibility upon us. Must be, because if the law of negligence were exclusively a set of policy arguments as to the social utility of the imposition of liability, the very foundation of the law as it recognizes our personal responsibility to each other would be lost. Must be, because without some central argument as to why we owe duties to each other, we would have no way even of distinguishing between core cases of negligence and comparatively new and developing areas. Their distinction depends on their relative distance from some archetype in which responsibility can be justified.

Perre v. Apand acknowledges this on every page. Each of the judges (with the partial exception of Hayne J) explicitly declares that they must do more than explain to us why the practical reasons against holding the defendant responsible do not apply. They must equally articulate a positive argument in favour of a duty of care. As McHugh J says, the negative policy arguments are simply a hurdle before "community standards and the goals of negligence law, as an instrument of corrective justice" may impose a duty of care.[197] And this is precisely the question that neither incrementalism nor the policy arguments of the courts can ever hope to articulate or to dismiss. Neither, as we have seen, can an explanation in terms of mental states or consciousness – whether expressed in terms of reasonable foreseeability, reliance, or assumption of responsibility – ever properly ground such a justification.

I will return to the courts' attempt to rediscover some positive argument for responsibility in the following section of this chapter. Apart from Kirby J, they do so without express mention of proximity.[198]

But my argument has been that in the process they have rediscovered it. Deane J himself to the contrary, proximity is not a *limit* placed on responsibility understood in terms of foreseeability. Rather, as Levinas shows us, proximity is the positive argument that establishes responsibility for another in the first place – this is why it matters. It does so by reference to an experience of relationship characterized by your vulnerability, on the one hand, and my response ability, on the other – this is what it looks like. On both sides, one does not choose it; it chooses me: it is marked not by conscious intent but by subjection. The vulnerable are those who are hostage to another; the powerful, in their turn, find themselves hostage to their responsibility, weakened and subjected precisely by the passivity of the other – this is what it feels like.

... OR ONLY MISLAID?

The language of proximity, dimly perceived and poorly explained, has forced enormous change upon the High Court over the past twenty years. Reasonable foreseeability has become of trivial significance. Assumption of responsibility and reliance have been tried and found wanting. Policy arguments have been increasingly limited and defined. I venture to suggest that it is far too late for the High Court to "reject" proximity. They have already been contaminated. For there has been another language of responsibility that has gradually intruded on the deliberations of the Court, imposing itself with growing insistence. This language has centred on the experience of vulnerability and the capacity to control: precisely the features that I have argued give real and recognizable content to Levinas' description of responsibility. Ironically, the renunciation of proximity coincided exactly with its redemption. As the Court slowly discarded mental states, conceptual generalities, and fictions in favour of phenomenology, it thought it was turning away from proximity. In fact, a trace of its true nature was to be found at every turn.

This theme can be seen in almost every significant negligence case over the past twenty years, first as a minor element and then with growing vigour. In retrospect it forms the unspoken subtext even of those cases that did not explicitly address it. *Jaensch v. Coffey* is generally thought to form a separate area of liability requiring the application of discrete principles. But I have argued that the discussion of proximity can in fact be explained in terms of the distinct vulnerability of the plaintiff to a web of harm into which they had been drawn beyond their control.

In *Sutherland Shire Council v. Haymen,* Mason J subtly recognized that the question is not one of conscious knowledge or consent on either side. He phrased his argument in terms of "general reliance," since he understood the law of negligent omissions to require some kind of reliance by the plaintiff on the council's actions. In the form of general reliance, the concept was roundly criticized by the Court in *Pyrenees Shire Council v. Day.* There it was branded a "legal fiction" because it is not really a species of reliance. True enough. But it need not be formulated in those terms. Mason J envisaged situations in which a council or statutory body might be responsible for a harm even though they neither represented themselves as acting in a certain way nor were relied upon by the plaintiff to do so. Mason J speaks in terms of "a general *expectation* that the power will be exercised," on the one hand, and "a *realization* that there is a general reliance or dependence," on the other.[199] He speaks, in other words, in the language of consciousness and choice. His examples, however, are telling. "Reliance or dependence in this sense is in general the product of the grant (and exercise) of powers designed to prevent or minimize a risk of personal injury ... of such magnitude or complexity an individual cannot, or may not, take adequate steps for their own protection ... The control of air traffic, the safety inspection of aircraft and the fighting of a fire in a building by a fire authority ... may well be examples of this type of function."[200]

The common theme of these instances is better put by McHugh J in *Pyrenees Shire Council v. Day.* "Thus, it applies only in those situations where individuals are vulnerable to harm from immense dangers which they cannot control or understand and often enough cannot recognize."[201] Reliance is therefore simply a consequence of a predicament in which individuals are necessarily vulnerable to harm in ways that they cannot do anything about and subject perforce to some organization vested with more and particular power. As opposed to Heyman, who could have arranged for the inspection of his own house, we cannot inspect the planes on which we fly. That is a vulnerability commensurate to another's response ability.

The significance of this new language extends still further. The notion of proximity I have outlined makes particular sense of cases of what are normally termed "nondelegable duties." The term refers to circumstances in which the courts have imposed positive duties of care that cannot be satisfied by the employment of a competent independent contractor. The employer or institution must go further and ensure that care is taken. Standard examples include the responsibility of a hospital for its patients, employers for their employees, schools for their pupils, or a parent for his or her children.[202] In the past, these responsibilities have been understood in terms of prior relationships that justify the imposition of "special duties," including duties of positive action. In *Kondis*, Mason CJ describes in each case the special responsibility as arising from "an undertaking." "In these situations the special duty arises because the person on whom it is imposed has undertaken the care, supervision or control of the person or property of another or is so placed in relation to that person or his property as to assume a particular responsibility for his or its safety, in circumstances where the person affected might reasonably expect that due care will be exercised."[203] But it makes better sense to understand these, too, as arising from the dynamic of vulnerability and control, and not from some consensual origin. The nondelegable duty arises because "the employer has the exclusive responsibility for the safety of the appliances, the premises and the system of work to which he subjects his employee and the employee has no choice but to accept and rely on the employer's provision and judgment in relation to these matters. The consequence is that in these relevant respects the employee's safety is in the hands of the employer; it is his responsibility."[204] This is a powerful argument. But it speaks to a responsibility arising out of the vulnerability of a particular situation and not out of any "undertaking" evinced by a contract of employment. Indeed, although in legal taxonomy the situation is quite separate, Mason's language here is redolent of nothing so much as his earlier argument for general reliance. A nondelegable duty is simply a private-sector corollary to the public-sector doctrine of general reliance. Both are better understood as establishing special duties of positive action that arise out of a circumstance of distinct vulnerability (on one side) and unique control (on the other). Both concern the true application of proximity.

In its 1994 decision of *Burnie Port Authority*, perhaps the most significant in the Australian common law of torts since *Jaensch*, the court moved towards a general theory of liability covering these situations.[205] The court sought to articulate the general duty that arises from a relational environment and not a specific duty arising from behaviour. Thus, in *Burnie Port Authority* the owner of premises authorized work to be done by an independent contractor. The contractors were welding in the roof space of Burnie Port Authority (BPA) when the insulation materials there combusted. In the conflagration that ensued, not just property owned by BPA but a frozen-goods company that occupied part of the premises was destroyed. The question before the Court was whether the authority should have prevented the accident. Although BPA was not vicariously liable for the negligent welding, the High Court nevertheless held that they remained responsible for the environment in which the welding took place. They had not just a duty to take care themselves but also "a duty to ensure that reasonable care is taken."[206] But what are the features of the relationship that justified the Court in treating the environment of the port as equivalent to a school, a factory, or a hospital? Here the language of the majority judgment is both precise and prescient. In "the principal categories of case in which the duty to take reasonable care under the ordinary law of negligence is non-delegable ... [t]he relationship of proximity ... is characterized by such a central element of control and by such special dependence and vulnerability."[207] So, in *Burnie Port Authority* itself,

One party to that relationship is a person who is in control of premises ... The other party to that relationship is a person, outside the premises and without control over what occurs therein, whose person or property is thereby exposed to a foreseeable risk of danger ... In such a case the person outside the premises is obviously in a position of special vulnerability and dependence. He or she is specially vulnerable to danger if reasonable precautions are not taken in relation to what is done on the premises. He or she is specially dependent upon the person in control of the premises to ensure that such reasonable precautions are in fact taken.[208]

This analysis explains not a particular legal rule but the very meaning of "the relationship of proximity" itself. Ironically, *Burnie Port Authority*, which came so close to perceiving this in the passage quoted above, marked a turning point in the Court's deliberations. Although the Court could have developed its instinct as to the essential features that mark a proximate relationship, it did not. From then on, the High Court began to emphasize the elements of control and vulnerability, albeit inconsistently, while backing away from the language of proximity. They did not appreciate what is, with the benefit of hindsight, obvious: one explains the other.

The characterization of proximity in the terms articulated by the Court in *Burnie Port Authority* explains the difference between the majority and the minority in *Pyrenees* itself. In that case, the local council failed to follow up an inspection of a faulty chimney. A later tenant used the fireplace, and the entire premises burnt to the ground, destroying not only property owned by their family company Eskimo Amber but the shop owned by the Days, with whom they shared a common wall. McHugh and Toohey JJ, who dissented, both supported the doctrine of general reliance rejected by the other judges. But why did that lead them to conclude that the Days were entitled to succeed where Eskimo Amber were not? If one focuses simply on what the council knew or ought to have known, the two cases are indistinguishable. That was the approach the majority took.[209] But from the point of view of the actual experience of vulnerability, the two plaintiffs were differently situated. The tenants could have protected themselves – it was their fireplace. The neighbours could not. They could neither prevent the fireplace being used nor protect themselves from the consequences. They had no rights of access or inspection. They were, then, vulnerable, as Eskimo Amber were not, dependent solely on the council's actions, as Eskimo Amber were not.

Just like Vicki Coffey in *Jaensch*, or like the plaintiffs in any other of the long series of cases that followed it, the Days were distinctly exposed to harm. The language of general reliance merely obscures this insight. Nondelegable duty and general reliance are merely further instances of the general principle of proximity. If one understands proximity as the way in which vulnerability and response ability constitute one another, relative to each other, then it is neither indeterminate nor unclear to conclude that the Days alone were proximate to the council.

Pyrenees and *Sutherland* are thought, within the incremental approach, to raise discrete tests of negligence liability, since the former deals with physical loss and the latter with "pure economic loss." Brennan CJ is categorical (so to speak) about the distinction.[210] My argument has been that in fact they share an underlying theme of proximity as the determinant of a duty of care: proximity understood as a moral relationship stemming from an unavoidable vulnerability to harm and a unique capacity to help. Such an approach began to assume increasing prominence in those cases where reliance was notably absent. In *Hawkins* and later in *Hill*, precisely as proximity came to be criticized, the language of vulnerability and control began to replace it. In *Hill*, it will be recalled, the question before the Court was whether a solicitor who negligently draws up a will rendering it void owes a duty of care to a thwarted beneficiary. Dawson J regards as "crucial" two elements: first, that only the defendant solicitor can normally discover or remedy an error in the construction of a will; second, that the error is apparent only at the very moment – at the client's death – that it becomes too late to do anything about it. This speaks both to the unique control exerted by the solicitor, and to the "particularly vulnerable" circumstance of the beneficiary.[211] Gaudron J, still more clearly, states "that by reason of her position of control ... there was a relationship of proximity between Ms Hill and Mrs Van Erp."[212] The exclusivity of knowledge forms a key element that constitutes both distinct control and distinct vulnerability, as it did in *Hawkins v. Clayton*[213] and also in *Shaddock v. Parramatta City Council*.[214]

If *Burnie Port Authority* marks the turning point of the High Court's analysis, *Perre v. Apand* is its apotheosis. A potato farmer in rural South Australia was unable to sell his potatoes as a result of the negligent contamination of a neighbouring farm with bacterial wilt. The potatoes themselves were uninfected, but the operation of Western Australia's farm quarantine laws prevented their sale in that market regardless and so caused the farmer to suffer pure economic loss.[215] Again in this case there was no reliance or conscious relationship between those responsible for the introduction of the disease and the farmers who suffered loss. The Court explicitly severs vulnerability from reliance.[216] Although there is a diversity of approaches in the judgments, no less than three of the judges are at pains to emphasize the unavoidable vulnerability of the farmer to the actions of the disease, his inability to protect himself, and, conversely, the control exercised by the contaminator over the farmer's livelihood.[217] Vulnerability, says McHugh J, "is likely to be decisive and always of relevance."[218] Indeed, His Honour goes further in making sense of the logical trajectory of the High Court's approach to the determination of duty in the past twenty years.

Like proximity, reliance and assumption of responsibility are neither necessary nor sufficient to found a duty of care. In my view, reliance and assumption of responsibility are merely indicators of the plaintiff's vulnerability to harm from the defendant's conduct, and it is the concept of vulnerability rather than these evidentiary indicators which is the relevant criterion for determining whether a duty of care exists. The most explicit recognition of vulnerability as a possible common theme in cases of pure economic loss is found in the judgment of Toohey and Gaudron JJ in *Esanda Finance Corporation Ltd v. Peat Marwick Hungerfords* ... In terms of a duty of care, however, it is not reliance that is relevant, but its consequence, vulnerability.[219]

The argument should be extended. It is not just in pure economic loss but throughout the literature that the features identified by McHugh and Gaudron JJ have proven determinative. Suitably modified, the argument applies equally well to cases as disparate as *Pyrenees*, as *Jaensch*, as *Sutherland*, and as *Hill*, as well as to BPA and to *Perre*. It is fair to say that the question of control by the defendant has been the predominant feature of Gaudron's analysis in several of these cases,[220] while McHugh J for his part has paid greater attention to the vulnerability of the plaintiff.[221] But as Levinas has made clear – and as was explicitly articulated in *Burnie Port Authority* – it is their mutuality that creates an obligation of responsibility. A distinct capacity to control particularizes the defendant, while a distinct vulnerability to harm particularizes the plaintiff. Both are needed to found a duty, because each position constitutes and individualizes the other.

We are singled out by the hostaged gaze of the other, made vulnerable by their very vulnerability and made unfree by the other's unfreedom. The relationship is not symmetrical or reciprocal, says Levinas, because one is not free to choose or to reject responsibility: on the contrary, it chooses us. This distinguishes privity and contract from proximity and tort. In contract we are all, at least in formal terms, on a level playing field; in Levinas' terms, we are each of us to each other a "thou," or a *tu*, that is, an other person with whom we are on good speaking terms. Not so in tort. Levinas' metaphor of "height" – particularly in *Totality and Infinity* – is purposefully ambiguous.[222] How can the other be "at once higher and poorer than I"? What does it mean to say "the I is distinguished from the Thous, not by any sort of 'attributes,' but by the dimension of height"?[223] The law of negligence shows us exactly how, for it is the very poorness and vulnerability of the other that calls forth our ability and demands a response. And the greater the differential, the higher the standard of care demanded: the poorer the higher.[224]

Taken together, these requisite asymmetries, identified so clearly in recent cases, are not simply features like proximity: they *are* proximity. And neither is this a limitation on the duty of care. It is how and why the duty emerges. Proximity does not come after this relationship with another, to describe or delimit it. It is the moment that births the relationship, and us with it. Without such an understanding neither the law nor our own sense of self could have any normative justification. So Levinas' remark amounts to the foundation of a jurisprudence, as well as an ethics: "My responsibility for the other is the *for* of the relationship."[225]

SUMMARY

I have sought to establish the distinctness of Levinas' argument for proximity as the crucial element in his ethical theory of responsibility. I have then attempted to show the relevance of this approach to the common law question of the nature of the duty of care in negligence. The well-rehearsed weaknesses in the High Court's use of the concept stem from those moments where they have misunderstood or misapplied it and where a reading of Levinas might have, and might still, help. Moreover, while in recent years the High Court has rejected the language of proximity, in reality their analyses have moved on occasion, though not all the time, towards it. Proximity is, in effect, indispensable to the duty of care and central to the courts' remarkable trajectory in recent years. The courts may eschew the word, yet it connotes the normative aspirations of their project, the phenomenology of asymmetry that constitutes it, and its distance from consciousness and choice. Neither can they entirely roll back the directions in which all these aspects have taken them.[226] Like some intellectual virus, proximity has contaminated the law, "which nothing could rejoin and cover over."[227]

It is not an adequate response to insist that proximity has no place in the law because it is not a rule. It is true that "if judicial decisions are to be based on more than a judge's sense of justice, like cases must be decided alike and in accordance with a principle that transcends the immediate facts of the case."[228] We have seen, however, two things pertinent to this critique. The first is that something more can and has been said about the nature of proximity, both in the philosophical and in the judicial literature. The second is that the problem of indeterminacy is ever-present within the common law and cannot be solved simply by mandarin decretals enjoining us all to treat like cases alike. As Kirby J writes, the application of "labels" to necessarily particular and changing facts is the very stuff of law. "But, equally, negligence itself is a 'label.' So are the criteria or 'principles' ... Labels are commonly used by lawyers. They help steer the mind through the task at hand."[229]

Kirby's point is well made. Legal language does not determine the outcome of legal disputes. Rather, it "steers the mind through the task at hand," directing practitioners and thinkers in an ordered way towards various factors and particular ways of presenting their arguments. The common law is, in short, a discourse and not a machine. It is exegetical in the sense of continually teaching us something new about the world and ourselves, and not in the sense of being objective and definitive. That is one sense in which it shares a strong affinity with that other great exegetical tradition, the Talmudic.[230] Using the work of Emmanuel Levinas, I have tried to give some distinct content to the terminology of proximity so that it might fulfil that function. To expect more of it would be as impossible as it would be ultimately undesirable. Jorge Luis Borges might even have been talking about the common law of negligence when he wrote: "Thus we begin to see the book's general scheme: The insatiable search for a soul by means of the delicate glimmerings or reflections this soul has left in others – at first, the faint trace of a smile or a word; toward the last, the varied and growing splendours of intelligence, imagination, and goodness."[231] Each case within the common law is but a glimmering or reflection of a meaning that can never be entirely found or pinned down. Like proximity itself, the law of duty will never be defined but only *approached*, through the mirrors and traces it leaves behind. Each case points to a final goal that we will never reach. The strength of the law is that this restless quest, in case after case, offers us an adaptive capacity well suited to the protean world.

For Levinas, of course, language could not be pinned down in this way. Some meaning would always escape its reduction to themes and definitions. He called this "the interval between the saying and the said."[232] Like Borges, he believed in the power and necessity of the "trace" that opens up between the two and that he described as "the veracity of the approach, of proximity."[233] Levinas uses terms like "the knot as a diremption in the order of intelligibility," "the interruptions of discourse," and "the trace of a diachrony."[234] What he means is that if language could be defined in a completely determinate way, nothing new could be discovered, and we would be reduced to an understanding of the world that we already had. This intellectual stasis he called totality. But our relationship with others is infinite and irreducible to any expectation or experience we might have of it. The very polysemy and ambiguity of language allows experience to enter into it; allows us to learn and appreciate and acknowledge something new. The saying always exceeds the said.[235] The trace thus permits the infinite and the changeable to *shock* the little world of the closed and known. If this is true, then there must be some way of touching without appropriating, of hearing without simply translating. This Levinas calls by many names, foremost amongst them proximity. Consequently, proximity not only cannot be fully determined, fully reduced to rules – it must not be. To do so would destroy its very power to discover our responsibility anew. This is surely a truth about ethics and a truth about the common law. Both are necessarily explorations, discursively open and normatively incomplete. That is not their failure but their nature.[236]

Levinas therefore relates a theory of responsibility to a theory of meaning. The two go together, and proximity relates to both. Language exists only through our capacity to engage empathetically and imaginatively with something outside our prior experience and substitute, by means of a symbol system, something known for it – without thereby reducing the former to a mere term of the latter.[237] Difference becomes not sameness but non-indifference; we learn and we change. So too responsibility exists only through our capacity to engage empathetically and imaginatively with someone outside our prior experience and to substitute, by means of a legal system, someone known (our very self) for it – without thereby reducing the former to a mere term of the latter. "Proximity, difference which is non-indifference, is responsibility."[238]

The relative openness of the common law is therefore no scandal. Just like Borges, the structure is the message: the common law of negligence rightly exemplifies in its form and its approach the notion of responsibility – fluid, responsive, open-ended, ongoing – which it articulates. Seen in that light, it just might be the case that there are, paradoxically, structural resources within the common law that give real recognition to the "surprise and anarchy of inter-subjectivity."[239] It might even be that part of our responsibility as law teachers is to help our students to see that these resources offer the possibility of a growing and organic justice that is socially indispensable, even though it is incapable of reduction to the mere rules that students often initially imagine the law to be.

Proximity must be understood to capture a distinct and crucial, though imprecise, element of the constitution of responsibility. It is a goodness that exists not as an answer but as a question to be spoken of in certain ways but not ever to be finally answered. The gradual expansion of proximity over the past thirty or forty years therefore demonstrates not the failure of this approach but its success. Proximity describes a responsibility that ramifies the more we become conscious of it. The courts have themselves been agents and arbiters of this growing awareness of our obligations to those who are close to us. If we are faced, then, with mounting responsibilities that seem to continually outstrip our expectations, that growth is part of its organic nature.[240] Responsibility, like goodness, is not fulfilled but deepened.[241]

And proximity, likewise, does not fulfill or define this search, like a rule, but actively deepens and encourages a continuous and – it is devoutly to be hoped – unceasing discourse on it. Proximity is the language that encourages the discourse to go on. It might be translated as "He who goes in quest of aid."[242] Proximity invites and describes our non-indifference, but it does not do so by the finite application of a rule that already exists, enclosed within itself like a heart of stone and simply awaiting its predestined application. Proximity is instead the place in law and in ethics wherein we learn. "The other," as Levinas often said, "is my teacher."[243] Surely that is true. Surely that matters. What is at stake, then, is whether the law will have the courage to position *itself* as a student or will instead claim to be merely the didactic instructor of the rest of us. So proximity is that attractive and necessary ghost, always behind a screen, approached but never reduced to the familiar, always inciting us on, never resolving itself into a definitive and dogmatic form: the great student Al Mu'tasim himself.

6

Here I Am

God did tempt Abraham, and said unto him, "Abraham": and he said, "Behold, here I am." And God said, "Take now thy son, thine only son Isaac, whom thou lovest, and get thee into the land of Moriah; and offer him there for a burnt offering upon one of the mountains which I will tell thee of"... And Isaac spake unto Abraham his father, and said, "My father," and he said, "Here am I, my son." And he said, "Behold the fire and the wood: but where is the lamb for a burnt offering?" And Abraham said, "My son, God will provide himself a lamb for a burnt offering": so they went both of them together. And they came to the place which God had told him of; and Abraham built an altar there, and laid the wood in order, and bound Isaac his son, and laid him on the altar upon the wood. And Abraham stretched forth his hand, and took the knife to slay his son. And the angel of the Lord called unto him out of heaven, and said, "Abraham! Abraham!" and he said, "Here am I."[1]

Genesis 22:1–12

A light is needed to see the light.[2]

Emmanuel Levinas, *Totality and Infinity*

FROM SAID TO SAYING: RESPONSIBILITY AND WORDS

My purpose in this chapter is to pursue the interrogation of our case study into what might broadly be called areas of limitation. That is, if responsibility is in law (at least) not universal and unbounded, how does the law deal with the making of boundaries in this respect? This drawing of lines – judgment – has proved a difficult question, particularly in those areas in which there has been no immediate physical connection between the parties – areas in which, for example, words and not actions caused harm, in which the harm was purely economic and not physical, or in which the actual physical injury inflicted on the victim was occasioned by a third party. In all these circumstances – and perhaps surprisingly, given the way in which Levinas has often been read – we will find that Levinas' language of "infinite responsibility," understood by reference to the experience of proximity, is not without resources to help us understand where and how to think about these boundaries.

We will see, indeed, that questions of language, loss, and our responsibility for the acts of others take us to the heart of some of the most difficult aspects of Levinas' work. The limitation of the ethical impulse, its need to be constrained by the pragmatic and political compromises of "the middle," was a question that Levinas himself found intensely troubling. We will have to be critical of Levinas' own understanding of the relationship of ethics, politics, and law if we are to remain faithful to the core of his project. In this, then, the legal framework that I have been exploring is not to be imagined as simply subservient to Levinas' ethical ideals. The two offer a critique and a reconstructive potential to each other.

Language is central to how Levinas imagines the inauguration of responsibility. A friend clears his throat: "Can I ask you a question?" The phone rings and we answer it. The door knocks and we open it. A child is born, demanding without words.[3] In none of these cases do we know the content of the demands to be placed upon us, but we put ourselves forward in order to establish the condition for such a relationship to commence. These are all examples of that little phrase, *me voici*, here I am. Levinas' emphasis on the reflexive or accusative tense emphasizes the way in which *me voici* means more than simply "here I am," but implies already a kind of relationship with another: here I am for you. For Levinas, this statement of responsibility and vulnerability – of responsibility *as* vulnerability – consecrates and makes possible our relation to others. It "opens me to the other before saying what is said ... Here I am! The accusative here is remarkable: here I am, under your eyes, at your service."[4] To greet is to open oneself to whatever perils lie in the path of this responsibility and to do so without prior knowledge of "what is said," of the direction in which the content of that responsibility might ultimately lead.

Levinas draws here on the way in which we find the phrase "Here I am" in the Bible depicting the essential response of man's relationship with God. Since God himself is unknowable, *me voici* describes a radically asymmetric relationship marked by an openness to possibility,

on the one hand, and mystery, on the other. Thus, when Abraham
answers God's call and says "here I am, here am I" he cannot know
what is being asked of him or even who it is who truly speaks. *Me
voici* is the opening gambit that merely declares itself ready to take on
this unknown responsibility – a statement of presence as a promise of
duty. "It is without words, but not with hands empty."[5] Now, for
Levinas the danger is that any description or definition of this responsibility, by reducing the experience to a form of words, is a kind of
policy-making or system-building in which the initial nature of this
relational openness is lost. In other words, one might say that Levinas
applies the Marxist idea that alienation is inherent in commodity form[6]
to language itself, our oldest and most ubiquitous commodity. We
exchange words as we exchange coins, comparing them to each other
and to earlier uses of the same words, and in the process the singularity
of the situation before us is likewise commodified. This at least was
the upshot of Derrida's powerful criticism of Levinas in "Violence and
Metaphysics."[7] So Levinas had to face the problem that his own language – and any language that attempted to explain it – would in the
process fall foul of his own critique of corruption.

Levinas' response was not to abandon the key role that the trope of
the "voice," like that of the "face," plays in allowing us access to the
treasured and incomparable singularity of the other. In "Language and
Proximity"[8] and then in *Otherwise than Being* Levinas focuses on the
distinction between the "saying" and the "said."[9] All language betrays,
by its reduction to specific, abstract, and generalizable signifiers, the
unique relationship that first gave rise to it. Nevertheless, behind the
words that we use lies a "trace" of that initial gesture of welcome, like
a blackboard that can never be entirely wiped clean.[10] "In this 'said,'
we nonetheless surprise the echo of the saying."[11] The ethical structure,
then, is not a system of rules and principles that can be reduced to
writing; it is rather "a sign given of this giving of signs."[12] *Me voici* is
not for Levinas a thing we say or do not say; it is the voice that makes
all those other things, ideas, plans, and relationships possible.

Thus language – the voice – matters a lot to Levinas, but only in a
certain way. In "Language and Proximity," he had this to say:

Is language the transmission of and a listening to messages which would be
conceived independently of this transmission and of this listening, independently of communication? ... Or on the contrary, would language involve a
positive and antecedent event of communication which would be an *approach*

to and a *contact* with the neighbour, and in which the secret of the birth of thought itself and of the verbal statement that bears it would lie?

The contact in which I approach the neighbour is not a manifestation or a knowledge, but the ethical event of communication which is presupposed by every transmission of messages, which establishes the universality in which words and propositions will be stated. This contact transcends the I to the neighbour, and is not its thematization; it is the deliverance of a sign prior to every proposition, to the statement of anything whatever.[13]

The distinction between the saying and the said is itself highly suggestive. Let us look then at an unusual case in which the Australian High Court was asked to attribute meaning to the words and gestures of a child, the very crucible of vulnerability and therefore of responsibility. It is a case that remains the law on the duty of care owed by an adult to a child, though much has changed in the courts' approaches to the idea of responsibility since it was decided, in 1971.

Hahn v. Conley[14] concerned a little girl called Anne. Just over three, she was staying on her grandparents' farm in South Australia one weekend. It was getting on for twilight on a summer's evening, and her grandfather had strolled across the quiet country road to chat with a neighbour. Anne had wandered off from the "womenfolk"[15] in the house, and, now she found herself alone and cried out. Her grandfather called to her, saying exactly this: *"Here I am."* So Anne set out for him, first walking and then, as she drew near, in a trot. At the last moment, her grandfather sensed her peril and set out to intercept her. But it was too late, and Anne was struck and badly injured by a car travelling over forty miles an hour. The driver of the car was sued, for he had clearly been negligent. He in turn argued that the grandfather ought to bear a proportion of the damages, since he too was responsible for the child's injury.[16]

The majority excused the grandfather from all culpability. The blood relationship, though perhaps in some situations important, was not definitive. Rather, whether or not the grandfather had "assumed the charge and control of the child" was treated as a matter of fact in the specific circumstances.[17] Barwick CJ, in particular, proceeded to analyse the unfolding drama moment by moment, parsing each utterance and fragment of time to determine if anything in the relationship between the two had changed. Most significantly, Barwick dismissed the relevance of the grandfather's *me voici*. "I doubt if there is really any evidence that the appellant did call the child to him [he says]. I think the predominant conclusion from the evidence is that the appellant's response to the child's cry was no more than a reassurance to her that she was not alone."[18]

For Barwick, an utterance is something said whose meaning lies in the objective propositions it contains. Believing that responsibility cannot be imposed unless it is first actively assumed, he focuses exclusively on the intention of the utterer. It is a fairly naïve theory that equates meaning with intention. Yet the Supreme Court of South Australia approached the matter similarly, differing principally in their interpretation of the redolent phrase "Here I am." Bray CJ insisted that there was nothing in the words that could have constituted "an invitation to the plaintiff to cross the road," while Hogarth J insisted that "Here I am" was precisely a call to the child to come to him.[19] On all these views, the relationship is determined by the objective meaning of the actual words used. "Here I am" must mean something in particular: our job as judges is to work out what it is. It is that objective meaning that determines the relationship. And even the dissenting judgment of Menzies J in the High Court (with whom Walsh J agreed) conceded that the call of the grandfather founded no duty of care: "She was not in his charge. Had he then called the child to cross the road to him, that would have been negligent because, by so doing, he would both have exercised control over her and exposed her to danger. His calling would both found a duty of care and constitute a breach of that duty. Here there was no call to cross the road. The appellant's early call to the child has not that character."[20]

So according to a majority of the High Court, "Here I am" was not a promise or an undertaking to which the child obviously responded; it was simply a statement of fact about the world. Perhaps they did not remember the story of Abraham and Isaac. But even on purely semantic grounds, there is a poverty of imagination here. Justice Windeyer, whose concurring judgment we will come to shortly, puts his finger on it when he remarks, "it seems to me to be a mistake to treat the appellant's intention in calling as he did as a critical consideration. His words are not significant because of the meaning that he intended them to convey, but for what might be the reaction of his three-year-old granddaughter when she heard them."[21]

Why, exactly, was the child crying though "not," apparently, "weeping or in distress"?[22] The Court seems to treat this as a question with no possible answer, though a modicum of imagination might provide one. After all, Barwick CJ himself describes the grandfather's response as "no more than a reassurance to her that she was not alone."²³ Reassurance against what? Against the sense of vulnerability that Anne undoubtedly felt when she thought, in some inchoate way, that she had been abandoned. Anne did not want to know simply as a fact that she wasn't alone; she wanted the fear that accompanied it to be taken away. She wanted to feel safe again. Otherwise, her movement towards her grandfather, first a walk and then a trot, makes no sense. She wanted to be closer because she wanted to be safe, and there was therefore already a promise of some kind inherent in the grandfather's statement. The word "reassurance" already implies as much. Anne's grandfather may or may not have meant to inaugurate an act of responsibility, but the responsibility came toddling towards him, nonetheless.

What makes the story so compelling from a Levinasian perspective is not just the way in which those very words *"Here I am"* vividly enact the innocent and accidental, but neverthless authentic, inauguration of responsibility. It is also the way in which we must understand the meaning of the phrase quite apart from the semantic content of the words. We see here the actual effect of the "saying" (*dire*) of language on a child who is unlikely to have the kind of linguistic competence that Barwick believed was the only possible way to approach the case. Is there a comfort that language first provides? Just this: the presence of another to take care of you; another who can be trusted; another who can welcome you and keep you safe. Just to say *here I am* – just to say anything at all, the fact of speech – is already to invite a movement in response to a promise. Anne was a child of three. She probably understood only the saying, and not the said. And it was that saying, that voice, that quite literally drew her to the other. To speak, to clear one's throat and begin, is already a responsibility that cannot be reduced to a specific signification.

The troubling aspect of this conclusion was not the argument but its consequences. The Court was no doubt mindful of one momentous implication that they were careful never even to mention. The driver had insurance; the grandfather, in all probability, did not. So a decision that the grandfather was to some degree responsible for the child's injuries had the perverse effect that more of the burden, not less, would fall on Anne's family. True or false, such an allocation of responsibility was not in Anne's interests. Justice Windeyer attempted to circumvent the invidious problem in another way. He argued that the grandfather did have a responsibility for the child. "It was the relationship of 'proximity,' the facts of the occasion, which made the appellant's little

granddaughter his 'neighbour.' Prominent among those facts was that
he was not merely an onlooker, as for example was the man with whom
he was conversing. He was known to the plaintiff as her grandfather
and as the man who had called to her. He was aware of her presence
and he knew she was aware of his."[24] But Windeyer concluded that the
grandfather's behaviour, though in this sense a cause of Anne's injuries,
was reasonable in all the circumstances. "There is no evidence that
motor traffic on the road was so frequent that any crossing must have
been hazardous [he concluded]. If the appellant had gone to the child
when he first saw her, she would not have been hurt. When he decided
to do so it was too late. But he is not to be said to be a tortfeasor
simply because he did not prevent the accident."[25] A duty of care was
owed, but not breached. Admittedly there is still some sleight of hand
at work here, for if we accept that the grandfather was responsible for
the child, having called to her, then surely a reasonable person, mindful
of such a responsibility, would at least have made sure the road was
safe for her to cross. The chance of a car coming was perhaps not so
far-fetched as to allow a three-year-old to cross it unsupervised. But the
point is at least arguable, and though Windeyer might be said to have
stretched his reasoning to reach the desired outcome, he does not
destroy the entire structure of tort law in the process. Barwick CJ came
to the same result, but by a process that misunderstands the very nature
of the duty of care.

The difference between the two approaches can be readily appreciated
if we transfer the setting from a country road to a busy city street. For
Barwick, since there is no duty of care in relation to the child in the
first place, the result is the same, while for Windeyer the inaction is
this time surely negligent. Yet it cannot be the case that a grandfather
– or indeed, a nursemaid or a friend or a stranger – who calls to a
little child in such a situation owes no responsibility to her. Barwick's
reasoning distorts the whole relationship in order to get the answer he
wants, with far-reaching consequences for our understanding of it.[26]
This might not matter if the law of negligence were simply an instrument to allow the compensation of injured parties, but it is not. Its
value, if it has any, is as a social and public discourse by which the
nature of our responsibility to others is explored and deepened. The
court's judgments about the extent of that responsibility matter, not
only to the parties before the courts and not simply as legal formulae.

If we accept this approach to negligent words, then certain opacities
that have endured since the path-breaking House of Lords decision in

Hedley, Bryne & Co v. Heller can be clarified.[27] Despite the range of reasons suggested in that case, the fundamental notion persists that a responsibility for words, in order to be recognized by the law, must have been consciously accepted by the defendant. In that case, the bank's advice was clearly headed "without responsibility on the part of the bank" and that alone was ultimately enough to abrogate any duty to its recipient that might otherwise have followed. Thus Lord Devlin: "A man cannot be said voluntarily to be undertaking a responsibility if at the very moment when he is said to be accepting it he declares that in fact he is not."[28]

Yet the categorical distinction suggested here has become progressively harder to maintain. In *Shaddock*,[29] although the Australian High Court continues to speak of responsibility as something assumed or voluntarily undertaken,[30] Justice Stephen expressly indicates that in some circumstances a local council might still be held responsible for their advice even were they to deny any responsibility for it. "The information in question was of a kind which was known by all to be of great importance to those seeking it and it was largely inaccessible through other channels. Moreover, much of the information sought would concern the Council's own actions ... Were a council expressly to qualify its answers, stating that they might be subject to errors for which it accepted no responsibility, the present practice would be rendered largely worthless."[31]

Of course, it is not to be supposed that one would always be held responsible for the provision of bad information. It would hardly be negligent to indicate ignorance or uncertainty before or instead of expressing an opinion. But it will be otherwise if the information sought lies within the sole power of the defendant to discover or reveal. It would have made no sense to withhold liability in such circumstances simply because the council had decided to preface its remarks with various disclaimers. It is the saying and not the said that establishes the proximity of the parties. The council, having placed itself in the position of saying, in effect, "here I am," cannot fall back on the strict construction of their words, because behind those words necessarily lay a relationship of promise and of dependence. That is the lesson of *Hahn*, on the one hand, and of *Shaddock*, on the other. In that light, *Hedley, Byrne & Co v. Heller*, too, might be open to criticism as having paid insufficient attention to the relational context of the two parties – a context that the bank's saying set up and that was surely not entirely without relevance – and treating as conclusive its purely semantic content.

To insist on the priority from the point of view of duty of the saying over the said emphasizes the same factors that in other circumstances have proved determinative, such as the power to control information on one side, and the vulnerability to it, on the other. The question is whether, having been given advice or information, one is really in a position to take it or leave it. The situation in *Sutherland Shire Council v. Heyman*,[32] which we have looked at previously, was very different, for there the council did not say, "here I am" at all or offer to provide information except under certain defined circumstances that were not set in motion; and the purchaser of the land was able to make their own inquiries.

The difficult feature of the negligent provision of information by an agency like the Bureau of Meteorology, for example, is not the vulnerability of those who might have no real choice but to depend on it (such as the sailors being alerted to storm conditions) but, rather, the very large number of people who, via radio or TV, might ... like the weather service, by way of comparison, no doubt also offers speculative interpretations. Yet this is not by itself reason to deny the existence of a duty. In *San Sebastian v. The Minister*[33] it was not the voluntary and public provision of information that told against the plaintiffs. While the gesture of openness implied by "here I am" is much clearer and more direct in a case like *Hahn* than in a statement made to all the world, this is not an insuperable obstacle.[34] The problem in that case was, rather, that the "study documents" and "development plan" that the plaintiffs took to be binding promises of future government action with respect to the redevelopment of an inner Sydney suburb were no such thing. As the Court says, "there are, accordingly, two relevant characteristics of a development plan of the kind in question. First, there is the element of impermanence and capacity for modification and revocation. Second, the plan does not diminish the overriding discretion of the responsible authority to depart from the proposals incorporated in the plan when determining individual applications for development approval."[35] The government was not making a statement of fact relating to matters within its own competence. It was outlining possibilities that were necessarily speculative. An organization like the weather service, by way of comparison no doubt also offers speculative interpretations. But it also presents and guarantees the accuracy of specialized date on which such speculations are based. The failure to give or update a storm or hurricane warning is hardly the same thing as a faulty prediction of a sunny day, and one can well imagine those who might be seriously injured by relying on the Bureau's not merely wrong but dangerous or negligent information. The question in such cases is whether there has been an initial offering of communication – *me voici* – and, if so, to whom. Both for Levinasian ethics and in the common law, the question remains one of establishing a requisite closeness.

MATTERS OF LIMITATION:
RESPONSIBILITY AND ECONOMIC LOSS

The courts have been particularly concerned to placate the spectre of indeterminate liability that hovers over the whole field of negligent misstatement. As Lord Pearce said, "Words are more volatile than deeds. They travel fast and far afield ... Yet they are dangerous and can cause vast financial damage."[36] So, much of the concern has therefore derived not from the nature of the words that generate the relationship but rather from the nature of the loss. Indeed, negligent misstatement was traditionally understood as a species of economic loss.[37] But this is not always the case. The meteorological example shows this very clearly, for in that case an imagined misstatement in the form of a public announcement, while not directed to a particular individual or individuals, might still cause physical, not economic, loss. Yet both areas raise the same concern, which relates to the limits to be placed on proximity. One "facet of the problem arises from the propensity of negligent statements to generate loss which is purely economic. The recovery of economic loss has traditionally excited an apprehension that it will give rise to indeterminate liability. And there is also an apprehension that the application of the standard of reasonable foreseeability may allow recovery of economic loss of such magnitude and in such circumstances as to provoke doubts about the justice of [it]."[38]

The problem is almost always one of excessive abstraction, for in an abstract sense a chain of events started by some careless action can set in motion a vast and ever-expanding chain of financial events, eventually to engulf whole communities. If I negligently damage a road or a bridge, then eventually not only commuters but the whole economy of the city will suffer. Economic loss is in this sense strictly speaking unbounded – so the question of how far *I* should be held responsible for such ripples in the economic pond becomes extremely difficult to determine. Levinas would wholeheartedly concur with this concern, for the essential characteristic of proximity is that it is specific and not universal; "contact" and "touch" are the foundations of proximity and not a kind of knowledge about consequences; "sensibility not cognition" is the characteristic form of its recognition.[39] The real beauty of Levinas' appreciation of "saying" is that he understands it as the physical spark that language ignites. Language establishes "a proximity between me and the interlocutor and not our participation in a transparent universality. Whatever be the message transmitted by speech, the speaking is a contact. One must then admit that there is in speech a relationship with a singularity located outside the theme of the speech ... The contact in which I approach the neighbour is not a manifestation or a knowledge, but the ethical event of communication which is presupposed by every transmission of messages."[40]

If anything, then, Levinas' approach to proximity suggests rather more restrictive boundaries around the categories of economic loss and of negligent misstatement than the courts now tolerate. Nevertheless, the intimacy of this contact, which is the necessary limit of proximity – understood as a foundational concept in ethics – is distinct in its own terms. It is not, on the one hand, as pedantically narrow as whether I knew the plaintiff "by name." The name of something, after all, is just what Levinas means by the "said" that can exist only *after* the "saying" has constituted a relationship that then makes such knowledge and information possible. The relationship of responsibility preexists, and makes possible, our naming of it.

In fact the "who is it?" is not a question and is not satisfied by a knowing. He to whom the question is put *has already presented himself*, without being a content ... To be sure, most of the time the *who* is a *what*. We ask "Who is Mr. x?" and we answer: "he is the President of the State Council," or "He is Mr. So-and-so" ... To the question *who?* answers the non-qualifiable presence of an existent who *presents himself* without reference to anything, and yet distinguishes himself from every other existent.[41]

On the other hand, neither is the intimacy of proximity as conceptually broad as a mere causal link between the defendant's behaviour and the plaintiff's loss, as we have already seen in observing the vast economic effects that sometimes flow from our behaviour. For Levinas, a judgment of causation is a consequence of our social values, whilst a judgment of proximity is what constitutes the social in the first place. So to define proximity in terms of whether x caused y, a kind of strict liability, misses the point.[42]

In economic loss, the relevant question is therefore not whether one could identify the plaintiffs "individually, and not merely as a member of an unascertained class."[43] In *Perre v. Apand*,[44] a much larger group of claimants – potato farmers within a twenty-kilometre radius of an outbreak of bacterial wilt – was held entitled to succeed in an action brought against a negligent manufacturer who was responsible for the outbreak. The operation of law prevented them from selling in the Western Australian market whether or not their plants had actually succumbed to the disease: that is, these farmers suffered economic loss even though their potatoes were physically unharmed. McHugh J is surely right to emphasize that the guiding principle here must be the vulnerability of the defendant and not these semantic considerations. "In my view, reliance and assumption of responsibility are merely indicators of the plaintiff's vulnerability to harm from the defendant's conduct, and it is the concept of vulnerability rather than these evidentiary indicators which is the relevant criterion for determining whether a duty of care exists."[45] *Perre v. Apand* provides a good example of a group of plaintiffs who found themselves uniquely vulnerable to the careless actions of the defendant in circumstances where they could take no action to prevent or minimize the consequences of that negligence. They could not prevent the manufacturer's conduct; neither did it matter if they took their own steps to prevent the disease taking hold on their farms, since it was not diseased potatoes that were prohibited but all potatoes in the region.

Suppose, in contrast, we imagine an update to the shop-worn hypothetical of Mrs O'Leary's cow and the Chicago fire of 1871.[46] Let us think instead about the solitary animal in Alberta with "mad cow's disease" (BSE)[47] that led to the closure of export markets to Canadian beef during 2003, thereby inflicting enormous damage on the whole Canadian economy. (Instances involving the destruction of vast herds of cattle as a result of outbreaks of foot and mouth disease or BSE in the United Kingdom, for example, could readily be provided). It is hardly a question of whether the class of persons harmed by some hypothetical act of negligence could be accurately defined or determined: "every person in Alberta" is a perfectly ascertainable class, albeit there are three million members of it. Neither is it a question of foreseeability, since such damage is entirely predictable. Nor yet is it a matter of cause, since the sick cow was without doubt the precipitating cause of the whole catastrophe.

It is, rather, a question of proximity. What is lacking, as Levinas shows us, is the intimacy of the relationship between plaintiff and defendant. This is not just a question of knowledge or names or numbers but of a relationship that specifically connects the vulnerability of the one to the capacity of the other to effect the situation. Even if we focus simply on the farms that had to destroy their herds, the economic damage suffered in Alberta was a function of a range of factors including the state of u.s.-Canadian relations, the effects of NAFTA on the integration of the beef industry right across North America, the sensitivity of the Japanese government's response, and even, one might suggest, the way in which the crisis was exacerbated by fear of other diseases at the time, such as SARS or West Nile virus. The class of persons harmed by this mad cow was made vulnerable not simply by the (hypothetical) negligence of the defendant but, in addition, by a wide range of other circumstantial factors.

It is not that these factors were unforeseeable but that there was no special or distinctive vulnerability in the plaintiff or plaintiffs that was capable of *singling out* the defendant's control over circumstances – of saying, you alone are the one who can make a difference. For Levinas, the foundation of responsibility is vulnerability, and vulnerability in turn is an event that singles me out. *Me voici*, I say, announcing my presence and acknowledging my responsibility at the same time. In contrast, the example we have been exploring clearly demonstrates a vulnerability that is radically over-determined by other events. And the more distant the economic effects, no matter how predictable the causal connection, the more impossible the claim for some proximity to bind together *this* defendant with *this* plaintiff.

In *Perre v. Apand*, McHugh J clearly points to the importance of vulnerability,[48] though he does not perhaps emphasize well enough its particularizing capacity. It is not the simple fact of my vulnerability to harm, but my *subjection to you* that draws forth your responsibility. This is what is meant by proximity and what confines its operation. "[T]he responsibility to which I am exposed in such a passivity does not apprehend me as an interchangeable thing, for here no one can be substituted for me ... It obliges me as someone irreplaceable and unique, someone chosen ... Irreplaceable in responsibility I cannot, without defaulting, incurring fault ... escape the face of a neighbour."[49] I cannot escape the uniqueness of my responsibility, which is to say, the uniqueness that responsibility finds in me. It is abundantly clear that this responsibility is at times an enormous burden. Particularly in *Otherwise than Being*, Levinas speaks of responsibility as causing us discomfort,[50] and elsewhere he speaks of "wounds and outrage."[51] It is a kind of suffering. But it is no less a gift for that, because it alone is capable of giving meaning to suffering. Responsibility is not just pain: it is a suffering, or at least a sacrifice, small or large, *for* another. And perhaps in a world in which suffering and pain are such an inherent part in life, this is the greatest gift of all.[52] It undoes "the substantial nucleus of the ego"[53] and in the process forms us as unique subjects.

We do not become "better" individuals by caring for others, by trying, in other words, to "be otherwise." It is, rather, that this is how we become individuals at all. That is what Levinas means by "otherwise than being." Consciousness, after all, is the very bedrock of individuality, and it requires not so much a sense of ourselves as a sense of something outside ourselves, a sense of time and memory and otherness. For Levinas, it is the approach of the other that coalesces us, just as the caress of the other makes us aware of our skin.[54] The other, by singling us out – by holding us hostage[55] or, to put it more positively, by entreating our hospitality[56] – breaks the eternal slumber of dull self-referentiality and makes us, at last, distinctly individual, fully conscious human subjects. Subjectivity is not the purpose of responsibility, but it is the consequence.[57]

Yet Levinas' argument here makes apparent that the very idea of proximity, although it demands a great deal of us – may command of us that we rescue a person with whom we have no prior relationship or obligation at all – nevertheless imports a singularity that is neither absolute nor unlimited: the supplicant "yet distinguishes himself from every other existent."[58] It is on this point that Levinas is often misunderstood. When Levinas speaks of responsibility as infinite, he does not mean that it extends equally over everything it encounters, like some kind of monstrous sump of duty. He means that it continues to demand from us in ways that fuel our aspirations and our striving while giving us no grounds for complacency. It is infinitely deep, not infinitely wide. In just the same way, when Levinas refers to the infinity of others, he does not mean anything to do with their quantity but, rather, with a quality within every single one of them that takes them forever out of reach of our knowledge of them. We are never done with responsibility, we are never responsible enough. Responsibility is infinite in the sense that it is insatiable, so to speak, but not in the sense that it is indiscriminate.[59] This is the point that makes Levinas relevant to law, and not merely another homily in favour of the universal brotherhood of man.

As we have already seen, Levinas provides a strong philosophical foundation on which to sustain a duty to rescue, such as we find in the Quebec Charter of Rights and Freedoms: "Toute personne doit porter secours à celui dont la vie est en péril, personnellement ou en obtenant de secours, en lui apportant l'aide physique nécessaire et immédiate."[60] This goes beyond the common law, as we have seen, because neither here nor in Levinas' meditations is the act/omission distinction important. What matters is not whether I have *caused* your vulnerability but whether I am uniquely placed to do something about it. "I am obliged without this responsibility having begun in me."[61] But we can immediately see here that this *is* a vulnerability that particularizes us, each of us who find ourselves in such a situation, and crucially identifies us as "irreplaceable and unique, someone chosen." Welcome or unwelcome though the attention may be, here I am, "under your eyes, at your service."[62] But, as we have seen, this responsibility is not unlimited. For example, the call for charity, though it is made by or on behalf of persons who are in their own situation just as vulnerable, cannot operate to single me out in such a way. I am statistically responsible, socially implicated, but that is precisely the kind of reasoning that, relevant though it is in certain circumstances, does not form the basis of an ethical (or tortious) obligation.

On the other hand, the more influence or power I have, the more irreplaceable my position and the more responsibility will make demands upon me. Such a logic would certainly apply to the kinds of situations in which the courts have expanded liability by reference to categories like "non-delegable duties" or its misnamed public sector counterpart, "general reliance." An employer is responsible for the system of work prevailing in a factory, because they are in an irreplaceable and exclusive position to control the conditions of work.[63] "That such an element exists in the relationship of employment is beyond serious challenge. The employer has the exclusive responsibility for the safety of the appliances, the premises and the system of work to which he subjects his employee and the employee has no choice but to accept and rely on the employer's provision and judgment in relation to these matters."[64]

Yet the same is no less true of public authorities. In some circumstances our vulnerability to the actions of governments or their agencies is inescapable, just as their capacity to act is incomparable. We simply cannot control air traffic or fight city fires by ourselves. It is not a question of fictional reliance or some hypothetical social expectation or some special or exceptional doctrine. This fictional or hypothetical nature caused the idea to be misunderstood in *Sutherland Shire Council*, and eventually led to its hasty dismissal in *Pyrenees Shire Council v. Day.*[65] It is not a question of imagined attitudes or concepts, and most especially it is not a question of "reliance," fictional or actual, general or specific, but of real phenomena: vulnerability and the unique or singular responsibility that it identifies in relation to it. It is a question, in other words, of proximity.

MATTERS OF LIMITATION: RESPONSIBILITY FOR THIRD PARTIES

If *me voici* defines a relationship that chooses us, does it matter if the harm done as a consequence of my omission is actually realized by the actions of a third party? The courts have been especially cautious not to overburden the extent of our responsibilities not just *to* others but *for* the actions of others, circumspectly confining liability to cases in which there was some preexisting relationship of control over the actual actors. In *Smith v. Leurs*, Sir Owen Dixon emphasized that these relationships, such as, for example, parents' responsibility for certain of the activities of their children, were to be characterized by means of that uniquely Dixonian signifier, "special."[66] Indeed, in *Dorset Yacht Company v. Home Office*, the House of Lords characterized such relationships as involving not merely actual control but the *right* to exercise control.[67] In that case, the Home Office was held liable for damage done by a group of escaped juvenile delinquents. The legal rights the government exercised over the confined children founded their responsibility. "What distinguishes a Borstal trainee who has escaped from one who has been duly released from custody is his liability to recapture."[68]

In the Australian High Court, matters came to a head in the recent case of *Modbury Triangle Shopping Centre v. Anzil,*[69] a case that powerfully illustrates the cautious and perhaps retrograde approach to responsibility that has begun to characterize the Court's reasoning since the demise of proximity. The employee of a video store at a suburban shopping centre was severely injured when three men assaulted him. Tony Anzil had finished business at ten o'clock and then proceeded to close the till and lock up. Around 10:30 P.M., on the way to his car, he was attacked, probably in the course of a robbery. Despite consistent complaints from the manager of the video shop as to the safety of the premises at that time, the shopping centre management had set the automatic timer that controlled the car park lights to go off promptly at 10:00 P.M. By the time that Mr Anzil began to leave, the shopping centre was dark, deserted, and dangerous. He was accosted in the ten metres that separated the shop from his car. The High Court rejected the responsibility of Modbury Triangle despite what appears to have been their disregard for the safety of their tenants. Kirby J's dissent expresses a certain outrage: "Rushing to the rescue of the respondent was not what the law required of the appellant. Reprogramming a simple light switch in the face of numerous requests to do so was scarcely an onerous burden. I do not accept that the law of negligence in Australia sanctions such obdurate indifference to the safety of persons."[70]

There were, undoubtedly, considerable problems affecting Anzil's claim. The question of causation was one. It is by no means obvious that if only Modbury Triangle had left the lights on, the attack would necessarily have been averted. The lower courts had, in line with current practice, simply asserted that causation had been established as a matter of "common sense."[71]

Nevertheless, the issue cannot just be dismissed: how do we know that if the area had been adequately lit, the attack would not have taken place? This concern troubles the judgments of the majority. Callinan J, in particular, appears entirely unconvinced by the idea that "common sense" could be used to predict behaviour that is by its nature uncommon and nonsensical.[72] The High Court's reflections are not without nuance. First, Justice Hayne is concerned to point out that this was not a case in which the defendant company could have controlled access to the premises altogether. He suggests that if it could have, different considerations might have applied.[73] Clearly, a properly secured car park would have been sufficient to prevent the attack. But that was not possible. Neither did the victim argue that security guards should have patrolled the premises (although that too would have been a much more effective measure), presumably because Modbury Triangle was in no better position to provide such security than the video shop itself. In short, Modbury Triangle could discourage the attack but not prevent it.[74] Second, it was not even clear just how much of a disincentive proper lighting might have been. Both Hayne J and Gleeson CJ likewise acknowledge that matters might rest differently if "there is a high degree of certainty that harm will follow from lack of action."[75] These are important caveats and might have formed an alternative basis on which to deny liability. There was, after all, little but

assertion before the Court to establish causation as to the sufficiency
of the duty, if performed, to avert the harm.

Justice Kirby appears to make the argument as well as he can. He
writes of the general consensus that "good lighting discourages criminals," and refers to general practices of perimeter lighting, movement
detectors, and the like, in homes and businesses.[76] "Common sense"
is a language that encourages such generalizations. But the point here
was surely that Tony Anzil's vulnerability was not merely statistical but
particular. One small point in Kirby's judgment seems worthy of rep-
etition: "It was accepted by the trial judge that the respondent, before
leaving the store, would have looked out the window to his car to see
if there was anybody suspicious near the car."[77] Perhaps Callinan J was
right: perhaps there were other places for the assailants to hide; perhaps
they were intent on using that baseball bat, come what may. Nevertheless, it seems far more likely that with a good view of the car park,
able at last to see all those who were loitering in it and all those who
were passing through it, Mr Anzil would have safely made those ten
steps – no more – to his car. That would be one way of approaching
the question of causation.

Instead, the majority of the Court treated causation as very much a
secondary issue and chose to build their case on a much broader
ground that expressly rejects any supposed "duty to control the criminal conduct of others"[78] and largely affirms the principles of *Dorset
Yacht Co.* and *Smith v. Leurs.* "In those cases where a duty to control
the conduct of a third party has been held to exist, the party who owed
the duty has had power to assert control over that third party. A gaoler
may owe a prisoner a duty to take reasonable care to prevent assault
by fellow prisoners. If that is so, it is because the gaoler can assert
authority over those other prisoners. Similarly, a parent may be liable
to another for the misconduct of a child because the parent is expected
to be able to control the child."[79] The reasoning of the court, particularly in the judgment of Gleeson CJ, focuses once again on the idea
of an "assumption" (that is, a free and prior acceptance) of responsibility. As Gleeson CJ explicitly argues, the fact that the shopping centre
had the capacity to make the environment safer does not mean that
they had assumed the responsibility to do so.[80] Neither can it be said
that Modbury Triangle had the least "control" or "knowledge" over
the criminal behaviour that actually caused the injury.[81] Hayne J, with
whom Gaudron J agreed, likewise insists that the appellants "did not
control what happened to the first respondent," which was, rather, the

result of "deliberate criminal wrongdoing by a third party. By its nature that conduct is unpredictable and irrational."[82]

The majority's reasoning represents another instance of the High Court's turn away from the broader ambit of responsibility that had derived from its development of themes of proximity. The Court is right to insist upon the paramount question of control. But here the Court's steadfast refusal to couch the question in the language of proximity leads them seriously astray. The Court focuses on the shopping centre's control – or lack of it – over the criminals.[83] Hayne J insists that the fundamental principle in this case is that "there is no duty to control the criminal conduct of others except in very restricted circumstances."[84] After all, Modbury Triangle didn't hit anyone with a baseball bat. This completely miscasts the use of the word control in the context of our duties to others. No one expected *Modbury Triangle* to control the criminal conduct of others. They were asked to control their own environment, in order to protect those who were singularly vulnerable to it. So, too, no one would suggest that the installation of proper air conditioning for the height of an Australian summer was an attempt to "control the weather," only to recognize the need to respond to it.

Proximity is a *relationship* that gives rise to a duty of care, and the relationship in which the language of control and vulnerability ought to be raised is that between the employee and the shopping centre – not between the criminals and the shopping centre. The High Court insists that the shopping centre is not to be held responsible for the conduct of criminals. That is not the question. They could control the environment and, in particular, Mr Anzil's experience of it. Modbury Triangle's exclusive ability to control the lighting of the car park made Mr Anzil vulnerable to attack in a situation in which he was himself powerless to do anything about it. He could not avoid that vulnerability. Neither he nor, indeed, the video shop could protect him. And it is this relationship that *singles out* Modbury Triangle. The High Court, in forgetting the relational nature of the duty of care that proximity served to foreground, abstracted the question of control from the very person over whom it was exercised.

This failure to properly consider the relevant relationship likewise led the High Court to ignore what was indeed, to recall Dixon's language, "special" about it.[85] The judges were concerned that if Modbury Triangle were responsible for Mr Anzil, then they would be obliged, at the very least, to "leave the lights on all night."[86] After all, the shopping centre was also home to an automatic teller machine that might attract customers much later than 10:30 in the evening. "If the appellant owed [Anzil] a relevant duty of care, it was to take *whatever* steps were reasonable in all the circumstances to hinder or prevent *any* criminal conduct of third persons which injured the first respondent or *any* person lawfully on the premises."[87] Gleeson CJ approaches the matter similarly[88] and so too does Callinan J: "There was, in the circumstances, no relevant difference between the duties owed to other lawful entrants upon the car park and the respondents."[89] So the Court sees nothing distinctly vulnerable in the situation of Tony Anzil and nothing to connect that vulnerability to the areas under Modbury Triangle's control. Not so. As we have seen, proximity *is* about the special closeness of particular persons. But what makes it special has nothing to do with any prior relationship between the parties. Responsibility is a fact, prior to principles and commitments, deriving from the immediate experience of vulnerability that identifies a unique subject.[90] The vulnerability of an employee in a work environment has this nature, as has long been recognized. It is easy to see its relevance here. The automatic teller machine's customers can always decide to get their money somewhere else. They can always decide to come back in the daylight. They can have their friends or family come with them, late at night, if they wish. They have a freedom to come or to go that attests to the fact that Modbury Triangle is on no account in control of their fate. But an employee is quite differently situated. He cannot, realistically, choose to work elsewhere (unless, of course, one agrees with Posner that a worker in a dangerous job is merely "marketing his taste for risk").[91] He cannot decide to wait until the morning to leave. There was only one way out and he had to take it, and he had to take it then. Mr Anzil was vulnerable in a way quite different from others who might come and use the shopping centre's facilities, and the only one who could allay that vulnerability was Modbury Triangle.

Yet none of the judges, not even Justice Kirby in his dissent, appears to me to have fully appreciated the extent of the respondent's utter vulnerability in the circumstances created by the appellant. And this lies at the heart of the majority's systematic refusal to acknowledge any special proximity between Modbury Triangle and the victim. That danger stemmed not just from Modbury's failure to leave the lights on, which might indeed have affected every visitor to the shopping centre equally, but from the relationship between darkness and light in which the victim of this brutal attack unwillingly found himself. Mr Anzil was trapped. He was a spot-lit target, all too easy to observe as he completed his work in a pool of light, surrounded by a darkness that readily concealed both the observers and their conduct. He could not see them as they waited, but they could see him, a problem that was only exacerbated when he left Focus Video for the low light to which his eyes had not yet adjusted but that suited his attackers admirably. It was, in fact, the perfect environment for a lying-in-wait. There was only one way home: through the darkness that Modbury Triangle had created, that they alone could remedy, and about which, apparently, they could not have cared less.

The Court's failure is therefore primarily imaginative, not conceptual. Proximity has been rightly criticized for its over-generalized logic, but that was never its real value. Certainly, for Levinas, proximity founds responsibility not on logic but on experience. It offers not one rule amongst others, as indeterminate as all the rest but, instead, a necessary moment in which to understand our relationship to others as coming from a phenomenal connection between persons that arises out of a particular predicament that binds together the vulnerability of one to the response ability that singles out another. Without reference to proximity, it is not our law's reasoning that will suffer, but its empathy – and that, says Levinas, is what makes reasoning possible.

ME VOICI: POLITICS AND THE CHALLENGE OF RESPONSIBILITY

The real implications of such a broad understanding of responsibility are not always palatable. Even Levinas has been guilty of political hesitancy when confronted with the specific implications of his arguments in circumstances whose parallels with the questions confronted by the High Court in *Modbury* make for an interesting comparison.

September 16, 1982, was a Thursday. Israeli Defence Forces (IDF) had occupied West Beirut forty-eight hours previously in response to the assassination of the president of Lebanon, in order to "prevent any possible incident and to secure quiet." Yet according to the Israeli government's commission of inquiry, that same evening groups of Lebanese Phalangist militia were in fact permitted to enter the Palestinian refugee camps of Sabra and Chatila, supposedly in order to clear out suspected terrorists and *fedayeen*. The IDF did nothing to prevent the indiscriminate violence that occurred that night and all the next day. Despite growing reports of atrocities and discussions at the highest level of the Israeli government, the IDF stood back and refused to intervene until

Saturday morning. By then, upwards of seven hundred people had been killed.[92] The figure may have been as high as two thousand.[93]

There is no dispute as to the perpetrators of the massacre. Neither is there any dispute as to the conditions under which the killings took place. The question was ethical, and it sent shock waves through Israeli society. On one side stood the government, disclaiming all responsibility. Prime Minister Menachim Begin declared that "No one conceived that atrocities would be committed ... Simply, none of us, no minister, none of the other participants supposed such a thing."[94] Ariel Sharon, then minister of defence, insisted that "the hands of the IDF are clean ... We never imagined in our worst dreams that these same Phalangists would do the worst thing possible."[95] On the other side, a wide range of critics in Israel and around the world stood prepared to hold the IDF, and Begin and Sharon, in particular, themselves responsible for the massacre. As Labour Party leader Shimon Peres said, "Whose was this stupid idea, to send the Phalangists to the refugee camps to find the terrorists? ... Is this surprising? This was something unprecedented? ... Where was your supervision? Where were your reports? Where was your follow through? The television photographers had to unearth this?"[96] There are good reasons to doubt the Likud government's protestations of innocence. The Commission of Inquiry chaired by the Supreme Court president, Justice Yitzhak Kahan, revealed clear evidence of knowledge at the highest levels, from as early as Thursday evening, of what was going in the camps.[97] Cabinet itself had already been assured that the IDF would not themselves venture into Sabra and Shatila, leaving the Phalangists to proceed "with their own methods."[98] Furthermore, the government's expressions of surprise sit uneasily with the rationale for the IDF's invasion of West Beirut, which was precisely aimed at protecting the Moslem population, largely sheltering in the refugee camps, "from the vengeance of the Phalangists."[99] It can hardly be true that "no one had imagined that the Phalangists would commit such acts," while at the same time "we made them swear, not one oath but thousands ... that the kind of actions that were committed would not be committed."[100] "Thousands of oaths" suggests an acute level of distrust in their bona fides. It would appear, then, that the real possibility of these atrocities was on everyone's mind exactly at the time that the conditions were established that allowed them to be carried out unhindered. These are the facts that led the Commission of Inquiry, which conducted its work with unstinting honesty, to hold responsible, and ultimately force the resignation of, Ariel Sharon.[101]

But the central question was not factual. It was about the nature of responsibility. Was the IDF responsible notwithstanding that it did nothing except fail to intervene? If one were to adopt an approach similar to that advanced in *Modbury Triangle*, one might wonder. There we have seen the Court insist that only exceptional circumstances impose a "duty to control the criminal conduct of others."[102] The court inquires into the relationship – in *Dorset Yacht*, the legal *right* to control – between the defendant and the third party, and not their control over the environment in which the criminality takes place. Clearly, no such relationship existed here. There was, of course, no right to control the actions of the Phalangists, and indeed the IDF's entire strategy consisted simply in permitting them to enter the camps "with their own methods." One might certainly argue that the defence forces, in entering West Beirut avowedly in order to maintain control of a volatile situation, had in some measure assumed responsibility over the situation: they had taken charge by force. But the emphasis in *Modbury* would appear to suggest that the right question to ask is whether they had assumed responsibility over the criminal conduct, and here the IDF clearly and expressly did not.

It is true that the inactions of the IDF in Sabra and Shatila were, in principle no less than in their tragic and incomparable consequences, a great deal more egregious than those of Modbury. In Beirut the IDF had the capacity to secure access to the area. At the same time, despite the expressions of shock and surprise voiced by Sharon and Begin, the likelihood of harm consequent on their action was close to a certainty.[103] It will be recalled that these two provisos form the principal exceptions to the general rejection of liability in *Modbury*. As opposed to that case, the IDF could have prevented the harm altogether and not just lessened its probability. But I cannot help feeling that a theory of liability that finds itself uncertain as to the correct response to the events of September 1982 and that looks to create out of those events an *exception* has started from the wrong premise. Sabra and Shatila ought to offer us a paradigm for the nature of responsible action, and not an exception. It ought to be exemplary. If instead it looks like a "hard case," then I think that what has gone wrong is our initial theory of the origin and direction of that responsibility.

It was in this climate of shame and accusation that Emmanuel Levinas was interviewed by Radio Communauté. It was unusual for Levinas thus to be confronted by a specific political event. And he is quite clear in acknowledging the "ethical reaction" of responsibility "on the part of ... the majority of the Jewish people," which "constitutes every man's responsibility towards all others, a responsibility which has nothing to do with any acts one may really have committed."[104] At the same time, there is a perfectly comprehensible emotional struggle in Levinas against "all those who attack us with such venom [and] have no right to do so."[105] In other words, the defence of Israel and of the Jewish people requires not only an ethics but a politics: the former an "unbounded responsibility" to others, the latter a balancing of interests as between neighbours whose interests clash. The ethical demand, which is uncompromising, contradicts the political demand, which entails nothing but balance and compromise.[106]

As the interview proceeds, Levinas appears to become increasingly confused as he struggles to weigh up the ethical responsibility that attaches even to those "who have done nothing," against the political responsibility for the difficult survival of Israel. Shlomo Malka asks, "Emmanuel Levinas, you are the philosopher of the 'other' ... and for the Israeli, isn't the 'other' above all the Palestinian?" But Levinas' response prevaricates. "My definition of the other is completely different. The other is the neighbour, who is not necessarily kin, but who can be. And in that sense, if you're for the other, you're for the neighbour. But if your neighbour attacks another neighbour or treats him unjustly, what can you do? ... We are faced with the problem of knowing who is right and who is wrong, who is just and who is unjust."[107]

The implication would appear to be that this is no longer a question of ethics but of politics and that the two inhabit fundamentally irreconcilable realms, unmixable as oil and water. But is this good enough? The application of Levinas' writings to questions of politics has been a central task of recent scholarship. And the question of what it means when faced with particular institutions with their own logics and agendas – Parliaments, the army, the law – to apply an ethics of infinite responsibility has proved exceptionally difficult. Neither has this been helped by Levinas' own ambivalence. At least according to Howard Caygill, this ambivalence stemmed from a deep horror of political engagement as such, born of "the presentiment and memory of the Nazi horror,"[108] coupled with a relationship with the State of Israel that was sometimes cautious and yet often passionately committed.[109] Between the critique of the State in "Place and Utopia" and his enthusiastic support in "The State of Israel and the Religion of Israel," not to mention the Zionist elements to be found in certain essays in *Difficult Freedom*, there is clear evidence that Levinas found no easy reconciliation between his ethical and political impulses.[110] Indeed, several of his other attempts at political commentary are disturbingly simplistic and at times unpleasantly close to racism.[111] At the very least we can conclude that Levinas found the transition between the two no easier than the rest of us.

Levinas certainly concludes that "there is also an ethical limit to this ethically necessary political existence,"[112] and he locates this limit in our souls, in the light of which "a person is more holy than a land, even a holy land."[113] This is a fierce argument and one that the hawks of the Israeli cabinet, then and now, could hardly have welcomed. But there is an *aporia* here through which Levinas does not so much pass as side-step. It is the question of judgment, of how we are to discriminate between our doing nothing here and our doing nothing somewhere else, between this neighbour and that neighbour, the other and all the "other others."[114]

It is dangerous to continue to speak in terms of Israeli innocence or of a culpability that relates simply to having "done nothing." Levinas does not entirely avoid this danger. Every time he speaks of responsibility as generalized "towards all others," as limitless, or as implicating even "those who[m] we call innocent," he appears to be effacing the distinction that proximity insists upon. The problem with insisting that "you personally are implicated each time that somewhere ... humanity is guilty"[115] is that it appears that *all* those who have done nothing are to be held equally guilty. When Levinas goes so far as to say that "the more innocent we are, the more we are responsible,"[116] he might be taken to be implying a kind of martyrdom or self-sacrifice.

For if Levinas asks us to accept our own responsibility for the state of the world – nothing but a universal *mea culpa* – without accepting as part of that the grave responsibility of judging others and evaluating their response ability, then he is of no use to the project of law at all. As many critics of Levinas have pointed out, the problem with such a global responsibility is that it incites to irresponsibility. I do not want to say that the leadership of the Israeli Defence Forces was responsible for all the suffering in the world, for that would place them as no more or less responsible than everyone else. I want to say only that they were responsible for the suffering that occurred in the refugee camps of West Beirut between that Thursday evening and the following Saturday morning. Their doing nothing had a different character from their inaction elsewhere – or from yours or mine – and that difference is intrinsic to their responsibility. Ariel Sharon was not innocent. To speak of

Sabra and Chatila as "the place where *everything* is interrupted ...
where *everyone's* moral responsibility comes into play, a responsibility
that concerns and engages even *innocence*, unbearably so"[117] serves
only to efface these distinctions. "Everyone's responsibility," says Levinas,
a two-word sentence to punctuate the point.[118] But responsibility is not
everyone's. It singles us out by our capacity.

That was surely Levinas' point throughout his ethical writings,
though he comes close to evading it here. And it is a point that those
who insist on the unassimilable nature of ethics also do not entirely
accept, since any such singling out must involve a judgment of others
and not the kind of self-reflection and self-questioning that Levinas
asks of each of us, only for our part and for all the time.[119] The incommensurability of ethical notions of personal responsibility means that
one cannot ever *stay* with ethics, as Derrida pointed out.[120] That is
when we move from asymmetric ethics to symmetrical judgment. It is
for this reason that we will always need recourse to "laws and – yes
– courts of law, institutions and the state."[121] One might even say that
judgment itself, in its severity, its balance, and its haste, is inherently
unethical. Yet in taking seriously an ethics that does not put *our* priorities and paradigms first but instead forces us to consider the actual
vulnerability of others to our actions and omissions, we nevertheless
immediately trouble the standard ways of thinking about political ends
and means, about power and responsibility – including the standard
ways in which the Israeli army thought about just these questions –
and we open it to a more inclusive perspective once and for all.[122] We
break the string of seamless logic that no knot can perfectly retie. And
in this way, though we do not stay with ethics, our politics is troubled,
questioned, and finally transformed by it. As Wendy Farley writes,
"ethics is an exteriorizing mode of relationship to the other. Rather
than importing the other into the same, ethics carries the same beyond
itself to the other. Ethics does not think the other, it welcomes the other
or desires him."[123]

The purity of such a vision cannot long be maintained. We are once
again destined to betray our ethical ideals the moment we try to operationalize them or put them into practice, the moment we are called
upon to judge and to decide. That is yet another responsibility from
which we cannot hide. But the safe haven of a pure ethics is undesirable, and its betrayal is welcome if we are not to totalise our ethics as
much as we totalise our politics. Partiality, imperfection, and pollution
are part of the troubling power of ethics.

The language of proximity is notable for its absence in Levinas' interview, yet this is what allows us to do what Levinas sometimes seems to suggest is impossible, which is to weigh up our responsibilities and to recognize their urgency. Certainly there are intimations, even in this cautious text, as to what is involved in such a judgment. If Levinas appears to suggest sometimes that we are all neighbours, all indistinguishably "close to me," yet he also insists here on our obligation to "those closest to us." The very idea of close*ness* and of neighbourhood, implies something relative. When he claims that "you personally are implicated each time that somewhere humanity is guilty," he adds, crucially but parenthetically, "especially when it's somewhere close to you."[124] This subservient clause is key. The word "especially" ought not to be treated as an afterthought that highlights the proximity of the moment; on the contrary, it expresses the condition that summons it into existence.

It is certainly true that for Levinas proximity is a phenomenon to be experienced, not a concept to be imagined. The proximity of the IDF was not a function of their knowledge or the foreseeability of the harm that followed. One cannot hide behind ignorance. "Close to you – as if one could anticipate that!" remarks Levinas.[125] But our study of proximity as it has been illuminated both by Levinas' discussion of it and by the explorations undertaken by the Australian High Court should by now make it abundantly clear why the IDF were responsible: not generally, not ontologically, but specifically and uniquely. Those in the camps were utterly vulnerable. They had no capacity to escape or modify their destiny. They were, in short, trapped. And while it ought never to be forgotten that the Phalangist gunmen inflicted their deaths, they were able to do so only because of the control or lack of control exercised exclusively by the IDF – *pace Modbury*, a control over the environment, not over the gunmen. It is probably even true to say that so out of control were the Phalangist militia that no one of them was in a position to prevent the unfolding tragedy. It does not lessen the moral culpability of all those who pulled the triggers that night to note that the camps of Sabra and Shatila were a tinderbox awaiting a spark. What distinguished those in the camps was the capacity of Ariel Sharon, and of Ariel Sharon alone, to altogether prevent the fire that instead he chose to fan. There they were: *here I am.*

No doubt the IDF appears to have done rather more than just stand by. Once again, it was a question not a darkness but of light, not of concealment but of exposure. The IDF provided illumination of the refugee camps all through Thursday and Friday night.[126] This is a telling point, but we must be careful to think about exactly what it is telling us. The fact seems to go to the degree of Sharon's culpability and implies behaviour that was not just negligent but reckless or, even worse, wilful. It is not a matter of trivial importance when we come to evaluate what the IDF did and why. But the lights that they shone did not transform their inaction into a kind of action. Neither is it the case that in thus assisting the work of the Phalangists, the army was choosing to accept a responsibility over the camps. Rather, as Levinas would say, it dramatizes for us a responsibility that was already present in the fact of the disproportionate vulnerability of the refugee camps and the power exercised by the Israeli army over them. It is the capacity to light, and not the lighting itself, that matters: on or off, a floodlit camp or a pitch-black shopping centre, they establish to our satisfaction the extent of that power, for good and for ill: the power to shelter and the power to expose. The nightlights of the IDF gave the residents of Sabra and Shatila nowhere to hide, enforcing and enhancing their awful vulnerability. But these lights finally illuminate the defence forces themselves, singling them out as uniquely response-able.[127] The light says what responsibility always says: here I am, at your service. They tell us not that a responsibility has been assumed, but that it has been clearly recognized.

What one saw thereafter, particularly in the bitter recriminations and intense parliamentary inquiry that followed the massacre,[128] was just how ethics *can* work to hold politics to account; just how it can it sweep away the expedient logic and excuses that typically shield callous indifference from light and demand an acknowledgment – even in the political realm – of a deeper and abiding sense of responsibility. No doubt this ethical crisis cannot be said to have transformed the conduct of the Israeli army. Still, it is abundantly clear that, haunted by Sabra and Shatila, these ethical scruples are frequently used to scrutinize the army and to hold it to standards of justice, as well as of mere effectiveness. There is a long, long way to go, but I do not think it right to say that the radical discourse of ethics has made no difference at all.[129] No one in the IDF today can claim to be immune from the ghosts that haunt it or to have forgotten the knots that bind it.

Furthermore, the ethical relationship with the vulnerable is the very condition of trust that must begin before trust is established and, indeed, necessarily in the absence of trust. A political community must start with a sacrifice before any political negotiations are even possible.

Ethics, then, begins with a pledge, not a contract.[130] The saying – nothing more than that little phrase "here I am" for you – precedes the said and puts us in relation with the other. This entails its own risks. Yitzhak Rabin, prime minister of Israel, was assassinated in November 1995 precisely because he seemed prepared to sacrifice pride on the altar of peace, and not the other way around.[131] But the ethic of sacrifice and of responsibility is a necessary precondition for the foundation of what we might call normal politics. It proceeds asymmetrically,[132] and not as a by-product of any contract theory of mutual agreement.[133] In the absence of a sense of responsibility that is not in return for anything at all, that is ungrounded and unjustified, there is absolutely nothing to distinguish a pattern of exchange from a pattern of reprisals. Under the logic of contract, there can be no end to violence, for every reprisal merits its exchange, and every exchange demands a further reprisal. The newspapers are full of such a logic; so are the morgues. Instead, it is proximity, not privity, that connects us.[134] In this relationship, one neither assimilates the other nor attempts to build walls. It is instead a "non-allergic relation, an ethical relation."[135] Such a relationship, as we have seen, is not formal but particular, not conceptual but experiential, not equal but unequal. It begins with those few words that light us up as human subjects, subjected to responsibility, and that give tort law its distinct ethical framework and its point of departure: Here I am.

7

All the Others

Henry Moore's *Moon Head* has about it a sense of unconsummated longing.[1] One can see the connection, no doubt, to those many other sculptures in which Moore explored the relationship of form to negative space. But there is a figurative and immediately human quality to the *Moon Head* that sets it apart from many of these. Two concave bronze lozenges face each other on small plinths, smooth and blank and featureless. In one, a minor excision on the side is enough to suggest an open mouth and convert the disk to the form of a speaking face. In the other, a slightly larger cut on the top transforms it into a hand, mittened in bronze. Close to each other – only an inch or two apart – but not quite touching, they create a space between them that is charged with the energy of their absence, like the breath of desire. The face speaks, but we cannot hear it. The hand grasps, but we do not know what. Like the moon and the earth itself, these bodies appear caught in the thrall of each other's gravity, never to be joined, never to be free.

This remarkably intense work seems to me to speak directly to Levinas' theory of ethics and particularly to what one might call the more phenomenological, less metaphysical work to be found in *Totality and Infinity*. The language of gravity is itself redolent. At the end of that book Levinas refers to "the curvature of inter-subjective space,"

Henry Moore, *Moon Head* (1964). Reproduced by kind permission of the Henry Moore Foundation.

so as to capture the sense in which the weight of others itself constitutes our own mass, so as to suggest that the presence of the other does not just impinge on me but forms my gravity and bends the very space between us.² Our orbits draw us to each other, mould and shape our trajectories, congeal our mass without destruction. The notion of a "space between" is crucial to Levinas' understanding of proximity. This is just what he means by *infinity*: "a distance more precious than contact, a non-possession more precious than possession, a hunger that nourishes itself not with bread but with hunger itself."³ Our proximity to the other must be understood as a closeness that never destroys the other or translates it into *our* terms or attempts to convert it into another version of *me*. Only on these terms is responsibility – or love – possible. "Desire does not coincide with an unsatisfied need; it is situated beyond satisfaction and non-satisfaction. The relationship with the Other, or the idea of Infinity, accomplishes it."⁴

To explain all these ideas, Levinas has recourse to many examples. The most prominent of them are the face and the hand. The grasping hand begins life for Levinas as the apotheosis of totality. It is the agent of possession. The hand reaches out and grasps, takes something over and then converts it into an object usable, consumable, or otherwise functional for my needs. "The hand accomplishes its proper function prior to every execution of a plan, every projection of a project, every finality that would lead out of being at home with oneself. The hand's rigorously economic movement of seizure and acquisition ... is not a transcendence. Labor conforms with the elements from which it draws the things. It grasps matter as raw material."⁵

What is it that can slip through this primordial and acquisitive grasp? The face: the epiphany of infinity.⁶ It presents to us something wholly unequivocal: a presence and an otherness and a vulnerability beyond dispute. "The face resists possession, resists my powers. In its epiphany, in expression, the sensible, still graspable, turns into total resistance to the grasp."⁷ But this resistance is not a mode of violence, the opposition of one totality (or force, or ideology) to another. Ethical resistance is, on the contrary, an entirely passive movement – "the resistance of what has no resistance."⁸ Precisely by *appealing* to us "in the total nudity of his defenceless eyes,"⁹ the face makes completely clear the impossibility of ever overcoming the distinctness of another and the responsibility that this founds and justifies in us. To look in "the face of the neighbour"¹⁰ is to be aware, beyond argument, of a soul that cannot be acquired and used. "The impossibility of killing does not have a simply negative and formal signification; the relation with infinity, the idea of infinity in us, conditions it positively. Infinity presents itself as a face in the ethical resistance that paralyses my powers and from the depths of defenceless eyes rises firm and absolute in its nudity and destitution. The comprehension of this destitution and thus hunger establishes the very proximity of the other."[11]

Anyone who has studied civil disobedience will understand what Levinas is getting at. Terrorism, which attempts to prove the "feebleness of my powers,"[12] does not change anything. On the contrary, it provokes greater power against it: two warring ideologies, two totalities that cannot stand together, each mauling the other. Ethical resistance does not attempt to undermine power but affirms instead power's "capacity,"[13] demonstrating against this both what cannot be subjected to power, remaining forever outside its economy, and what is able to benefit by its operation. The limits of power are thus established not by a countervailing strength that can issue only in further struggle but, on the contrary, by "this most passive passivity."[14] This very weakness *proves* the limits of power's ability to destroy the other and at the same time highlights its ability to create. Gandhi's notions of passive resistance clearly drew on just this point.[15] Or, for example, think about the apartheid regime in South Africa, which was surely brought down not only by civil war but equally by the imprisonment of Nelson Mandela and the murder of Steve Biko.[16] Mandela proved by his imprisonment, as Biko proved by his death, that a certain dignity and resistance could never be obliterated and indeed would only be enhanced by the violence that sought to wipe it out. Instead, Mandela offered to F.W. de Klerk the possibility of using his capacity for power positively, as a sacrifice.

Proximity does not annihilate the other: it heals the self. While terrorism and violence incite us to redouble our efforts to destroy it, true resistance does something quite different. It invites us to find new powers within us: "powers of welcome, of gift, of full hands, of hospitality."[17] This alone does not confront and entrench the ego but transfigures it. The face and the hand are therefore not in opposition. They are different stages of development. The face – and above all the speech that issues from it – transforms our possessive reflex into a compassionate one. The hand becomes an agency for giving not taking, for caressing not grasping. "The caress consists in seizing upon nothing, in soliciting what ceaselessly escapes its form ... It is not an intentionality of disclosure but of search ... Anticipation grasps possibles; what the caress seeks is not situated in ... the light of the graspable."[18] The caressing hand senses and cherishes the proximity of another without holding on to it or taking it over. As Levinas remarks, though many are they who have not yet understood it, "nothing is further from *eros* than possession."[19]

These, then, are the elements of Moore's sculpture. Face and hand depict infinity, responsibility, and love. Their proximity, which is to say their closeness and at the same time their ineradicable distance, turns out to be the condition of a nonallergic relationship. Finally, the images themselves are delicately poised between particularity and abstraction, or rather as both particularity and abstraction at once. *Moon Head* is a singular object, itself and nothing else. But the featureless forms do not permit us to recognize someone familiar, someone we already know. It is not a portrait. Our empathy must be engaged, if it is engaged at all, on behalf of anyone in the formal position of proximity. *Moon Head* could be anybody and everybody, but only one at a time. So, too, Levinas insists that responsibility derives from the specific call of the other but not from the call of the specific other. Our responsibility comes from the saying that precedes the said, the face that precedes and exceeds all knowledge we might have of it. "The way in which the other presents himself, exceeding *the idea of the other in me*, we here name face ... The face of the Other at each moment destroys and overflows the plastic image it leaves me ... It does not manifest itself by these qualities ... It *expresses itself*."[20] It does not matter who you are, your name or the colour of your eyes, or your kinship to me. This is already a kind of knowledge that our ethical relationship makes possible and of which it is not in any way a consequence. We do not reason towards ethics but the other way around.[21] The essential point is that the other to whom we find ourselves proximate, our neighbour, is "irreducible to the representation of the other, irreducible to an intention of thought."[22] This is of course what makes him or her infinite but also what founds our responsibility prior to our knowledge of them. I do not believe this is a vague abstraction; it resonates deep within me and perhaps within you too. We feel before we know. "In representation presence is already past ... The contact in which I approach the neighbour is not a manifestation or a knowledge, but the ethical event of communication which is presupposed by every transmission of messages, which establishes the universality in which words and propositions will be stated. The contact transcends the I to the neighbour and is not its thematization."[23] Moore depicts our relationships in their embryonic state. This captures precisely the way love and responsibility, no doubt in different ways, impinge upon us well before we are aware of their extent and implications. "Consciousness is always late for the rendezvous with the neighbour."[24] Do we not have neighbours before we meet them?

We should not be surprised at the juxtaposition of these two works, of the Levinas of 1961 with the Moore of 1964. It is not a question of intention, the conscious appropriation and interpretation of the ideas of others to serve our purposes. But neither is the juxtaposition of artist and philosopher a coincidence. It is an instance of proximity itself, of a breath that one feels before one is conscious of its presence.[25] Proximity does not work by providing us with a new piece of information that we can use to reconstruct our knowledge of the world. Levinas' whole point is that knowledge comes from outside and can make a home in us only by its conversion into the language of the already familiar.[26] That is the problem and the paradox that leads Levinas to subtitle *Totality and Infinity* "an essay on exteriority." True difference, true innovation, is both an imposition and an impossibility. Levinas' solution lies in conceiving of our ethical relations as a way of transforming us from the inside out, thereby allowing us to discover this responsibility as within us already. We feel this our quickening before we know it. The connection between the perspectives of Emmanuel Levinas and Henry Moore – between the discoursing mouth of the one and the sculpting hand of the other – lies in their proximity: the head and the hand have contaminated each other infinitely, not totally.

ETHICS/POLITICS: "THE THIRD PARTY" AND
THE PROBLEM OF LAW IN LEVINAS

One of the problems in engaging in such speculations is that our world has vastly more influences in it than just these two, and any influence their work has exerted has been governed and mediated by many others, around it, before it, and after it. There is something very romantic in imagining a world of only two, just as there is something tragic in imagining a world of only one.[27]

Moore's *Moon Head* appeals to that romance directly, evoking a sense of privacy, intimacy, and exclusivity. So too does Levinas, and not only in his discussions of love, birth, parenthood, childhood, and so on.[28] The whole tenor of Levinas' ethical theory forsakes all others. And this, as has often been pointed out, is the problem. For in law and otherwise, it is very often the case that our responsibilities do not concern one other person alone. We must balance our obligations, weigh up the help a stranger calls from us against our duty to our families and the loved ones who are waiting for us at home. We live in a society in which needs invariably clash, in which budgets and resources are limited for each of us and all of us, and where more help is sought than can ever possibly be given. This, for Derrida, is the real question. What then? "I cannot respond to the call, the request, the obligation, or even the love of another without sacrificing the other other, the other others ... I am responsible to any one (that is to say to any other) only by failing in my responsibility to all the others, to the ethical or political generality. And I can never justify this sacrifice."[29] For Derrida, there can be no solution to this problem, for in the process we would reduce the ethical demand to a legal formula, a matter of equations and a hierarchy of norms and rules. And as we have seen, this defeats both the urgency and the pre-cognitive nature of proximity altogether. Proximity cannot ever be reduced to a rule. Moreover, if "every other is absolutely other" – "tout autre est tout autre"[30] – how could such a comparison even take place? How could incommensurable obligations ever be subject to measurement?[31] "Adhering absolutely to any one duty inevitably leads to my sacrificing another absolute duty, and this I do without any means of justifying my choice. And yet I choose. I choose to follow one and neglect another, to align myself with one and fight against another."[32]

Levinas is entirely mindful of the problem, and both in *Otherwise than Being* and elsewhere, he tries to address it.[33] Indeed, he concedes the unsustainability of his romance. "If proximity only ordered me to the one other, there wouldn't have been any problem ... it is troubled and becomes a problem when a third party enters. The third party is other than the neighbour, but also another neighbour, and also a neighbour of the other, and not simply his fellow. What then are the other and the third party for one another? ... Which passes before the other?"[34] The recognition that the third party is also my neighbour brings with it the need for balance and equality.[35] For Levinas, this is why we need "justice," which he would appear to use here to encompass the rule of law. But the entry of law into Levinas' world seems a lot like the demise of ethics. Justice, he concludes, is all about "comparison, co-existence, contemporaneousness, assembling, order, thematization ... the intelligibility of a system."[36] "In proximity the other obsesses me according to the absolute asymmetry of signification ...

The relationship with the third party is an incessant correction of the asymmetry of proximity in the face that is looked at. There is weighing, thought, objectification ... Justice requires contemporaneousness of representation. It is thus that the neighbour becomes visible and, looked at, presents himself, and there is also justice for me. The saying is fixed in a said, is written, becomes a book, law and science."[37] Levinas therefore seems to conclude that the entry of "the third" marks the moment at which "I am no longer infinitely responsible for the other, and consequently no longer in an asymmetrical, unequal relation."[38] Law takes over, since, as we have already seen, we cannot stay with ethics.[39]

This is not, perhaps, quite the post-metaphysical Gallic shrug it at first appears to be. At the very beginning of this essay I wrote about inspiration, a term that provides a suggestive metaphor for the ways in which things that are not ours and are not subject to our control can nevertheless touch us. An inspiration is a breath from beyond, filling us with something strange and new as we go about our lives. This breath does not arise in us, and we do not choose to receive it: it comes to us and makes its transformative demands whether we will have it or no. The question for this chapter is not, how does law operationalize ethics? but, how does ethics inspire law?

The first way in which ethics inspires law is this: in establishing the primacy of ethics over politics, Levinas offers an important foundation from which our understanding of justice might begin. "Justice remains justice only, in a society where there is no distinction between those close and those far off, but in which there also remains the impossibility of passing by the closest."[40] Let us notice in passing that in connecting ethics to the clos*est*, he assumes that it is possible and necessary to distinguish between the two. He continues, "The forgetting of self moves justice."[41] He does not mean that the abstraction or impartiality of the self leads to just judgment. He means that the sacrifice of self interest drives us to just action. Under the former model, indifference is a way of applying justice. Under the latter model, nonindifference is a way of moving or transforming justice and, indeed, of desiring it.

Recent work on what Levinas calls "the third" has insisted that our need to take into account "the other others" should not lead us to give up on the relationship of ethics and politics. Sarah Roberts, for example, argues that the institutions of the third (institutions such as courts of law and public services and even what is, to my mind, suggestively called "third-party insurance") enable us to fulfill our responsibilities to these

others. These institutions bridge our relationships with others: they do
not necessarily abandon the ethical insight but witness and testify to
it.[42] And finally, it is surely true that the reality of my relationship with
others in society is given meaning and depth by my feelings of ethical
proximity, without which "citizenship," or "social obligation," would
remain a purely abstract and probably unimaginable concept. "My relationship with the other in proximity," Sarah Roberts writes, "gives
meaning to my relationship to all others as 'citizens' or abstract members of a moral community. It is the face-to-face encounter with the
other which is the moving force, demanding political justice." What is
it that motivates the McCartney sisters – Donna, Catherine, Gemma,
Paula, and Claire – to take on the IRA within their own community,
after the murder of their brother? In a striking echo of Antigone,
Gemma says "Love. Basic love for my brother. Only now I'm in this
situation do I realize how essential justice is ... Otherwise he would
have died in vain."[43] Thus, justice doesn't eliminate my personal, asymmetrical responsibility but is motivated by it, and draws its authority
from it.[44] The primacy of the ethical over the political is not just an
abstract ontological point: it tells us something about how we find
meaning and legitimacy in our everyday lives. Ethical proximity is not
replaced by social justice but motivates and critiques it.

While Levinas concedes that on some level "there is a direct contradiction between ethics and politics," he insists that "there is also an
ethical limit to this ethically necessary political existence."[45] In other
words, justice must proceed from certain assumptions about the ineradicable nature of our duties to others, and these starting points make a
considerable difference to the contours of the law. This is why the
present essay has focused up until now on the question of the duty of
care in the law of negligence. The language of neighbourhood and duty
and proximity marks the contact point or hinge – Lacan might say the
"quilting point"[46] – that most clearly connects the philosophy of ethics
to the jurisprudence of torts. Just as importantly, the question of the
limits of duty establishes the framework on which that jurisprudence
will be constructed.

TOTALITY/INFINITY: FROM DUTY TO BREACH AND THE STANDARD OF CARE

The second way in which ethics inspires law is this: in establishing
the primacy of infinity over totality, Levinas seeks to emphasize the

importance of the preservation of distance in the fulfillment of responsibility. In previous chapters I have perhaps unduly emphasized the importance of proximity as a kind of closeness; but as Moore's sculpture illustrates, this closeness cannot ever convert the other into a species of the same. To be subsumed in a category is to be smothered and to die. Proximity – and this is one of the points that has proved most influential in the development of later writers such as Derrida – is not a presence capable of completion or perfection or closure but a necessary absence or imperfection.[47] To be proximate is to be juxtaposed but not together. The gravitational field of another draws us close but pushes us away: in short, neighbourhood.

I have said little about the standard of care in the law of negligence, except to indicate that it provides the opportunity to balance the contradictory demands that responsibility lays upon us. It is the venue wherein the law – as a means of "comparison, coexistence ... order" – moves from an absolute language of yes/no by which we determine those to whom we are responsible, to a language of reasonableness by which we determine whether we have fulfilled our responsibility. But reasonableness imports a social judgment, which means that it attempts to balance what we might have done against our other obligations and expectations and demands. In other words, reasonableness is a question of balancing the needs of the one who was injured against our own desires and against everyone else's needs too. As we have seen in case after case, one can decide that a responsibility was owed without necessarily concluding that it was breached.

What might these two frameworks have to do with each other? – totality/infinity, on the one hand, and the standard of care, on the other? One answer can be readily seen by reference to the classic U.S. case on the standard of care, *United States v. Carroll Towing*.[48] There, Justice Learned Hand attempted to convert the balancing act of the law into an algorithm. The standard of reasonable care requires us, he argued, to take into account the probability of an action causing harm, the gravity of the injury that might result and against that to weigh "the burden of adequate precautions."[49] "Possibly it serves to bring this notion into relief to state it in algebraic terms: if the probability be called P; the injury, L; and the burden, B; liability depends upon whether B is less than L multiplied by P: i.e. $B < PL$."[50]

The text has become a staple of both the law of obligations and of the economic analysis of law.[51] Let us put aside its obvious insufficiency as a formula and focus instead on its power as a metaphor. The standard of care is to be determined as if it were a matter of mathematical commensurates: as if risk and inconvenience were able to be placed on the same scale against one another. Of course, in the real world such a balance is complex and thoroughly imperfect, but the algebraic metaphor suggests to us the perspective towards which we ought to strive. Accordingly, the interests of each side are to be measured up in the light of some third party or neutral term, "reunited under a single gaze."[52] My B (the difficulty and cost of avoiding an accident) and your L (the injury you thereby suffer) both become quantities of x in the same juridical equation. This is the fundamental tenet of all forms of utilitarianism, and it is precisely the kind of totality-thinking that Levinas contrasts so forcefully with infinity. The effect is that as a society we can decide that my burden (the inconvenience of driving slowly, for example) is greater than your injury. Your injury becomes a cost that society will deem reasonable in proportion to the advantages that accrue to the rest of us from it. This is, of course, the mainstay of politics: the judgment of effects in terms of comparative statistics generalized across masses, in pursuit of collective goals such as efficiency or progress. There are prices to be paid to achieve our social ends – houses must be torn down so that airports may sprout up – but it is precisely its comparative reasonableness that justifies the imposition of that price on particular individuals. In deeming that your injury (and others like it) was reasonable, you are compelled to sacrifice something against a greater good that has been measured and weighed and judged.

Not only does this absorb the two parties into the midst of a social evaluation that consumes their personal relationship. It ultimately allows the unwanted imposition of a risk on another person if the inconvenience not just to society but to the defendant would prove too great an intrusion on their freedom. That too would be "reasonable." If the burden on me of avoiding a certain course of conduct is unreasonably great, Learned Hand's calculus allows the harm to reasonably befall you. So here, too, the two sides of the equation are treated just as if they both shared the same interests and values, as if the relationship was symmetrical and commensurable. In *Hahn v. Conley*,[53] for example, Justice Windeyer's judgment that the grandfather's responsibility to Anne was not breached amounts to the following: that the danger inherent in her crossing that road was small enough to permit her to suffer it in the interests of protecting his freedom. There is no proximity at this stage of the analysis, since there is no recognition of the incompatibility of their interests. Instead, the two are treated as if they were two halves of the same whole. That is the essence of Learned Hand's calculus. Yet surely it misses the very essence of responsibility, at least according to the argument I have been advancing. We are liable to another not because the benefits and detriments of our actions are commensurable but only because they are *not*.

Being both social and comparative, the judgment of the standard of care appears to move us out of the realm of the ethics of responsibility entirely. Reasonableness might be thought of as the domain of politics. When Levinas acknowledges the necessity of comparison and order,[54] the necessity, in other words, of the delimitation of reasonable care, does he thus abandon us to totality? Certainly there are moments in which he seems to. Levinas' own brief discussion in *Otherwise than Being* suffers from his own carelessness in running together, with little thought for their distinctiveness, "justice, society, the State and its institutions."[55] For him, this is all the same: not-ethics. But law is not politics, although there are elements of politics in it. It is true that reasonableness will always involve calculations of social and personal utility. But at the same time, the common law of negligence insists on taking the romantic duality of the world of responsibility – just he and I – seriously. In this, the law of torts is already a little closer to ethics than perhaps Levinas imagines. The question for the law of negligence is always particular, always shorn of some of its elements of expedience. We are to forget the framework of insurance or of social welfare and focus just on this singular moment and this singular relationship. It is no longer about me or about we but about you. For many, that gives to the legal argument an air of unreality. But it also properly recognizes the foundational quality of that relationship and provides it with a distinct voice. Very often, no doubt, it is just to support that recognition with comprehensive insurance and equality of care. But sometimes that recognition and that voice is the only justice possible.

There are alternatives to the totalizing calculus of *Carroll Towing*. It is possible to preserve a trace of Levinas' defence of proximity even within the socialized judgments embedded in the standard of care. I have been particularly influenced by Stephen Perry's remarks on the calculus of negligence. He writes that "the conception of fault which emerges here involv[es] not a balancing of interests, but rather a consideration of whether the creator of the condition in question ... imposed a certain *level* of risk upon others."[56] Perry is here drawing on the famous case of *Bolton v. Stone*,[57] in which a cricket club was sued for the damage it caused when a ball flew out of the ground and struck Miss Stone, standing one hundred yards away. The orthodox view was expressed by Lord Oaksey. "The standard of care in the law of negligence is the standard of an ordinarily careful man, but in my opinion, an ordinarily careful man does not take precautions against every foreseeable risk ... Many foreseeable risks are extremely unlikely to happen and cannot be guarded against except by almost complete isolation."[58] But Lord Reid has more to say on the subject of how to determine the behaviour of a reasonable man in fulfilment of his responsibility: "I do not think it would be right to take account of the difficulty of remedial measures. If cricket cannot be played on a ground without creating a substantial risk, then it should not be played there at all."[59] Lord Reid therefore rejects the relevance of the size of the burden in determining whether one's responsibility to others requires one to modify one's conduct.

A familiar example will demonstrate Lord Reid's argument. The notorious Ford Pinto was introduced in 1970 with very poor protection for its fuel tank. According to the exposé by Mark Dowie that appeared in *Mother Jones* in 1977, in every test carried out by Ford involving a rear-end collision at greater than twenty-five miles an hour, the tank ruptured. Said one engineer, "It's a catastrophic blunder ... It's almost designed to blow up – premeditated."[60] The consequence of this design flaw was a large number of preventable deaths and burns: estimates range from 180 deaths up to 900. Dowie's report won the Pulitzer Prize and led to the recall of one and a half million vehicles. It disclosed an internal investigation conducted by Ford as early as 1973 that had concluded that vehicle modification would require a complete retooling of the assembly line and was therefore not cost-effective. Taking a figure of $200,000 as the value of a human life (a rather arbitrary number that had been adopted by the U.S. National Highway Traffic Safety Administration),[61] Ford determined that the cost of vehicle adjustment was $137 million and the benefit in injuries foregone and lives saved only $50 million.[62] $B > PL$: QED. But the point does not depend on exactly how many people died or on how much a human life is worth, actually or actuarially. Neither is the point – which has been subject to some debate – whether the engineers or designers knew of the danger in 1970 or in 1973 or never. The point is, rather, that according to the logic of Learned Hand's formula, it was entirely proper for the company to have carried out such reasoning. For Learned Hand, that is just what responsibility asks of us.

Clearly, for most people something has gone wrong in simply undertaking such a calculation. It is not merely undignified. It is not merely impossible. It has missed the point. The burden to you of fixing a problem is not to be weighed against the injury to me of leaving it, for that treats us as if we somehow shared these burdens and benefits. It is not that these things cannot be weighed but that they should not. Responsibility for another asks us to respect the concept of proximity, by which is meant a requirement to preserve the distance of another from appropriation in the interest of some imagined joint project.

As Levinas himself concedes, whether we have breached our duties necessarily involves questions of balance; the point must be made more finely than Perry suggests. Responsibility entails striking a balance between the social and the individual: we do not demand that our vehicles are as safe as they could possibly be, because of certain established expectations concerning everything from price to speed. In law, responsibility entails striking a balance between the individual and the other – since, as Levinas says, we are ourselves an other to the others. The duty to rescue finds its natural limit in this balance. And in the interests of preserving our individual freedom, therefore, we are prepared to run certain risks that are neither large enough nor grave enough to warrant our attention. That, after all, was the logic of *Bolton v. Stone.*

Furthermore, responsibility entails striking a balance between our obligations to one other and to all the others. The existence of third parties "is of itself the limit of responsibility and the birth of the question: What do I have to do with justice?"[63] Particularly in dealing with government agencies, the need to balance a whole range of responsibilities may limit the kind and extent of intervention that it will be reasonable to undertake.[64] That has clearly been the animating concern of the courts in their attempts over recent years to control the expanding liability of local councils and the like. In *Romeo v. Conservation Commission of the Northern Territory,*[65] the Australian High Court was asked to reconsider the broad liability imposed on such authorities in *Nagle v. Rottnest Island.*[66] It might be said that this was another case in which, post-proximity, the Court has begun to view the question of responsibility more narrowly than before. While the majority affirmed the duty of care owed by the Conservation Commission to the users of a scenic car park overlooking a cliff-top near Darwin, the Court divided on whether its failure to provide some kind of fence breached that duty. A young woman had stumbled off the edge late one night, having had too much to drink. The commission was held not liable, not simply because it would have cost too much to put up the fence but rather because of the range of other responsibilities and associated costs the commission faced. In the competititon for resources, such organizations must constantly balance one "other" against all the others. Although Hayne J simply argued that the risk was in the circumstances too minimal to bother about, Kirby J articulates a question of balance that also appears to have concerned Toohey and Gummow JJ. "Demanding the expenditure of resources in one area (such as the fencing of promontories in natural reserves) necessarily diverts resources from other areas of equal or possibly greater priority. Whilst this consideration does not expel the courts from the evaluation of what reasonableness requires in a particular case, it is undoubtedly a factor to be taken into account in making judgments which affect the operational priorities of a public authority."[67]

The question of how to act responsibly will admit of different alternatives – more or less expensive, more or less extensive.[68] In many cases, a warning sign erected by a council may well prove reasonable enough.[69] Indeed, the difference between the majority judgments in *Romeo* and the dissents of McHugh and Gaudron JJ rest precisely on the future resource implications across the range of the commission's responsibilities of holding in favour of Nadia Romeo.[70] The existence of alternative responsibilities and claims upon a council's resources lies at the heart of the so-called distinction between "policy" and "operational" factors.[71] The council worker who comes to inspect your home finds herself in no conflict in determining the exercise of her responsibility, for it is specific, limited, and singular; the question as to whether the council ought to institute a system of inspection in the first place is, on the other hand, just such a matter of balancing finite resources amongst multiple responsibilities. All this reflects the ways in which the question of breach changes with the entrance of the third party. While "the Other's hunger – be it of the flesh, or of bread – is sacred ... the hunger of the third party limits its rights."[72]

But – and this is the point that Levinas forces us to confront – responsibility does not entitle us to think of ourselves at the very moment when we should be thinking of the other. Levinas goes on: "the only bad materialism is our own."[73] Responsibility will not permit us to do nothing when we ought to be doing something, simply because doing nothing relieves us of a burden. It is not up to us to "trade off" the other against ourselves. That would remove the distance between us altogether and destroy the experience of proximity that it must preserve. That burden, which Learned Hand suggests can be reasoned away, is the very fact of responsibility. Responsibility, like hospitality, means the welcoming of inconvenience. This is what Lord Reid means when he states that if a certain activity cannot be undertaken without creating a substantial risk, it ought not to be undertaken at all.[74] We are not at liberty to decide that our cricket is more important than Miss Stone's security in circumstances in which that security is the very essence of our responsibility. That is what Learned Hand suggests and what *Bolton v. Stone* rejects. Our courts have not surrendered reasonableness to the internal calculus of cost and benefit.[75] As in the Pinto case, it would be fundamentally wrong to attempt to balance out costs and benefits when there is a "substantial risk" to which the plaintiff has been exposed. In such a case, the inconvenience or cost of protecting the safety of another is your responsibility, not just an element to be considered in deciding how far it extends.[76]

Responsibility is not a question of contract, in which one *uses* another person in ways that advance some project or interests we have decided to share.[77] We cannot possess the other, appropriate their interests to advance ours, or turn them into an object of knowledge. There is a distance between us, and a "height" that, at exactly the moment that it recognizes my power, demands of me a sacrifice in order to preserve that distance and that radical and irreconcilable heterogeneity of beings.[78] Responsibility requires a sacrifice in order to preserve something unshared and unique (so do all sacrifices). Perhaps that was what Ford's rational system did not allow for. Instead, they traded off those who burned, in the interests of efficiency. And this is no less violent than a war in which bodies are traded off to serve some expedient goal.[79] On the other hand, the unchosen and unexceptionable – and no doubt inconvenient, irritating, and inefficient – obligations of responsibility are not violence but the possibility of peace.

Much writing on legal responsibility attempts to define what it is for – efficiency or progress or whatever. But this is to get it upside down. Responsibility is the birth of purpose; it is what makes possible the society in which we can have purposes and the persons who can have them. It is not for something; it is what something is for.[80] Responsibility is truly responsible only when it is against my interests, against "our" interests, beyond all such calculations. If one is responsible for something – for the safety of others on the roads, or the welfare of the child in your care – one is not responsible up to a point. One does not cease to be responsible when it is no longer "worth it" *to you*. To think of responsibility in those terms is already to be irresponsible. That is what Levinas means by contrasting "the hunger of the third party," which limits responsibility, with "our own bad materialism," which does not.[81] It is what Lord Reid meant too, and it strongly contrasts with what is commonly and revealingly called "the calculus of negligence." Even when it is reduced to a legal system through the operation of the standard of care, responsibility thus preserves something of its essential character, interrupting our general rules with specific instances and providing depth, meaning, and desire to our search for justice.[82]

SAYING/SAID: PROXIMITY AND THE PROBLEM
OF JUSTICE IN LEVINAS

The third way in which ethics inspires law is this: in establishing the primacy of the saying over the said, Levinas means to suggest that the moment of fixing ethics in a theme or a system, of turning it into a book of law or a code of rules, does not inevitably signal the complete loss of ethics. Simon Critchley emphasizes the fact that the "said" is continually "informed and interrupted by the trace of the Saying."[83] Levinas, in a direct response to Derrida's critique in "Violence and Metaphysics," talks about how the "oblique rays" of the saying of ethics – that moment of revelation in which we experience our ineradicable responsibility for an other – are not captured by the said, but only "reflected" in it.[84] There is always a danger in reading Levinas of letting his rhetorical intensity trick us into believing that he has answered questions more convincingly than he really has.[85] This is rather ironic, since Levinas himself maintained his fervent distrust for rhetoric, for metaphor, and for poetry on more than one occasion.[86] Nevertheless, we are not much closer to understanding what this trace or interruption looks like if it is not reducible to the said and yet somehow affects us all the same.

The notion of disruption might take us rather closer.[87] Levinas associates saying, as an event of language, with "infinity," as an event of existence. Both indicate the outside – uncodifiable, incomprehensible – that nevertheless affects us. The whole message of Levinas is that this outside is the necessary remainder or supplement to any system of meaning whatsoever. What from the point of view of a system of law that is attempting to build rules that are certain and predictable would be described as a waste or surplus – or perhaps merely a nuisance – is from the point of view of proximity "an excellence, an elevation, the ethics before being."[88]

We cannot reduce language to the things-that-language-says any more than we can reduce another person to the things-the-person-is. In each case, there is something left over: the field or relationship that makes these things possible. This relationship affects us and, most importantly, continually demands something more of us. Our responsibility grows as we find our complacent norms disrupted by "the extraordinary event ... of [our] exposure to others."[89] Thus it is that we can never be entirely settled in our duties or comfortable in our obligations. Instead one is "ill at ease in one's own skin."[90] Responsibility is not a contract: we *always* get more than we bargained for.

There is nothing particularly mystical about this. Levinas could be describing the operation of the common law of torts over the past century or so. The growth of a complex sense of responsibility has emerged, gradually but inexorably, precisely in response to the exposure to others irreducible to the prior "said" of the law. Each time the law's response is to create a new book, a new law, but never adequately or permanently. There is always some new remainder or loose end waiting for a further event to challenge and to press it. Casuistry, the methodology of the common law, embodies the recognition that no code can ever capture the true experience of responsibility. The phenomenon of our relationship to others is destined to catch us out. Concerning each of us and in relation to the system of the common law as a whole, the duty of care is not some thing we choose. It just happens to us.

To some this will come as a disappointment. Time after time the critics of proximity have attacked its indeterminacy and have appealed to the common sense view that law is a system of rules.[91] "If negligence law is to serve its principal purpose as an instrument of corrective justice, the principles and rules which govern claims in negligence must be as clear and as easy of application as is possible. Ideally, arguments about duty should take little time with need to refer to one or two cases only instead of the elaborate arguments now often heard, where many cases are cited and the argument takes days."[92] So, too, the English courts have frequently insisted that the "criterion of liability" must present an "ascertainable meaning" if it is to have "utility."[93] The many dissents of Brennan CJ surely address precisely this point, conceiving of law as a system of rules and proximity as a surplus or a waste – so much unnecessary verbiage. Perhaps proximity is not entirely predictable. Clients – again the perspective is most strongly associated with McHugh J – deserve to know in advance exactly what their obligations to their fellow man are.

But proximity *is* ethics. This is not to say that the requirements of law, and even of justice, ought to go unremarked or unrecognized: no one would suggest that we ought to get rid of rules and limits altogether. But Levinas insists that there is a necessary ethical register to law, too, one that neither cannot nor should not be entirely eliminated in the interests of personal comfort and social stability. In the law of negligence, proximity is that register. If, to recall a familiar objection, proximity is the "fifth wheel" of the duty of care, then it is a flywheel, storing and releasing the energy that permits forward movement. There is a certain productive antagonism between ethics and law. This is precisely the discomfiting, nagging role of proximity in negligence. If it fails as a rule, then it has succeeded as ethics.

Now Levinas makes this argument with regrettable vagueness. His understanding of law is, in this respect, simplistic (just as Deane's understanding of ethics was too simplistic to properly articulate the unsettling role that proximity fills). Not only does Levinas confuse law with politics, as we have already seen. So, too, he appears to equate law with justice, with a written code. Levinas does at times describe justice as "unethical and violent," saying "We must ... un-face human beings, sternly reducing each one's uniqueness ... and let universality rule."[94] This might lead us to read him as separating the legal from the ethical in a rather crude way. At stake, then, are two points: the narrow way Levinas understands law and the narrow way he understands justice. At this time we need to rescue Levinas from himself. As Roberts writes, "if one takes seriously Levinas' claim that asymmetrical ethical responsibility is the origin of justice, then one must also reject Levinas' suggestion that justice involves viewing persons and responsibility as comparable and symmetrical."[95]

The criticism of Levinas' conception of the meaning of justice and its relationship to law was first made in "Violence and Metaphysics" by Derrida, who suggested there that one of the reasons that one cannot stay with "an ethics without law" is because alterity is "already *in* the same," which is to say that ethics has already contaminated the allegedly rigid purity of the law.[96] He then offered an extensive exploration of the legal question twenty-five years later in "The Force of Law." For Derrida, there is a contrast between law – in the traditional sense of a stable body of rules – and justice: "law is the element of calculation, and it is just that there be law, but justice is incalculable, it requires us to calculate with the incalculable."[97]

But the tension is not just between law, on the one hand, and justice, on the other. On the contrary, it dwells within the idea of justice itself, itself internally riven between the operation of two mutually incommensurable impulses: equal treatment and singular respect.[98] Justice embodies both an aspiration towards "law or right, legitimacy or legality, stabilizable and statutory, calculable, a system of regulated and coded prescriptions"[99] and at the same time the desire for a unique and singular response to a particular situation and person before us. Justice is both general and unique; it involves treating everybody the same *and* treating everybody differently.[100]

What is more, this tension dwells within the idea of law too (although Levinas appears to have imagined otherwise).[101] It is not only that the legitimacy of the legal system demands rather more than historically established procedures for resolving disputes, although the justice of law is surely not irrelevant to its authority. More importantly, it is because the moment of every legal decision requires us to make a judgment as to the applicability of prior general norms to the necessarily different and singular situation before us. A judge trying to decide whether the current dispute fits within the established category must always confront the fact that there is a choice, and this choice can never be ignored. Although "hard cases" dramatize this choice, every case requires us to make the same kind of decision. We must still decide if *this* case is "the same as" or "different from" the past, and this decision of course involves the very choice that the past cannot ever help us with. Be it ever so slight, the burden of judgment is an ineluctable part of the choice that the specificity of a case – of any case – imposes on us. Indeed, a judge who acted as if there was no choice in the matter (as some claim to do), as if their role was purely mechanical, would be obedient, but not responsible.[102] Such a judge would be as incapable of making a "just" decision as a machine or the weather.

The paradoxical choice that judgment always opens up, then, is a necessary element of law as it is of justice. Both demand of us that we respect the rules in their utmost generality and at the same time the individual in his utter specificity, that we attend to the constructive power of the past as a way of controlling the future and the re-constructive power of the present as a way of reinterpreting the past. This complicated backwards-and-forwards dynamic is essential to all decision making and no rules could ever tell us exactly how to accomplish it. A rule is not a self-basting pudding. In short, in law the judge is bound to choose.

Human judgment requires us to be both accountable (to some norm for our actions) and responsible (to those before us, for its application at this very moment) – not a bit of one and a bit of the other, not one or the other or one and then the other, but entirely and simultaneously both. The argument is made by Derrida both clearly and succinctly in the following passage: "In short, for a decision to be just and responsible it must, in its proper moment if there is one, be both regulated and without regulation: it must conserve the law and also destroy it or suspend it enough to have to reinvent it in each case."[103] Thus the moment of judgment – the answer to the question of whether and how to follow "the rules," which must be singular and newly minted – is a crucial moment in which the judge is singled out and rendered irreplaceable, incapable of substitution by some mere procedure. The burden is his and his alone, an inescapable responsibility.[104]

We may describe this moment of suspension and reconstitution in terms of Levinas' trace, by which the incalculable or nonsystemic is capable of making a synaptic leap across the cells of the world.[105] The trace, it will be recalled, is the moment of connection between incommensurable orders that Derrida pushed Levinas into elaborating in *Otherwise than Being* and then adopted as a central element of the project of deconstruction.[106] What Derrida initially described as "impossible – unthinkable – unutterable"[107] is embraced in his later work as all that ... and necessary too.

But the crucial move that Derrida makes is to situate this trace as part of the inevitable operation of justice (and not as separate) and justice as part of the inevitable operation of interpreting law (and not as separate). Ethics demands an element of incalculability, an element irreducible to formal rules, an experience that continually unsettles our established categories of thinking and forces us to reconsider the meaning of our rules at the very moment we apply them. If Levinas shows us the necessity of this instability, Derrida shows us how it is already part of something as mundane as legal reasoning. Gillian Rose accused Levinas of abandoning "the broken middle" through which our ethics and our institutions might actually communicate with each other.[108] As relevant as this criticism may be of Levinas, I do not see that it can fairly be applied to Derrida.[109] In Levinas justice is admittedly treated as an order, "giving the self over to calculus" no less, and in that sense "comparison, measure, knowing, laws, institutions – justice" all amount to the same thing.[110] But neither justice nor law in Derrida are capable of being reduced to "juridical-moral rules, norms or representations, with an inevitable totalizing horizon,"[111] some one-way track by which the past stops us thinking in the present about what it's for and what it means. For Derrida, in law as in language, this dictatorship is simply not possible. The necessary passage of time between enactment of a norm and its application and the necessary uniqueness of the present case by comparison to prior norms inevitably opens up what Julius Stone called a "lee-way," to be taken or not as the judge chooses. The "road less travelled" might be easy to find or not, attractive or not, significant or not. But nothing can erase the crossroads itself. If Levinas "includes in justice [and law] almost everything he rejected in his description of asymmetrical responsibility," thus creating an impassable barrier between the two, Derrida does not.[112]

The common law of negligence, for all its faults, is a vehicle that remains deeply committed to an engagement on these terms. Its failure as a collection of rules amounts to its success as an ethical foundation for the law: the idea of proximity then serves as a crucial bridge beyond the ways in which we have already explored its day-to-day operation. From Justice Deane onwards, the word "proximity" and all the discussions that have swirled about it have suggested precisely the operations of a judgment that cannot be entirely settled in advance and that remain sensitive to the particular and the experiential – the place of the ethical *in* law, "the other *in* the same." Proximity is best understood as a kind of predicament that gives rise to responsibility and that stems from a surprising moment of being-already-in-relation-with-another. Its central insight is that we feel before we know. Certainly, proximity's phenomenological nature provides what we might call an anti-rule, the haunted house of undecidability in the law, or, to put it in a way that will be familiar to members of the High Court from the lectures delivered by Julius Stone at the University of Sydney in the 1950s and 1960s, a "category of indeterminate reference."[113] It was the insight of the American legal realists, a school to which Julius Stone could be said to have belonged, that such indeterminacy is inevitable.[114] The argument formed the basis of the wholesale attack on legalism launched by "critical legal studies" in the 1980s.[115] But Derrida is not of a piece with this kind of nihilist critique. Indeterminacy is both an inevitable function of language and a stroke of luck for our capacity to be touched by something new and to change in response to it.[116]

No doubt such inescapable uncertainty makes the judicial role very much harder. "This moment of suspense ... is always full of anxiety, but who pretends to be just by economizing on anxiety?"[117]

This is what Derrida means when he declares, in so many words, "Deconstruction is justice."[118] This is neither "a mystical equation between justice and deconstruction" nor yet a "provocative metaphysical formula," and only a very careless reading could have drawn such epithets.[119] It is something we experience every day of our life, in our teaching and our reading and our speaking: justice is not a thing but an attitude, not an answer but a way of approaching questions. Justice is the questioning itself. Once we decide that we *have* justice, that we know it and only need to put it down on paper and enforce it, we are already well on the way to dogma and injustice. Justice is not to be attained under any circumstances by realizing a system or implementing a policy. This is not to say, of course, that we can do without policies or systems altogether: like memory and intention or the conscious and subconscious minds, the calculable and the incalculable exist in different registers, doing different things, or, in Levinas-speak, they exist "diachronously."[120] Justice is attainable only if we resist such simplifications and if we thereby allow for the possibility of our own growth.

In the law of torts, proximity is the structural site in which a receptiveness to the experience of others has been purposely kept open, an institutionalised and unstable force for change. It is the part of the "third," or social, realm that witnesses our rendezvous with the other, providing a space for a "never-ending oscillation" between ethics and politics.[121] It is the moment in our judicial reasoning wherein the "saying" of responsibility may still surprise the "said" of law. Proximity identifies the possibility of a non-appropriative relationship with the neighbour, or *le prochain*, and at the same time it articulates the conditions under which we find ourselves with a responsibility to respect it. And the nature of this responsibility, indeed the nature of responsibility per se, which is intrinsic to ethics in Levinas and was then introduced to law and legal interpretation by Derrida, cannot be settled in advance. After all, the application of rules or methods is just what our response ability cannot hide behind and just the kind of a priori reasoning that circumstance always exceeds. Proximity represents then the site of a kind of judgment, unavoidable and indeterminate, that lies at the heart of both writers.

Despite the abuse and sloppy use from which it has suffered over the years, the legal instantiation of proximity within negligence does

not merely "mask ... policy preferences."[122] On the contrary, it is also
an ethics, an anti-policy, in Levinasian terms. Through its judgments,
the court's constant re-articulation of the duty of care is not just a way
of "changing its mind" or "changing the law": in the process of trial
and judgment, it is finding out something new about ourselves, something, perhaps, that was not there before. Proximity is the legal structure that accommodates the saying while no doubt attempting, always
unsuccessfully, to pin it down in the form of the said. These two levels
– ethical singularity and the legal past – are in constant oscillation,
each attempting to refute the other: they too are neither the same as
nor different from each other but non-indifferent. How is coexistence
even possible when the instability that remains so important to ethics
and justice is always trying to be erased by law?[123] Levinas rather
helpfully provides us with a metaphor of knots that "interrupt the
discourse" of law.[124] "The interruptions of the discourse found again
and recounted in the immanence of the said are conserved like knots
in a thread tied again, the trace of a diachrony that does not enter into
the present."[125]

Levinas criticizes the State as attempting to cut out the knots of
discourse and thus to repress or suppress the interstices of ethics. Statute law and codification have something of that character, preserving
"law" only in an eternal and coherent present. Indeed, in many jurisdictions amendments to statutes are now placed on-line. In theory, this
is said to acknowledge the increasingly changeable nature of modern
acts of Parliament, some of which are amended many times a year.[126]
In practice, because the process of amendment is concealed by a product that is always perfectly up-to-date, it becomes ever more difficult
to access a history or, ironically, to experience law as a temporal phenomenon. In cyberspace, the visible law belongs to a seamless present
that seems to have been formed out of whole cloth.

But judicial decision making is different. Precedent remembers and
continues to worry over that knotty problem of the past. It builds knots
upon knots, imperfections upon imperfections. Certainly the High
Court, faced with such interruptions in its supposedly seamless thread
of rules, will always attempt to gather up the loose ends and retie the
thread over and over again. That is how our institutions work. But the
knots thus formed conserve the memory of that disruption and autho-
rize the possibility of new ones to further unsettle a purely internal and
conceptual system of order.[127]

The great strength of the role of proximity is that it recognized those knots, worried over them remorselessly, and at the same time actively demonstrated why they remain necessary. Proximity is law ... deconstructed. On one level the law of proximity spoke of the recognition of citizens' responsibilities for each other and the dimensions that such a response ought to take. And as we have seen, the articulation of such responsibilities is necessarily – ethically – imperfect and subject to amendment. Sometimes, the call of others will put the responsible citizen on the spot. On another level, the question of proximity operated as the forum for law's recognition of its own response ability. The law, too, finds itself reminded here that a responsible judgment cannot be rendered in advance, that it must acknowledge the imperfection of its doctrines and their openness to amendment and reflection. Sometimes the call of others will put the responsible judge on the spot. As a legal principle, then, proximity provided a meditation on the ethical engagement that connects persons – while as a legal discourse, proximity provided the moment for an ethical engagement between those who speak the law and those who supplicate themselves before it.

The danger of the present trend away from proximity is that it represents a narrower view of the nature of legal responsibility and a narrower view of the nature of legal discourse, and no view at all of the relationship between them. The law of proximity set up a sympathetic resonance between the true meaning of our responsibility for others (unresolved, retrospective, nascent) and the structure through which that meaning ought to be explored (ditto). Neither should this parallel surprise us. Responsibility is always a kind of judgment in which we are confronted by difficult choices but with no choice but to make them; in the face of the other, we are indeed the chosen ones. Judges too are confronted by choices but with no choice but to make them; in the face of the parties, they too are the chosen ones.

So proximity offers us a structural resource through which to talk about the nature and approach we ought to take to the experience of responsibility. At the same time, it applies this methodology of singularity, predicament, and response not only to our everyday judgments and errors of judgment but to our institutional judgments about those errors. There is, therefore, a commensurability between how the law of negligence articulates our responsibility to others and how it understands its own responsibility to the development of the law. Proximity talks about responsibility, *responsibly.*

The responsibility that Levinas thus defends is, for each of us and for the law itself, a "difficult freedom," a "jurisprudence for adults."[128] It requires us to give up forever a concept of rule-fetishism and absolute obedience that tends to obsess six-year-olds, according to Piaget, though they grow out of it soon enough.[129] Instead, proximity provides us with a discourse and a structure through which to reflect on the *gap* between the general rules we elaborate to guide our conduct and the specific lives and experiences that are influenced by them. The reflection that this gap ought to inspire leaves it open to the law to respond and to continue to strive towards a justice that is always out of reach, never just enough. Proximity is the immanent possibility of an on-going rebellion against complacency "that begins where the other society is satisfied to leave off, a rebellion against injustice that begins once order begins."[130]

There is therefore something singularly fitting in the location of Levinas within proximity, within the duty of care, within negligence, and within the common law. All perform, on different levels, the ideas of responsibility and subjectivity that a commitment to ethics entails. We see here the structural recognition of an ethical principle that our law can ill afford to ignore.

PROXIMITY/PRIVITY: ON THE FOUNDATION AND SOUL OF LAW

The fourth way in which ethics inspires law is this: in establishing the primacy of proximity over privity, Levinas defends a concept of obligation and of the origin of responsibility and subjectivity that places the law of negligence as the foundational moment of law. Torts ceases to be either an imperfect graft upon the logic of natural rights or the expression of a State-defined and contingent social policy. It even ceases to be the outcome of a conception of justice and becomes instead the description of a relationship with the other that makes justice and fraternity possible.[131] In just the way that Levinas sees ethics as "first philosophy," so torts is "first law."[132] In all this we have, I think, a reason to respect the discourse of the law, to cherish and develop it, and not just to turn our back upon it. Neither is this discourse merely reflective of the understanding of responsibility we happen to have. That is not how discourse works. Discourse develops itself and develops our self-understanding at the same time.[133] The expansion of the duty of care over the past several years – at least until the High Court's turn away from proximity in recent years, notably in *Pyrenees Shire Council v. Day*[134] and later in cases such as *Modbury Triangle Shopping Centre v. Anzil*[135] and *Romeo*[136] – should not therefore be surprising. That is the nature of responsibility. The discourse between law and society establishes within us not just the obligations of responsibility but a desire for it that constantly takes us out of ourselves and towards the other.[137] "It is like goodness – the Desired does not fulfill it, but deepens it."[138] Development and change are intrinsic to such a law. "The infinity of responsibility denotes not its actual immensity, but a responsibility increasing in the measure that it is assumed; duties become greater in the measure that they are accomplished."[139] The point is that the legal system has not just responded to a changing social understanding of our duties to others. More than this, the legal system has been and continues to be itself a force in the evolution of that consciousness. The discourse of responsibility begets its own growth by and through a language that continually reaches out beyond its established parameters.

We would lose this if we were to give up on the common law either because it is proving too compassionate to defendants (and that is what is typically meant by the phrase "tort reform" in jurisdictions in the United States)[140] or because it is not proving compassionate enough (and that is what is typically meant by advocates of "no fault" schemes that prevail in jurisdictions such as New Zealand).[141] There is much truth to both these allegations, and I have sought to understand the structure of the duty of care rather than simply to defend it. Reducing tort law to a static series of principles or, worse, to codified rules or administrative arrangements may, no doubt, solve some problems. It will also deprive us of important opportunities. Such changes make sense if we are sure that by and large we know already what the "right outcome" ought to be; if we are confident that justice is something that can be set down and applied. But if we are not, then we have lost a prime forum through which to learn through judgment and reflection. Proximity, as I have insisted on several occasions, is that place in which the law is a student of the other and not its master.[142]

We might in the end lose something far more than a term of art if we have truly witnessed "the demise of proximity."[143] Everything it has come and could come to stand for is at stake: a language of hospitality and suffering; a law that "calls my spontaneity in question,"[144] not once and then resolved but over and over again. Recent cases and remarks of the members of the High Court, some of which I have discussed elsewhere, suggest at least the possibility of such a closure. Proximity stands above all as a beacon of the first philosophy and the ethical foundations of law.[145] In that sense, its loss would constitute more than a substantive loss or even a loss of methodology. It would constitute a loss of direction.

On the most general level, should the eclipse of proximity in fact be accompanied by a loss of the ideals of asymmetric response ability with which it has been associated, the law, and those whom the law instructs, will have settled down, closed the books, and ceased to remain open to the singular call of the other. We might return to concepts of choice, action, and the assumption of risk to determine our obligations; we might choose once and for all the paradigm of privity over the paradigm of proximity. In such a world, we will have rules, we will have obedience, and we will all, including the law, *know who we are*. One is accustomed to think of "settled law" as an ideal, but Levinas suggests that ethics asks of us never to be entirely settled, never to be at home in our world, always to be in movement and in question.[146] Every return home – "at last" – ends in an economy, a trade or pact, and a settled identity in all of which response ability is no longer possible. Against the Hellenic narrative of Ulysses, then, the wandering hero who finally comes home to rest, Levinas sets Abraham and the ideal of exile, a series of spiritual encounters that never ends.[147]

The open wounds that permit others to affect us must never be hardened into scar tissue.[148] We must never dwell anywhere too securely, too unchallengeably.[149] It is not, of course, that no laws should ever be settled; it is only that ethics asks also that we find a space from which to recognize and give effect to the necessary unsettlement of our obligations, since that unsettlement and openness makes responsibility possible. Proximity and the common law both work to keep these wounds open. They are not just rules: they are "an optics," a "rupture" that we ought to welcome in the law.[150] They are law's uncomfortable scruples.

If this seems threatening, it is in part because of the fear of interpretative uncertainty that the positivist and Western tradition has so potently invoked. Our understanding of interpretation has always sought to maximize the objective, the impersonal, and the fixing of "right answers."[151] Adjudication is a process of settlement and determination. But the Talmudic exegetical tradition from which Levinas clearly springs (and Derrida, too)[152] thinks otherwise and finds in the complex ambiguities of interpretation a rich source of dialogue, personal exploration, and change that likewise never returns home to rest. Ethically, man "lives in the desert and dwells in tents."[153] That which Athens sees as a fear,

Jerusalem imagines as an opportunity. It is not of course that there is some kind of choice here between the two. It is too late for that. "We live in the difference between the Jews and the Greeks."[154] Jewgreek and Greekjew, we are already contaminated, neither and both. But our theoretical resources seem often to get thinner the more thickly complex the lives we lead. The crisis in interpretation theory we face in law is in part due to the limited tradition upon which it has tended to draw. I have been defending in these pages an understanding of proximity as a site of interpretative response and endless dialogue. This understanding has the additional strength of drawing on a five-thousand-year-old interpretative model that captures the organic workings of common-law judgments in a way that seems rather closer to the reality of our judicial practices than the hierarchical and dogmatic approach to meaning that one finds so often in the law and the philosophy of law.[155]

One could therefore take this chance to find in our systems a contaminant, a trace of the other, that was always there and that allows us to expand the range of cultural voices that animate our laws. Not, it need hardly be said, in order to replace a faulty tradition with some perfect one, but simply to allow their proximity to enrich our self-discovery. What is at stake, it seems to me, is the soul of law, the breath of the other *in* me.[156]

CONCLUSION

The purpose of this long essay has been to bring together for the first time Levinas and the law of negligence: Levinas, who was relatively ignorant of the law, and most assuredly of the High Court of Australia; and the High Court of Australia, which is relatively ignorant of ethical philosophy, and most assuredly of Emmanuel Levinas. Yet despite their mutual ignorance, these two fields of writing represent two of the most extensive literatures on responsibility we have, and they speak in strikingly similar terms about the duty of care, about neighbourhood, and about proximity. In the process of bringing them together I have wanted not only to demonstrate the importance of the expansive vision of responsibility articulated within common law jurisdictions, and particularly in Australia during the 1980s and 1990s, but also to insist on its integrity.

That is, contrary to common arguments that have been used both to attack the expansionist era of proximity and to defend it, it is not the case that the court is simply in the business of choosing between different policies – some more individualist and narrow in outlook, some more collectivist and broader – with nothing to go on but their own sense of social justice.[157] Courts do not or should not choose policies just because they lead to outcomes they like or because they reflect a social ideology they happen to like; if they did, then there would be no particular reason why they could not as validly choose otherwise in order to achieve a different set of outcomes or a different social ideology. My argument has been that an expansive, organic, and self-questioning approach to proximity and the duty of care is simply a better understanding of how law really works. My argument has been that the court's focus on vulnerability, asymmetry, and unpredictability is simply a better understanding of what responsibility really means. And finally, my argument has been that there is a necessary connection between the true nature of law and the true nature of responsibility. Proximity embodies a kind of openness because law necessarily embodies a certain openness, because responsibility necessarily embodies a certain openness, and because law necessarily embodies a certain responsibility.

So negligence law and Levinasian ethics can each help us illuminate something intrinsically true about the other. I began this project confident that a sustained study of Levinas could teach the law a thing or two. I have been surprised at how much a sustained study of the jurisprudence of negligence has taught me a thing or two about Levinas, allowed me to understand and to test his theses, and, yes, to question them too. We are all students, all the time. I make no apologies if my approach to Levinas has become contaminated by the pragmatics of law. That is the point of ethics: it is necessarily governed by ingratitude and betrayal if it is to be spoken at all.[158] It is not that the jurisprudence of negligence and the philosophy of Levinas are the same thing. Neither is it the case that they are radically different, so that one might correct and take over the other, as knowledge succeeds ignorance or truth defeats falsity. The strength of the conjunction of these two discourses lies rather in their capacity to draw out the resonances that one can already detect each in each. The potential that might derive from the exploration of the duty of care in Levinas through and by an exploration of the duty of care in law lies in the possibility it offers of a mutually transformative encounter between two important and complex meditations on responsibility.[159]

In other words, the real reason for connecting law and ethics, negligence and Levinas, is not their amity or enmity but something infinitely more complicated: their neighbourhood, or put simply, their proximity.

Notes

CHAPTER ONE

1 Melville, *Moby Dick*, 36.
2 *Soul* itself is Germanic, and of uncertain etymology.
3 Hegel, *Phenomenology of Spirit.*
4 Foucault, *Discipline and Punish*, 29.
5 *New Yorker*, 2004.
6 Melville, *Moby Dick*, 49.
7 See, inter alia, Emmanuel Levinas, *Otherwise than Being.* "The psyche in the soul is the other in me, a malady of identity." Ibid., 69.
8 Melville, *Moby Dick*, 50.
9 Derrida and Dufourmantelle, *Of Hospitality.*
10 Emmanuel Levinas, about whom I shall have much more to say, writes: "On the hither side of or beyond essence, signification is the breathlessness of the spirit expiring without inspiring." *Otherwise than Being*, 14.
11 *Vaughan v. Menlove* (1837) 3 Bing. N.C. 467, 132 E.R. 490.
12 [1932] A.C. 562.
13 Ibid., 580 per Lord Atkin.
14 *Hargrave v. Goldman* (1963) 110 C.L.R. 40, 66–7 per Windeyer J.
15 Horwitz, *The Transformation of American Law.*
16 Hobbes, *Leviathan*, 223–9, 311–26, 183–93.
17 It is customary to spell "Lévinas" without an accent when writing in English, and that practice I follow here.

18 Critchley, *The Ethics of Deconstruction.*
19 Bauman, *Postmodern Ethics*; Diamantides, *The Ethics of Suffering*, 2, et seq.
20 This understanding of ethics governs Caputo, *Against Ethics.* See Duncan, *The Pre-Text of Ethics*, 141.
21 Adriaan Peperzak, "Emmanuel Levinas," 297, 302.
22 Bernasconi, "Deconstruction and the Possibility of Ethics," 131; Diamantides, "Ethics in Law," 209, 224–5.
23 Levinas, *Éthique comme philosophie première.*
24 Derrida and Dufourmantelle, *Of Hospitality.*
25 Rawls, *A Theory of Justice.*
26 Habermas, *Philosophical Discourse of Modernity*; Rose, *The Broken Middle*; Derrida, "Violence and Metaphysics."
27 Levinas, *Difficult Freedom*; Caygill, *Levinas and the Political.*
28 Bernasconi, "The Trace of Levinas in Derrida"; Bernasconi, "Deconstruction and the Possibility of Ethics"; Roberts, "Rethinking Justice"; Simmons, "The Third."
29 For example, the discussion of justice in *Otherwise than Being*; see also Simmons, "The Third," 93–7.
30 Dworkin, *Law's Empire.*
31 Roberts, "Rethinking Justice," 5.
32 Derrida, "Violence and Metaphysics"; Caputo, "Hyperbolic Justice"; Cohen, "The Privilege of Reason and Play"; Llewelyn, "Levinas, Derrida and Others vis-à-vis," and "Jewgreek or Greekjew"; Perpich, "A Singular Justice"; Raffoul "On Hospitality, between Ethics and Politics"; Srajek, *The Margins of Deconstruction.*
33 Derrida, "Before the Law," and "Force of Law."
34 Roberts, "Rethinking Justice"; Simmons, "The Third."
35 Of recent work drawing on Levinas and legal theory, see Fitzpatrick, *Modernism and the Grounds of Law*; Motha and Zartaloudis, "Law, Ethics and the Utopian End of Human Rights"; Motha, "Mabo"; Douzinas, *The End of Human Rights*; Douzinas, "Human Rights at the 'End of History'"; Douzinas, "Justice, Judgment and the Ethics of Alterity."
36 Diamantides, *The Ethics of Suffering*; "Ethics in Law"; "The Ethical Obligation"; "In the Company of Priests"; "The Subject May Have Disappeared."
37 Diamantides, *The Ethics of Suffering*, 23.
38 Ibid., 25.
39 Ibid., and see especially "Ethics in Law," 227.

40 Dworkin, *Law's Empire*; Weinrib, "Understanding Private Law"; Coleman, "Tort Law and Tort Theory," 183, 203.

41 Levinas, *Otherwise than Being*, 153–62.

42 Rose, *Judaism and Modernity*, e.g., at 23.

43 Derrida, *Adieu to Emmanuel Levinas*; Duncan, *The Pre-Text of Ethics*, 159.

44 *Hedley, Byrne & Co. Ltd v. Heller & Partners Ltd* [1964] A.C. 465; *Dorset Yacht Co. Ltd v. Home Office* [1970] A.C. 1004; *Anns v. London Borough of Merton* [1978] A.C. 728; *Jaensch v. Coffey* (1984) 155 C.L.R. 549; *Sutherland Shire Council v. Heyman* (1985) 157 C.L.R. 424; *Caltex Oil (Australia) Pty Ltd v. The Dredge "Willemstad"* (1976) 136 C.L.R. 529.

45 Levinas, *Otherwise than Being*, 100–1.

46 See, in particular, Levinas, *Otherwise than Being*, chap. 3, 63–97.

47 Levinas, "Beyond Intentionality," 112.

48 *Stevens v. Brodribb Sawmilling Company; Gray v. Brodribb Sawmilling Company* (1986) 160 C.L.R. 16 at 52–3 per Deane J.

49 *Donoghue v. Stevenson* (1932) A.C. 562 at 580 per Lord Atkin.

50 See, for example, McHugh, "Neighbourhood, Proximity and Reliance"; Amirthalingam and Faunce, "Patching Up 'Proximity.'"

51 *Pyrenees Shire Council v. Day; Eskimo Amber Pty Ltd v. Pyrenees Shire Council* (1998) 192 C.L.R. 330 at 414 [238] per Kirby J.

52 Ibid. per Kirby J.

53 Burggraeve, "Violence and the Vulnerable Face of the Other," 33.

54 Simmons, "The Third," 99.

55 See Critchley, *The Ethics of Deconstruction*, 20.

56 Gibbs, "The Other Comes to Teach Me," 219–20.

57 Cohen, *Ethics, Exegesis and Philosophy*, 225–45.

58 Goodrich, *Reading the Law*.

59 Gordon, "Critical Legal Histories"; Kelman, *A Guide to Critical Legal Studies*; Hutchinson, *Critical Legal Studies*, and "A Bibliography of Critical Legal Studies"; Tushnet, "An Essay on Rights"; Kennedy, "The Structure of Blackstone's Commentaries"; Gordon, "Critical Legal Histories"; Kelman, "Trashing"; see also special issues of *Stanford Law Review* and *Texas Law Review* published in 1984.

60 Derrida, "Before the Law" and "The Law of Genre," 181–220, 221–52; Foucault, *Power/Knowledge*; *Discipline and Punish*.

61 See Blackshield, Coper, and Williams, *The Oxford Companion to the High Court*, 486–9; Sturgess, "Murphy and the Media"; Blackshield, "The 'Murphy Affair.'"

62 Scutt, *Lionel Murphy*; Hocking, *Lionel Murphy*.

63 Mason, "Legislative and Judicial Law-making"; "The High Court of Australia"; "The Tension between Legislative Supremacy and Judicial Review."

64 Levinas, *Totality and Infinity*, 192.

65 See Cohen, *Ethics, Exegesis and Philosophy*, 224.

66 "Justice must be informed by proximity; that is to say, the equality and symmetry of the relations between citizens must be interrupted by the inequality and asymmetry of the ethical relation. There must be a certain creative antagonism between ethics and politics." Critchley, *The Ethics of Deconstruction*, 233.

67 Levinas, *Otherwise than Being*, 159–60.

68 Roberts, "Rethinking Justice," 9.

69 Manderson, "Modes of Law"; "Et lex perpetua"; *Songs without Music*; "Apocryphal Jurisprudence"; "From Hunger to Love"; "In the *tout court* of Shakespeare."

70 Cohen, *Ethics, Exegesis and Philosophy*, 224.

71 Peperzak, "Emmanuel Levinas," 305.

72 Levinas, *Éthique et Infini*, 115.

73 Cohen, *Ethics, Exegesis and Philosophy*, 263.

CHAPTER TWO

1 Fitzpatrick, *The Mythology of Modern Law*, considers in detail several interrelated strands of these myths, focusing in particular on the different aspects of Hobbes that I touch on briefly below. While wholeheartedly subscribing to this argument, I want to mention here the different myths that find resonance in the common-law legal system, even within Hobbes himself, while acknowledging their complementarity.

2 Locke, *Two Treatises of Government*.

3 Macpherson, *The Political Theory of Possessive Individualism*.

4 Locke, *Second Treatise*, para. 57.

5 Taylor, *Hegel*.

6 Nozick, *Anarchy, State and Utopia*; Weinrib, "Corrective Justice"; Weinrib, "Legal Formalism"; Weinrib, "The Jurisprudence of Legal Formalism."

7 Hobbes, *Leviathan*, chap. 15, "Of Other Lawes of Nature," 201–3 (spelling modified).

8 Ibid.

9 Freud, *Civilization and Its Discontents.*
10 Hobbes, *Leviathan,* chap. 13, 183–93.
11 Fitzpatrick, *The Mythology of Modern Law,* chap. 6.
12 Sophocles, *Antigone.*
13 Dworkin, *Law's Empire,* chaps. 5 and 6; Fish, *Doing What Comes Naturally.* For a critique of Dworkin's argument, particularly from the point of view of his analysis of family, see Réaume, "Is Integrity a Virtue?"
14 Fish, "Dennis Martinez and the Uses of Theory."
15 See Derrida, "Declarations of Independence."
16 Kelsen, *General Theory of Law and State.*
17 Even the High Court may be said no longer to rely on the self-evident words of the Constitution or the sovereignty of the English parliament for their authority but, rather, on the aspirations of the Australian community that stand behind and before it: compare Windeyer, "A Birthright and Inheritance," and Dixon, "The Law and the Constitution," with *McGinty v. Western Australia* (1996) 136 C.L.R. 140, and Williams, "The High Court and the People."
18 Sandel, *Democracy's Discontent.*
19 Geertz, "Local Knowledge," 217.
20 *Donoghue v. Stevenson,* 580 per Lord Atkin.
21 Levinas, *Otherwise than Being,* 192n20.
22 Levinas, *Totality and Infinity,* 215.
23 Levinas, *Otherwise than Being,* 5.
24 Benso, *The Face of Things,* points out (25) that it is not the other that is placed before the self but our relationship with the other.
25 Derrida, "Violence and Metaphysics," 131. The "grammatology" of responsibility is also discussed in Caygill, *Levinas and the Political,* 70, and forms the structure – from first person to second person to third person – of Duncan, *The Pre-Text of Ethics.*
26 *Zugswang* is a position in chess in which a player is obliged to make a move, but no such move can be made without disadvantage: it is game theory *aporia.*
27 Levinas, *Totality and Infinity,* 274.
28 Shakespeare, *Hamlet,* 3.1.56 (1600?); Descartes, *Le Discours de la Méthode* (1637).
29 Libertson, *Proximity,* 10–11.
30 Hand, Introduction to *The Levinas Reader,* 4.
31 Davis, *Levinas,* 40.
32 Libertson, *Proximity,* 313.

33 See Sandel, *Democracy's Discontent*; Rawls, *A Theory of Justice*; Kymlicka, *Liberalism, Community, and Culture*.
34 American Psychiatric Association, *Diagnostic and Statistical Manual of Mental Disorders*; Bartol, *Criminal Behavior*; Hare, *Psychopathy*.
35 Levinas, "God and Philosophy," 165.
36 Libertson, *Proximity*, 180–1.
37 Ibid., 313.
38 Levinas, *Totality and Infinity*, 215.
39 Levinas, *Otherwise than Being*, 117.
40 Levinas, *Justifications de l'éthique* (Bruxelles 1984), in *The Levinas Reader*, 86.
41 Ibid.
42 Caygill, *Levinas and the Political*, 77.
43 Davis, *Levinas*, 40.
44 Derrida, "Violence and Metaphysics," 157–9.
45 Davis, *Levinas*, 27.
46 Levinas, "Philosophy and the Idea of Infinity" (1957), in *Collected Philosophical Papers*, 54.
47 Bernasconi, "The Trace of Levinas in Derrida," 15.
48 Levinas, "God and Philosophy" (1975), in *Collected Philosophical Papers*, 162.
49 The nature of the "in" in in-finity and Derrida's remarks on it are subject to much glossing. See Derrida, "Violence and Metaphysics," 140–3. For different views, see Bernasconi, "The Trace of Levinas in Derrida," 26, and "Deconstruction and the Possibility of Ethics," 128.
50 See Bernasconi, "The Trace of Levinas in Derrida," 15; compare Atterton, "Levinas and the Language of Peace."
51 Davis, *Levinas*, 40.
52 Bernasconi, "The Trace of Levinas in Derrida," 15–16; Derrida, "Violence and Metaphysics."
53 Derrida, "Violence and Metaphysics," 189.
54 Davis, *Levinas*, 45.
55 Foucault, *The Order of Things*, 215. The lack of an Archimedean point is a problem that has beset many critics. Indeed, the comparison with skepticism formed a central part of Levinas' own response to this criticism in *Otherwise than Being*. Levinas notes that the logical refutation of skeptical arguments does not herald their defeat but only shadows their return. The continual return of skepticism "despite the refutation that put its thesis into contradiction with the conditions for any thesis would be pure nonsense if everything in time were

recallable, that is, able to form a structure with the present" (Levinas, *Otherwise than Being*, 171; see generally 165–71). On the contrary, though, for Levinas the resilience of skepticism points to the possibility of truths existing at different levels and in different ways.

56 See Cohen, *Ethics, Exegesis and Philosophy*, 218; Caygill, *Levinas and the Political*, 109–24.

57 Levinas, *Otherwise than Being*, 64.

58 Levinas, *Totality and Infinity*, 26.

59 This is, of course, a theme throughout the literature of and on Levinas. For one recent discussion, see Maloney, "Levinas, Substitution, and Transcendental Subjectivity."

60 Aristotle, *Nichomachean Ethics* 5.111–12.

61 Perelman, "Equity and the Rule of Justice."

62 For a virulent critique of the idea of "patterned systems of justice," see Nozick, *Anarchy, State, and Utopia*.

63 *Prohibitions Del Roy* (1607), 12 Co. Rep. Mete-wand = metre wand = ruler.

64 Bentham, *An Introduction to the Principles of Morals and Legislation*, chap. 17, sec. 1; see also Mill and Bentham, *Utilitarianism*.

65 See Postema, introduction to *Philosophy and the Law of Torts*, 4–6.

66 Coase, "The Problem of Social Cost," 1, 2.

67 Ibid.

68 Posner, "A Theory of Negligence."

69 Posner, "Utilitarianism, Economic, and Legal Theory," 103, 116.

70 *United States v. Carroll Towing Co.* 159 F 2d 173 per Learned Hand J.

71 See also Richard Epstein's discussion of *Vincent v. Lake Erie* in "A Theory of Strict Liability."

72 Coleman, "Tort Law and Tort Theory," 206.

73 Levinas, *Totality and Infinity*, 111.

74 Ibid., 114–16.

75 Ibid., 129.

76 Ibid., 139.

77 Ibid., 132.

78 Ibid.

79 Ibid., 149; see sec. 2, "Interiority and Economy," in general.

80 Levinas, *Ethique et Infini*, 53.

81 Libertson, *Proximity*, is particularly helpful at drawing out these connections. For the relationship between Levinas and Derrida's analysis of subjectivity, see Critchley, *The Ethics of Deconstruction*.

It is a shared heritage that is made more explicit in some of Derrida's later works: see especially *The Politics of Friendship* and *Adieu to Emmanuel Levinas*.

82 Levinas, "God and Philosophy," in *Collected Philosophical Papers*, 165.

83 Compare Heidegger, whose philosophy is relentless in its pursuit of "the thing in its thingness" and the being in its *Dasein* (or being-ness). Heidegger, "The Origin of the Work of Art," 19.

84 Levinas, *Totality and Infinity*, 177.

85 Ibid., 197.

86 Lingis, translator's introduction to *Otherwise than Being*.

87 Levinas, *Totality and Infinity*, 198–9.

88 Caygill, *Levinas and the Political*, 56–61.

89 Ibid., 183.

90 Levinas, *The Levinas Reader*, 90.

91 *Geyer v. Downs* (1977) 138 C.L.R. 91.

92 Benson, "The Basis of Corrective Justice," 549.

93 Aristotle, *Nichomachean Ethics* 5.111; see also the helpful elucidation of the principle in Coleman, "Moral Theories of Torts," 6–7.

94 *Hedley Byrne v. Heller* [1964] A.C. 465.

95 *Geyer v. Downs* (1977) 138 C.L.R. 91.

96 *Dorset Yacht Co. v. The Home Office* [1969] A.C.

97 *Nagle v. Rottnest Island Authority* (1993) 177 C.L.R. 423.

98 Menlowe and Smith, *The Duty to Rescue*.

99 Posner, "Epstein's Tort Theory," 463.

100 Fried, "The Artificial Reason of the Law, or What Lawyers Know" (1981) quoted in Cane, *Responsibility in Law and Morality*, 195. See also Keating, "Social Contract Concept of the Tort Law of Accidents," 30–3.

101 Honoré, *Responsibility and Fault*, 137.

102 Ibid., 128–30.

103 Ibid., 31.

104 Mackie, *Ethics*, 208.

105 Smith, "Responsibility and Self Control," 1; Pettit, "The Capacity to Have Done Otherwise."

106 Perry, "Responsibility for Outcomes, Risk, and the Law of Torts," 72–4.

107 Gardner, "Obligations and Outcomes," 134.

108 Cane, "Responsibility and Fault," 104.

109 It is the case that according to at least some theories, vicarious liability is not a theory of responsibility at all. On such an analysis, there is a

compensatory and structural reason for such rules, but no normative principle at stake. This line of reasoning strikes me as failing to capture our thinking on this question. A refusal to acknowledge one's vicarious liability surely displays an ethical shallowness and not just a legal misunderstanding.

110 *Palsgraf v. Long Island R.R. Co*, 248 N.Y. 339; 162 N.E. 99 (1928) per Cardozo CJ.

111 Cane, *Responsibility in Law and Morality*, 23, 25.

112 Ibid., 41.

113 For example, England, *The Philosophy of Tort Law*, 88; Postema, introduction to *Philosophy and the Law of Torts*, 8; Stone, "The Significance of Doing and Suffering," 152–4; Coleman, "Tort Law and Tort Theory," 208; Vines, "Fault, Responsibility and Negligence," 136; Coleman, "The Practice of Corrective Justice," 56–7.

114 Derrida makes the same point in juxtaposing the Heideggerian *mit* (which we might think of as cognate to distributive justice) and the Cartesian *cogito* (which we might think of as cognate to corrective justice): "Violence and Metaphysics," 112.

115 Levinas, *Otherwise than Being*, 117.

116 Derrida, "Violence and Metaphysics," 113.

117 Levinas, *Totality and Infinity*, 21.

118 Hobbes, *Leviathan*; Rawls, *A Theory of Justice*.

119 Levinas, *Otherwise than Being*, 159.

120 Levinas, *Ethique et infini*, 74–5.

121 Benson, "Corrective Justice," 557.

122 Ibid., 564.

123 Ibid.

124 Levinas, *Ethique et infini*, 79.

125 Derrida, *Of Grammatology*; "Différance"; *Writing and Difference*.

126 Levinas, *Ethique et infini*, 21.

127 Levinas, *Otherwise than Being*, 25.

128 Peperzak, "The One for the Other," 436.

129 Peperzak, *Ethics as First Philosophy*.

130 Benson, "Corrective Justice," 561.

131 Hobbes, *Leviathan* (1651), chap. 15.

132 I say "default position" because of course there are situations in which we do not presume the integrity of the speaker: a play or a game, for example. But this is understood to be exceptional and gains its strength precisely as an exception against a background of presumed honesty.

133　Levinas, *Totality and Infinity*, 181.

134　Ibid., 182.

135　Levinas, *Otherwise than Being*, 119.

136　Levinas, *Totality and Infinity*, 73.

137　Levinas, *Otherwise than Being*, 96–7.

138　For example, Levinas, *Totality and Infinity*, 27.

139　For example, Levinas, *Otherwise than Being*, 107–10.

140　Ibid., 151.

141　Ibid., 195n12, discussed in Maloney, "Levinas, Substitution, and Transcendental Subjectivity," 57.

142　Levinas, "God and Philosophy," in *Collected Philosophical Papers*, 167.

143　Levinas, *Otherwise than Being*.

144　Levinas, *Ethique comme philosophie première*.

145　Again, we see the dichotomy everywhere; for example in Vines, in which "collective responsibility" and "individual responsibility," the latter understood as embodying a concept of free will and agency, are again presented as two complete and exhaustive alternatives.

146　Caygill, *Levinas and the Political*, 152.

147　Coleman, "The Practice of Corrective Justice," 55.

CHAPTER THREE

1　W.B. Yeats, "Before the World Was Made," in *A Woman Young and Old*.

2　Levinas, *Totality and Infinity*, 28: "a deduction – necessary yet non-analytical."

3　For more on the "is" that grounds ethics, as opposed to the "ought" that grounds morality, see Peperzak, "Emmanuel Levinas," 302. And for a discussion of how this embodiment is utilised meta-phorically, see Maloney, "Levinas, Substitution and Transcendental Subjectivity," 55–7.

4　Levinas, *Ethique et infini*, 11.

5　Ibid., 50; *Totality and Infinity*, 21.

6　Peperzak, *Beyond: The Philosophy of Emmanuel Levinas*, 112–5.

7　Levinas, *Totality and Infinity*, part 2C.

8　Levinas, *Théorie de l'intuition dans la phénmonénologie de Husserl; En découvrant l'existence avec Husserl et Heidegger*.

9　Levinas, *Totality and Infinity*, 75.

10　Ibid., 177.

11 "The 'resistance' of the other does not do violence to me, does not act negatively; it has a positive structure: ethical ... The face resists possession, resists my powers." Ibid., 197.

12 Gormley, *Field for the British Isles* (1993).

13 Derrida, "Violence and Metaphysics," 125–6.

14 Reported, inter alia, in http://www.sbc.org.uk/home/newsroom/ sub_newsroom/main/archive/9746637.

15 Lingis, translator's introduction to Levinas, *Otherwise than Being*, xxxiii.

16 Levinas, *Totality and Infinity*, 195. The translation says, "the ethical relationship which subtends discourse." The word "subtends" in this context is obscure and is used in English only in specialized scientific contexts. The French *sous-tends* emphasizes this idea of holding under, like a support or a scaffold, but is closer to the root-word *soustenir*, which means to sustain or provide sustenance, than the English. See Levinas, *Totalité et infini*, 213.

17 See Levinas, *Le visage de l'autre*. For a recent discussion, Duncan, *The Pre-Text of Ethics*, 41.

18 Levinas, *Ethique et infini*, 82.

19 Ibid., 83–4. In order to replicate the casualness of the conversation, I have adopted a very flexible translation here.

20 Levinas, *Totality and Infinity*, 187–212.

21 Levinas, *Otherwise than Being*, 49.

22 Duncan, *The Pre-Text of Ethics*, 79–82. See Irigaray, "The Fecundity of the Caress"; de Beauvoir, *The Second Sex*; Chanter, *Time, Death and the Feminine*, and *Ethics of Eros*.

23 See Katz, *Levinas, Judaism, and the Feminine*, 56.

24 Levinas, *Totality and Infinity*, 265; see, generally, part B, "Phenomenology of Eros," 256–66.

25 Levinas, *Totality and Infinity*, 258–9.

26 See Lingis, introduction to Levinas, *Collected Philosophical Papers*, xvi.

27 Levinas, "Language and Proximity," in *Collected Philosophical Papers*, 116–18.

28 Levinas, *Otherwise than Being*, 90.

29 Levinas, "God and Philosophy" (1975), in *Collected Philosophical Papers*, 165.

30 Ibid.

31 For more, with particular reference to the anti-Hegelianism of this concept, see Derrida, "Violence and Metaphysics," 114–15.

32 Levinas, *Ethique et infini*, 104–5.
33 Ibid., 105.
34 Levinas, *Totality and Infinity*, 290–1.
35 Ibid., 200.
36 Kundera, *The Unbearable Lightness of Being*.
37 Caygill, *Levinas and the Political*, 51–2. See also Agamben, *Homo Sacer*; Messiaen, *Quartet for the End of Time* (also written in a German prisoner of war camp).
38 Levinas, *Totality and Infinity*, 27.
39 Levinas, *Otherwise than Being*, 117.
40 Levinas, *Totality and Infinity*, 101.
41 Levinas, *Otherwise than Being*, 158–60.
42 Levinas, *Ethique et infini*, 93–4.
43 Levinas, "God and Philosophy," in *Collected Philosophical Papers*, 170.
44 Recall Derrida, "Violence and Metaphysics": a dream that must "vanish at daybreak" (189).
45 Levinas, *Otherwise than Being*, 109.
46 Ibid., 151.
47 Ibid., 49. See, generally, 48–51.
48 Ibid., 108.
49 Ibid., 110.
50 Hobbes, *Leviathan*, chap. 13.
51 Levinas, *Otherwise than Being*, 50–1.
52 Levinas, *Time and the Other*, 69–80.
53 Levinas, *Otherwise than Being*, 51.
54 Ibid., 92–3.
55 For example, ibid., 64.
56 Ibid., 117.
57 I am thinking in particular of the work of Gillian Rose. The particular criticisms that Rose fires at Levinas I address in a later chapter: see "New Political Theology," in Rose, *The Broken Middle*.
58 On this point, see particularly Levinas, *Otherwise than Being*, 45–8.
59 For example, ibid., 138–9. See Libertson, *Proximity*, 190.
60 Levinas, *Otherwise than Being*, 128.
61 Ibid.
62 Ibid., 86.
63 Amongst other places, see ibid., 85.
64 Ibid., 157.
65 Ibid.
66 Derrida, "Violence amd Metaphysics," 185; see also 189.

67 Rose, *The Broken Middle*.
68 Diamantides, *The Ethics of Suffering*, and "Ethics in Law"; Caygill, *Levinas and the Political*, 2-5.
69 Roberts, "Rethinking Justice"; Simmons, "The Third"; Critchley, *The Ethics of Deconstruction*.
70 Levinas, *Ethique et infini*, 94.
71 Levinas, *Totality and Infinity*, 195.
72 Levinas, *Otherwise than Being*, 56.
73 Levinas, *Totality and Infinity*, 189–92.
74 Peperzak, "The One for the Other," 439.
75 Levinas, *Otherwise than Being*, 114.
76 Ibid., 170.
77 Levinas, *Totality and Infinity*, writes: "This 'beyond' the totality and objective experience is, however, not to be described in a purely negative fashion. It is reflected *within* totality and history, *within* experience" (23).
78 Lingis, introduction to Levinas, *Totality and Infinity*, 13.
79 Levinas, *Ethique comme philosophie première*.
80 Levinas, *Totality and Infinity*, 291, pursues this metaphor of "the curvature of inter-subjective space."
81 Kant, *Religion within the Limits of Reason Alone*.
82 *Bouleversement*, a useful word meaning something like topsy-turvy, is one of Levinas' favourites, unsurprisingly, since it forms such a central part of his intellectual method.
83 Newton, *The Fence and the Neighbour*, 88; Llewellyn, *Emmanuel Levinas*, 113.
84 Levinas, "Signature," in *Difficult Freedom*, 291.
85 Levinas, *Otherwise than Being*, dedication page.
86 Peperzak, "Emmanuel Levinas," 297–9.
87 Levinas, *Ethique et infini*, 14. See in particular Levinas, *Difficult Freedom*.
88 Peperzak, "The One for the Other," 430–2. See also Bennington, "Mosaic Fragment," 97.
89 Rose, *The Broken Middle*, 256–64, and *Judaism and Modernity*, 11–23.
90 Levinas, "The Paradox of Morality," 168.
91 MacDonald, "Jewgreek and Greekjew," 217–18.
92 Derrida, "Violence and Metaphysics," 191–2. For more, see Llewelyn, "Jewgreek or Greekjew," and Srajek, *The Margins of Deconstruction*.
93 Levinas, "Assimilation and New Culture" (an extract from "Zionisms," 1982) in Levinas, *The Levinas Reader*, 287. See also Levinas, *Difficult Freedom*, 200; Llewellyn, *Emmanuel Levinas*, 197.

94 See, for example, Levinas, *Otherwise than Being*, 200; *Totality and Infinity*, 232–3; and *Time and the Other*.

95 One can only express a profound skepticism at Levinas' claim that "I would never, for example, introduce a Talmudic or biblical verse into one of my philosophical texts, to try to prove or justify a phenomenological argument." Llewellyn, *Emmanuel Levinas, Genealogy of Ethics*, 113. The distinction between the "phenomenological" arguments and the metaphorical and narrative arguments that surround them is hardly tenable.

96 Levinas, *Difficult Freedom*, 10.

97 Cover, "*Nomos* and Narrative."

98 On the Levinasian priority of *aggadah* within the contested Talmudic tradition, see Newton, *The Fence and the Neighbour*, 13–20.

99 Katz, *Levinas, Judaism and the Feminine*, 18; and see Cohen, *Ethics, Exegesis and Philosophy*.

100 Cohen, *Ethics, Exegesis and Philosophy*, 243–50.

101 Ibid., 225–7.

102 Quoted in Bernasconi, "Different Styles of Eschatology," 16.

103 Levinas, *Difficult Freedom*, 135–7.

104 Levinas, *Proper Names*, 138.

105 Levinas, *Totality and Infinity*, 271.

106 Levinas, "The Poet's Vision," in *Proper Names*, 133–6.

107 Lingis, preface to Levinas, *Otherwise than Being*, xxxi.

108 Blaise Pascal, *Pensées*, 112, quoted in *Otherwise than Being*, vii.

109 See Caygill, *Levinas and the Political*, eg., 85–8, 171–6.

110 MacDonald, "Jewgreek and Greekjew," 217–18.

111 This quote is provided courtesy of Professor Peter Goodrich, whose remarks have been of great assistance to me here, as elsewhere. And again does not Habermas' pejorative image of a wandering in the desert display here a trace of intellectual antisemitism?

112 And see Peperzak, "Emmanuel Levinas: Jewish Experience and Philosophy."

113 Levinas, "God and Philosophy," in *Collected Philosophical Papers*; "The Consolations of Religion," in Levinas, *Ethique et infini*, 109.

114 Schneider, *Daniel Libeskind*.

CHAPTER FOUR

1 Levinas, *Time and the Other*, 61.

2 Genesis 25:34.

3 Rose, *The Broken Middle*.
4 Ibid., 284.
5 Ibid., 282.
6 Ibid., 283.
7 Rose, *Judaism and Modernity*, 16.
8 Ibid., 21, 45, 221. See also Newton, *The Fence and the Neighbour*.
9 Rose, *Judaism and Modernity*, 50.
10 Habermas, *The Philosophical Discourse of Modernity*.
11 MacDonald, "Jewgreek and Greekjew," 215–22.
12 Ibid., 222.
13 See Shils, *Tradition*; Manderson, "Apocryphal Jurisprudence."
14 Rose, *Judaism and Modernity*, 87.
15 Derrida, "Violence and Metaphysics"; Bernasconi, "Different Styles of Eschatology," 7–13.
16 Rose, *The Broken Middle*, 250.
17 Ibid., 285.
18 Ibid., 293.
19 Ibid., 307.
20 Rose, *Judaism and Modernity*, 220.
21 Ibid., 6.
22 Rose, *The Broken Middle*, 310.
23 This appears to be an overstatement that Derrida is sensitive to and does not pursue in his later responses: see Derrida, "At This Very Moment in This Work Here I Am"; Bernasconi, "Different Styles of Eschatology," 11–13.
24 Quoted ibid., 16.
25 Levinas, *Totality and Infinity*, 22.
26 Bernasconi, "Different Styles of Eschatology," 7.
27 Marquez, "The Curvature of Intersubjective Space," 348.
28 Levinas, *Totality and Infinity*, 143–9.
29 Levi-Strauss, *Myth and Meaning*.
30 Rose, *Judaism and Modernity*, 6.
31 Ibid., 5.
32 Levinas, *Otherwise than Being*, 153–62.
33 Ibid., 168.
34 Critchley, *The Ethics of Deconstruction*, 42.
35 Levinas, *Totality and Infinity*, 195.
36 Rose, *The Broken Middle*, 264, 263, 307, 285.
37 Rose, *Judaism and Modernity*, 220.
38 Levinas, *Otherwise than Being*, 171. Italics mine.

39 Duncan, *The Pre-Text of Ethics*, 139. See also Simmons, "The Third"; Roberts, "Rethinking Justice"; and Critchley, *The Ethics of Deconstruction*.

40 Levinas, *Totality and Infinity*, 246; Levinas, *Otherwise than Being*, 159; Derrida, "Force of Law."

41 Derrida, "Force of Law," 20.

42 Levinas, *Difficult Freedom*, 147.

43 Levinas, *Otherwise than Being*, 117.

44 *Donoghue v. Stevenson* [1931] A.C. 562, 580 per Lord Atkin.

45 Luke 10:25, 29–37.

46 Levinas, *Otherwise than Being*, 157.

47 Ibid., 128.

48 Levinas, "The Ego and the Totality" (1954), in Levinas, *Collected Philosophical Papers*, 44.

49 Ibid., 45.

50 Levinas, "On Jewish Philosophy," quoted in Simmons, "The Third," 97.

51 Lingis, Translator's introduction to Levinas, *Collected Philosophical Papers*, xxi.

52 Levinas, *Otherwise than Being*, 170.

53 See *The Others* (2001); see also the discussion of the metaphor of ghosts in Levinas' *Existence and Existents*, in Caygill, *Levinas and the Political*, 60–1.

54 Derrida, "Force of Law," 24–6.

55 Critchley, *The Ethics of Deconstruction*, 163; Caygill, *Levinas and the Political*, 162–3.

56 Critchley, *The Ethics of Deconstruction*, chap. 2.

57 Derrida, "Violence and Metaphysics"; Critchley, *The Ethics of Deconstruction*, 69–96.

58 Derrida, "Violence and Metaphysics," 151.

59 Levinas, *Totality and Infinity*, 287–97.

60 Levinas, *Otherwise than Being*, chap. 6, "Outside," 175–85.

61 Derrida, "Violence and Metaphysics."

62 Critchley, *The Ethics of Deconstruction*, 125.

63 Levinas, "Meaning and Sense" (1972), in Levinas, *Collected Philosophical Papers*, 75, 102–7.

64 Ibid., 104.

65 Ibid., 104–5. Italics added.

66 This, notes Levinas, is why it disrupts phenomenology (ibid., 104).

67 Derrida, "Violence and Metaphysics"; Bernasconi, "Different Styles of Eschatology," 11, "The Trace of Levinas in Derrida," 13, and

"Deconstruction and the Possibility of Ethics"; Simmons, "The Third"; Maloney, "Levinas, Substitution, and Transcendental Subjectivity." A view in which Derrida is rather more opposed to Levinas on this point can be found in Atterton, "Levinas and the Language of Peace," and Cohen, *Ethics, Exegesis and Philosophy.*

68 Derrida, "Violence and Metaphysics," 142–3; Bernasconi, "Deconstruction and the Possibility of Ethics," 130.

69 Derrida, "Violence and Metaphysics," 164–5; Bernasconi, "The Trace of Levinas in Derrida," 19.

70 Gibbs, "The Other Comes to Teach Me," 230; Bernasconi, "The Trace of Levinas in Derrida," 14–15.

71 Derrida, "Violence and Metaphysics," 158; Bernasconi, "The Trace of Levinas in Derrida," 26.

72 Thus, see Rose, *Judaism and Modernity,* 23.

73 It is Atterton's view, and Bernasconi's on occasion, that Derrida did not adequately appreciate the power of trace and proximity in "Violence and Metaphysics" and that it was only in his later work, such as *"Différance"* and "At This Very Moment in This Work Here I Am," that he began to incorporate these insights into his own thinking about meaning and social change. Atterton, "Levinas and the Language of Peace," 67; Bernasconi, "The Trace of Levinas in Derrida," 14.

74 See also Gibbs, "The Other Comes to Teach Me," 225.

75 Critchley, *The Ethics of Deconstruction,* 124, 125, 127, 146, 164–5; Simmons, "The Third," 89.

76 I think that the contaminating power of this proximity is treated with considerably less sympathy in Diamantides, "Ethics in Law."

77 Derrida, "Violence and Metaphysics," 185.

78 Levinas, *Otherwise than Being,* 157.

79 Bernasconi, "Deconstruction and the Possibility of Ethics," 122; Burggraeve, "Violence and the Vulnerable Face of the Other," 33.

80 Critchley, *The Ethics of Deconstruction,* 233.

81 Ibid., 222.

82 Derrida, "Force of Law"; Maloney, "Levinas, Substitution, and Transcendental Subjectivity," 59; Duncan, *The Pre-Text of Ethics,* 139. See especially the treatment of law and justice in Roberts, "Rethinking Justice," and Simmons "The Third," 93–7.

83 Critchley, *The Ethics of Deconstruction,* 231.

84 This argument about justice as a second step is further developed in Atterton, "Levinas and the Language of Peace," 64–7.

85 Levinas, *Otherwise than Being*, 159–60.
86 Ibid., 101.
87 *Henwood v. Municipal Tramways Trust* (1938) 60 C.L.R. 438, 462 per Dixon and McTiernan JJ.
88 *Jackson v. Harrison* (1978) 138 C.L.R. 438; *Cook v. Cook* (1986) 162 C.L.R. 376.
89 *Gala v. Preston* (1991) 172 C.L.R. 243.
90 Ibid., 263 *per* Brennan J.
91 *Progress and Properties v. Craft* (1976) 135 C.L.R. 651, 668 per Jacobs J.
92 *Hall v. Hebert* (1993) 101 D.L.R. (4th) 129; 2 S.C.R. 159 per Sopinka J (S.C. Canada).
93 *Gala v. Preston*, 252 per Mason CJ, Deane, Gaudron and McHugh JJ.
94 *Smith v. Jenkins* (1970) 119 C.L.R. 397.
95 *Gala v. Preston*, 254 per Mason CJ, Deane, Gaudron and McHugh JJ.
96 Ibid., 254–5.
97 Ibid., 254.
98 Ibid., 277 per Dawson J.
99 Ibid., 254 per Mason CJ, Deane, Gaudron and McHugh JJ.
100 The matter is otherwise if the passenger soberly accepts the risks of travelling in the car with a drunkard, but this "specific and exceptional relationship" does not apply if the passenger is also inebriated and not therefore in a position to choose, although the behaviour may still constitute contributory negligence: *Insurance Commissioner v. Joyce* (1948) 77 C.L.R. 39 *per* Dixon J (cf. Latham CJ); *Preston v. Gala* [1990] 1 Qd. R. 170; *Cook v. Cook* (1986) 162 C.L.R. 376.
101 *Hall v. Hebert,* per McLaughlin J (S.C. Canada).
102 *Gala v. Preston*, 273. See, in identical terms, 279 per Dawson J.
103 Ibid., 271 per Brennan J.
104 Ibid., 279.
105 *Hall v. Hebert*, 195 per Cory J (S.C. Canada).
106 Ibid.
107 *Nelson v. Nelson* (1995) 184 C.L.R. 538.
108 *Riggs v. Palmer* 22 N.E. 188 (1889) (New York Court of Appeals).
109 *Gala v. Preston* (1991) 172 C.L.R. 243 at 269 per Brennan J.
110 Ibid., 279 per Dawson J.
111 Ibid., 269 per Brennan J.
112 *Hall v. Hebert,* 182 per McLachlin J (S.C. Canada).
113 Ibid., 183.

114 Levinas, *Ethique et infini*, 74–5.
115 *Gala v. Preston*, 250 per Mason CJ, Deane, Gaudron, and McHugh JJ.
116 Ibid., 253.
117 Ibid., 254.
118 Kostal, "Currents in the Counter-Reformation."
119 See McHugh, "Neighbourhood, Proximity and Reliance"; Kramer,
     "Proximity as Principles: Directness, Community Norms and the Tort
     of Negligence"; Vines, "The Needle in the Haystack"; Yeo,
     "Rethinking Proximity."
120 *Stevens v. Brodribb* and *Cook v. Cook*.
121 Levinas, *The Levinas Reader*, 120.
122 Levinas, "God and Philosophy," in *Collected Philosophical Papers*,
     167.
123 Ibid.
124 Atiyah, *Accidents, Compensation and the Law*, 63–72; Shapo,
     The Duty to Act; Weinrib, "The Case for a Duty to Rescue."
125 *Jaensch v. Coffey* (1984) 155 C.L.R. 549 at 578 per Deane J.
126 *Wilmot v. South Australia* (1993) *Australian Torts Reporter* ¶81-259;
     Nagle v. Rottnest Island Authority (1993) 177 C.L.R. 423.
127 *Hargrave v. Goldman* (1963) 110 C.L.R. 40.
128 Honoré, "Are Omissions Less Culpable?" 44.
129 *Hargrave v. Goldman*, 67 per Windeyer J.
130 Ibid., 66 per Windeyer J.
131 *Dorset Yacht Co v. Home Office* [1970] A.C. 1004 per Lord Reid.
132 *Geyer v. Downs* (1977) 138 C.L.R. 91.
133 *Sutherland Shire Council v. Heyman* (1985) 157 C.L.R. 424.
134 See the discussion of responsibility as death and as gift in Burggraeve,
     "Violence and the Vulnerable Face of the Other"; Derrida, *The Gift of
     Death*.
135 See, in particular, the remarks of Chief Justice Gleeson and Justice
     McHugh in *Perre v. Apand Pty Ltd* (1999) 198 C.L.R. 180.
136 Levinas, *The Levinas Reader*, 120.
137 Levinas, "Language and Proximity," in *Collected Philosophical Papers*,
     109, 125.
138 Levinas, *Difficult Freedom*, 140.
139 *Lowns v. Wood* [1996] *Australian Torts Reporter* ¶81-376; and see
     L. Haberfield, "*Lowns v. Woods* and the Duty to Rescue."
140 *Lowns v. Wood*, 63,172 per Cole JA.
141 Ibid., 63,155 per Kirby P.
142 *Medical Practitioners Act* 1938 (N.S.W.), s. 27(2).

143 *Lowns v. Wood*, 63,155 per Kirby P.

144 *Hargrave v. Goldman*, 66 per Windeyer J.

145 *Lowns v. Wood*, 63,166 per Mahoney JA.

146 Levinas, "Language and Proximity," in *Collected Philosophical Papers*, 116.

147 *Lowns v. Wood*, 63,166 per Mahoney JA.

148 Derrida, *Positions*, writes of philosophical texts as carrying "the cicatrice of alterity."

149 *Lowns v. Woods*, 63,168–9 per Mahoney JA.

150 *Goldman v. Hargrave* (1966) 115 C.L.R. 458. In *Geyer v. Downs*, Stephen J categorically rejected the argument that a school's responsibility to its students could be limited by its resources. The school, said the court, has a choice as to the time at which it will open its doors and commence its duties. But here we are speaking of a responsibility that arises from a predicament or a crisis in which I find myself without action on my part.

151 Levinas, *Ethique et infini*, 92.

152 Davis, *Levinas*, 51.

153 Levinas, *Otherwise than Being*, 157.

154 Ibid.

155 Ibid., 128.

CHAPTER FIVE

1 Adapted from "Macavity the Mystery Cat," in T.S. Eliot, *Old Possum's Book of Practical Cats*.

2 Jorge Luis Borges, *Collected Fictions*.

3 See for example "The Masked Dyer of Merv," "The Circular Ruins," "The Library of Babel," "The Approach to Al-Mu'tasim," "Murdered in His Labyrinth," "The Two Kings and the Two Labyrinths," "Covered Mirrors," and "The Mirror and the Mask" (ibid).

4 Thus, see "The Approach to Al-Mu'tasim," "Pierre Menard, Author of the *Quixote*," "A Dialog about a Dialog," "The Plot," and "On Exactitude in Science" (ibid.) and, from his nonfiction writings, "The Analytical Language of John Wilkins," in *Labyrinths*.

5 See "Borges and I" and "The Other," in Borges, *Collected Fictions*.

6 Borges, *Collected Fictions*, 82–7.

7 "The Approach to Al-Mu'tasim," ibid.

8 Ibid., 87.

9 Kafka, "The Parable of the Law." The story begins: "Before the Law stands a doorkeeper. To this doorkeeper there comes a man from the country and prays for admittance to the Law."

10 Lingis, preface to Levinas, *Otherwise than Being*, xxxi.

11 Borges, "The Approach to Al-Mu'tasim," in *Collected Fictions*.

12 Levinas, *Totality and Infinity*, 110–17.

13 Levinas, *Autrement qu'être ou au-delà de l'essence*, 129–56. This section was originally published as "La Proximité" in *Archives de Philosophie* (1971): see Levinas, *Otherwise than Being*, xlvii.

14 Levinas, *Otherwise than Being*, 5.

15 Levinas, *Totality and Infinity*, 257–8.

16 The original French, I believe, is clearer: "La caresse comme le contact est sensibilité ... La caresse ne vise ni une personne, ni une chose." Levinas, *Totalité et infini*, 288–9.

17 Levinas, "Phenomenon and Enigma," in *Collected Philosophical Papers*, 61, 73.

18 *Caltex Oil (Australia) Pty. Ltd. v. The Dredge "Willemstad"* (1976) 136 C.L.R. 529.

19 *Jaensch v. Coffey* (1984) 155 C.L.R. 549.

20 Libertson, *Proximity*.

21 "Separation and Cogito in Levinas," in Libertson, *Proximity*, 30–41.

22 Ibid., 264.

23 Ibid., 217.

24 Ibid., 322–3.

25 Levinas, *Otherwise than Being*, v.

26 Levinas speaks of his biography as "dominated by the presentiment and the memory of the Nazi horror." "Signature," in Levinas, *Difficult Freedom*, 291.

27 Levinas, *Otherwise than Being*, 114.

28 Ibid., 59, 121. "A subject is hostage" (ibid., 112).

29 Ibid., 56.

30 Levinas, "Justifications de l'éthique" (Bruxelles 1984), in "Ethics as First Philosophy," in *The Levinas Reader*, 83. Italics mine.

31 Levinas, *Otherwise than Being*, 105–51.

32 Ibid., 157. Reference might also be made of the work of Charles Sandford Peirce, for whom the "third," with all its implications and complexifications was also a critical analytical stage. See Kevelson, *Peirce, Science, Signs*.

33 *Jaensch v. Coffey*, 583 per Deane J.

34 Ibid.
35 *Gala v. Preston* (1991) 172 C.L.R. 243 at 253 per Mason CJ, Deane, Gaudron and McHugh JJ; 260 per Brennan J.
36 *Gala v. Preston*, 261 per Brennan J.
37 *Pyrenees Shire Council v. Day; Eskimo Amber Pty Ltd v. Pyrenees Shire Council* (1998) 192 C.L.R. 330.
38 Ibid., 414 [238] per Kirby J.
39 *Caparo Industries PLC v. Dickman* [1990] 2 A.C. 605, 617–18.
40 The brief discussion of this case is based on Baker and Manderson, "*Boland v. Yates* Re-opens Case."
41 *Demarco v. Ungaro* (1979) 95 C.L.R. (3d) 385.
42 *Arthur Hall v. Simons* [2000] 3 W.L.R. 543 (House of Lords).
43 *Giannarelli v. Wraith* (1988) 165 C.L.R. 543; *D'Orta-Ekenaide v. Victoria Legal & McIvor* [2005] HCA 12.
44 Emmanuel Levinas, transcript of interview on Radio Communauté, 28 September 1982, originally published in *Les Nouveaux Cahiers* 18 (1982–83) and reprinted as "Ethics and Politics," in *The Levinas Reader*, 293.
45 Levinas, *Otherwise than Being*, 117.
46 Ibid., 160.
47 Ibid., 117.
48 See, for example, the conflict between patient care and medical training (the doctor's "overriding duty" to the medicine), articulated in Gawunde, "The Learning Curve," 52.
49 *Donoghue v. Stevenson* [1931] A.C. 562 at 580.
50 Levinas, *Ethique et infini*, 92.
51 Mackie, *Ethics*; see also the several discussions of Mackie's work in Cane and Gardner, eds., *Relating to Responsibility.*
52 Perry, "Risk, Harm, and Responsibility," in Owen, *Philosophical Foundations of Tort Law*, 345.
53 Perry, "Responsibility for Outcomes," 83–91; Vines, "Fault, Responsibility and Negligence," 135, discussing Perry and Mackie.
54 *Chapman v. Hearse* (1961) 106 C.L.R. 112 per Owen Dixon CJ.
55 Vines, "Fault, Responsibility and Negligence," 135, discussing Perry and Mackie.
56 (1984) 155 C.L.R. 549.
57 *Donoghue v. Stevenson* [1931] A.C. 562 at 580 per Lord Atkin.
58 Ibid.
59 Ibid.
60 *Vaughan v. Menlove* (1837) 3 Bing. N.C. 467; 132 E.R. 490.

61 *Leigh & Sullivan v. Aliakmon Shipping Co Ltd* [1985] Q.B. 350,
p. 397 per Robert Goff LJ (English Court of Appeals).
62 Transcripts to *Chapman v. Hearse* (1961) 106 C.L.R. 112, quoted in
Luntz and Hambly, *Torts*, 145.
63 *Sutherland Shire Council v. Heyman*, 495 per Deane J.
64 *Jaensch v. Coffey*, 578 per Deane J.
65 *Sutherland Shire Council v. Heyman*, 495, per Deane J.
66 Levinas "Language and Proximity," in *Collected Philosophical Papers*,
125.
67 Ibid.
68 Geertz, "Fact and Law in Comparative Perspective," 221.
69 *Palsgraf v. Long Island R.R. Co.* (1928) 248 N.Y. 339 (New York
Court of Appeals).
70 Ibid., per Cardozo CJ.
71 Ibid., per Cardozo CJ.
72 Ibid., per Cardozo CJ.
73 *Chapman v. Hearse* (1961) 106 C.L.R. 112.
74 Stone, *Social Dimensions of Law and Justice*.
75 Derrida, "Force of Law," 963.
76 *Mount Isa Mines v. Pusey* (1970) 125 C.L.R. 383, 403 per Windeyer J.
The remark was directed towards the test for remoteness of damage,
but the comment applies with equal force here.
77 *Palsgraf.*
78 See also ibid., 342: the wrong was "apparently not one involving the
risk of bodily insecurity."
79 For the English and Australian position, see *Re Polemis* [1921] 3 K.B.
560 (English Court of Appeal).
80 *Overseas Tankship (UK) v. Morts Dock & Engineering (The Wagon
Mound (No. 1))* [1961] A.C. 388.
81 *Mount Isa Mines v. Pusey* (1970) 125 C.L.R. 383; *Nader v. Urban
Transit Authority of N.S.W.* (1985) 2 N.S.W.L.R. 501.
82 *Blyth v. Birmingham Waterworks Co.* (1856) 11 Exch 781 per
Alderson B.
83 *Wyong Shire Council v. Shirt* (1980) 146 C.L.R. 40 at 47 per Mason J.
84 Levinas, *Otherwise than Being*, 157.
85 Ibid., 64.
86 Ibid., 13.
87 Levinas, "Language and Proximity," in Levinas, *Collected
Philosophical Papers*, 119.
88 *Chester v. Waverley Municipal Council* (1939) 62 C.L.R. 1.

89 Luntz and Hambly, *Torts*, 151.

90 *Chester v. Waverley Municipal Council*, 10 per Latham CJ.

91 *Jaensch v. Coffey*, 587 per Deane J.

92 Ibid., 590 per Deane J.

93 *Chester v. Waverley Municipal Council*, 11 per Rich J.

94 Ibid., 16 per Evatt J.

95 Ibid., 17 per Evatt J.

96 Ibid., 25 per Evatt J.

97 Ibid., 11 per Rich J. Emphasis mine.

98 *Palsgraf v. Long Island R.R. Co*, 350, 349 per Andrews J.

99 *Bourhill v. Young* [1943] A.C. 92, 108 per Lord Wright.

100 *Bottomley v. Bannister* [1932] 1 K.B. 458 at 476 per Greer LJ.

101 *Leigh & Sullivan v. Aliakmon Shipping Co Ltd.* [1985] Q.B. 350 at 397 per Robert Goff LJ (English Court of Appeals).

102 *Caltex Oil (Australia) v. The Dredge "Willemstad"* (1976) 136 C.L.R. 529.

103 *Cattle v. Stockton Waterworks Co.* (1875) LR 10 Q.B. 453.

104 Of course specific areas of negligence law had already been acknowledged as exceptions: for example, in cases of nervous shock and negligent misstatement.

105 *Candlewood Navigation Corporation v. Mitsui OSK Lines* [1986] A.C. 1 at 22.

106 The fact that Caltex's oil and the damaged AOR pipeline were actually in physical contact was the basis of Jacob J's judgment: *Caltex Oil (Australia) v. The Dredge "Willemstad,"* 594–605 per Jacob J.

107 Ibid., 575 per Stephen J.

108 Ibid.

109 *Jaensch v. Coffey*, 558, reported in Brennan J's judgment.

110 *Chester v. Waverley Municipal Council*, 7 per Latham CJ.

111 *Jaensch v. Coffey*, 612 per Dawson J.

112 Ibid., 584 per Deane J.

113 Ibid., 600 per Deane J.

114 *Coultas v. Victorian Railway Commissioners* (1886) 12 V.L.R. 895; (1888) 13 AppCas 222 (Privy Council); *McLoughlin v. O'Brien* [1983] 1 A.C. 410 (House of Lords).

115 *Jaensch v. Coffey*, 605 per Deane J.

116 Dworkin, "Rules and Principles"; Vines, "Proximity as Principle or Category."

117 *Jaensch v. Coffey*, 605 per Deane J.

118 Levinas, "Language and Proximity," in *Collected Philosophical Papers*, 119.

119 *Jaensch v. Coffey*, 591 per Deane J.

120 (1985) 157 C.L.R. 424.

121 Ibid., 495 per Deane J.

122 Ibid.

123 *Burnie Port Authority v. General Jones* (1994) 179 C.L.R. 520 at 543 per Mason CJ, Deane, Dawson and Toohey and Gaudron JJ.

124 *Cook v. Cook* (1986) 162 C.L.R. 376 at 382 per Mason, Wilson, Deane and Dawson JJ.

125 Levinas, *Otherwise than Being*, 120.

126 *Sutherland Shire Council v. Heyman*, 497 per Deane J.

127 Ibid.

128 Ibid.

129 Ibid.

130 *Wyong Shire Council v. Shirt* (1980) 146 C.L.R. 40 at 44 per Mason J, quoting Glass JA in the New South Wales Court of Appeal: (1978) 1 N.S.W.L.R. 641.

131 *Jaensch v. Coffey*, 549 per Deane J.

132 "Proximity is a question of law to be resolved by the processes of legal reasoning, induction, and deduction." *Sutherland Shire Council v. Heyman*, 498 per Deane J.

133 Peter Fitzpatrick, *Modernism and the Grounds of Law* (Cambridge: Cambridge University Press 2001), 87–8.

134 *Burnie Port Authority*, 543 per Mason CJ, Deane, Dawson and Toohey and Gaudron JJ.

135 *Chadwick v. British Railways Board* [1967] 1 W.L.R. 912.

136 *Wagner v. International Railway Co.* (1921) 133 N.E. 437 (New York Supreme Court), per Cardozo J.

137 *Ogwo v. Taylor* [1988] A.C. 431; *Frost v. Chief Constable* [1997] 1 All E.R. 540 (English Court of Appeals).

138 *Jaensch v. Coffey*, 567 per Brennan J. Emphasis mine.

139 (1985) 157 C.L.R. 424.

140 Ibid., 497 per Deane J.

141 Ibid.

142 McHugh, "Neighbourhood, Proximity and Reliance," chap. 2; Amirthalingam and Faunce, "Patching up 'Proximity': Problems with the Judicial Creation of a New Medical Duty to Rescue."

143 See, for example, Levinas, *Oherwise than Being*, 56.

144 Ibid., 49–54.

145 *Wagner v. International Railway Co.* (1921) 232 N.Y. Rep 176 (New York Supreme Court), per Cardozo J.

146 Ibid., 176–80.

147 *Jaensch v. Coffey*, 567 per Brennan J.

148 *Campbelltown City Council v. Mackay* (1989) 15 N.S.W.L.R. 501 at 503 per Kirby P.

149 Ibid.; but see *Andrewartha v. Andrewartha (No. 1)* (1987) 44 S.A.S.R. 1; *Spence v. Percy* [1992] 2 Qd R 299.

150 *Jaensch v. Coffey*, 567 per Brennan J.

151 Levinas, *Otherwise than Being*, 13.

152 McHugh, "Neighbourhood, Proximity and Reliance," 13, also 36–9. "The notion of proximity, used as a legal norm, has the uncertainties and perils of a category of indeterminate reference." *Hill v. Van Erp* (1995–6) 188 C.L.R. 159 at 238 per Gummow J.

153 *San Sebastian v. The Minister* (1986) 162 C.L.R. 341 at 368 per Brennan J.

154 *Gala v. Preston*, 277 per Dawson J.

155 *Jaensch v. Coffey*, 585 per Deane J.

156 *Bryan v. Maloney* (1995) 182 C.L.R. 609 at 654 per Brennan J.

157 *White v. Jones* [1995] 2 A.C. 207 at 274 per Lord Browne-Wilkinson, refers explicitly "to a conscious assumption of responsibility."

158 *Sutherland Shire Council v. Heyman*, 502 per Deane J.

159 *Shaddock & Associates Pty. Ltd. v. Parramatta City Council (No. 1)* (1981) 150 C.L.R. 225.

160 Ibid., 251 per Mason J.

161 Ibid., 242 per Stephen J.

162 *Sutherland Shire Council v. Heyman*, 464 per Mason J.

163 Ibid.

164 *Parramatta City Council v. Lutz* (1988) 12 N.S.W.L.R. 293, per McHugh J.

165 *Pyrenees*, 387 [163] per Gummow J; see also Brooking JA, [1997] 1 V.R. 218, 233.

166 Levinas, *Otherwise than Being*, 87.

167 *Hawkins v. Clayton* (1988) 164 C.L.R. 539; *Hill v. Van Erp* (1995–6) 188 C.L.R. 159.

168 *Hawkins v. Clayton*, 545 per Mason CJ and Wilson J.

169 Ibid., 597 per Gaudron J.

170 Ibid. 576 per Deane J.

171 Ibid., 593–4 per Gaudron J.

172 *Hill v. Van Erp*, 198 per Gaudron J.

173 Ibid., 184–5 per Dawson J, emphasis added.

174 *San Sebastian v. The Minister* (1986) 162 C.L.R. 341.

175 Ibid., 355 per Gibbs CJ, Mason Wilson and Dawson JJ. See also
' *Bryan v. Maloney.*

176 Ibid., 366 per Brennan J.

177 See also *Hill v. Van Erp*, per Dawson J; *Pyrenees*, 339 [9] per Brennan
CJ.

178 *San Sebastian v. The Minister*, 210 per McHugh J.

179 *Hill v. Van Erp* (1995–6) 188 C.L.R. 159.

180 *Pyrenees.*

181 Mason, "Legislative and judicial law-making"; Vines, "Fault,
Responsibility and Negligence in the High Court."

182 Stapleton, "Duty of Care Factors," 60–2.

183 *San Sebastian v. The Minister*, 369 per Brennan J.

184 *Hill v. Van Erp*, 177 per Dawson J.

185 (1999) 198 C.L.R. 180.

186 Ibid., 216–17 [93]–[94] per McHugh J.

187 *Hill v. Van Erp*, 199 per Gaudron J, citing Brennan J in *Hawkins
v. Clayton*, 555.

188 The standard reference is to Goodhart, "The *Ratio Decidendi* of
a Case."

189 Stone, *Legal System and Lawyers' Reasonings*, 267.

190 *San Sebastian v. The Minister*, 369 per Brennan J.

191 *Hill v. Van Erp*, 177 per Dawson J.

192 *Perre v. Apand*, 217 [94] per McHugh J.

193 *Hill v. Van Erp*, 180 per Dawson J.

194 *Perre v. Apand* 192 [5] per Gleeson CJ. See also Gaudron J at 199–
200 [31]–[33], McHugh J at 220–6 [106]–[119], Kirby J at 289–90
[297]–[302], Hayne J at 302–3 [334]–[335].

195 Ibid., per Gaudron J at 197 [25] citing Mason CJ, Deane and
Gaudron JJ in *Bryan v. Maloney*, 618.

196 *Donoghue v. Stevenson*, 580 per Lord Atkin. My italics.

197 *Perre v. Apand*, 220 [103] per McHugh J.

198 Kirby J's three-fold test, adopted from the House of Lords decision
in *Caparo*, separately distinguishes and analyzes foreseeability,
proximity, and policy: ibid., 275 [259]; *Pyrenees*, 419–20 [294] per
Kirby J.

199 *Sutherland Shire Council v. Heyman*, 464 per Mason J.

200 Ibid.
201 *Pyrenees*, 370 [107] per McHugh J.
202 See *Albrighton v. Royal Prince Alfred Hospital* [1980] 2 N.S.W.L.R.
     542; *Kondis v. State Transport Authority* (1984) 154 C.L.R. 672; *The Commonwealth v. Introvigne* (1982) 150 C.L.R. 258; *Hahn v. Conley* (1971) 126 C.L.R. 276; *Robertson v. Swincer* (1989) 52 S.A.S.R. 356.
203 *Kondis v. State Transport Authority*, 687 per Mason CJ.
204 Ibid., 687–8 per Mason CJ.
205 *Burnie Port Authority v. General Jones Pty Ltd* (1994) 179 C.L.R. 520.
206 Ibid., 550, quoting *Kondis v. State Transport Authority* (1984) 154 C.L.R. 672 at 686.
207 *Burnie Port Authority*, 550–2 per Mason CJ, Deane, Dawson, Toohey and Gaudron JJ.
208 Ibid., 551.
209 Ibid., and *Pyrenees*, for example, 427–8 [254]–[256] per Kirby J.
210 *Pyrenees*, 339 [9] per Brennan CJ.
211 *Hill v. Van Erp*, 216 per Dawson J.
212 Ibid., 199 per Gaudron J.
213 Per Gaudron J.
214 *Shaddock & Associates v. Parramatta City Council (No. 1)* (1981) 150 C.L.R. 225.
215 *Perre v. Apand*, 191 [2] per Gleeson CJ.
216 Ibid., 194 [11] per Gleeson CJ. In an illuminating analysis, Vines (2000) suggests that the battle in these and other cases is a question of "individual" and "collective" responsibility. For reasons that are I hope by now apparent, I do not think that this captures the notion of other-directed (but personal rather than collective or social) responsibility that vulnerability indicates. It seems to me that in *Perre*, in particular, the fact that the defendant could be singled out as uniquely capable of making a difference clarifies the issue and the reasoning much better. Responsibility is not here understood as collective, but neither is it grounded in autonomy.
217 Ibid., 194–5 [13] per Gleeson CJ, 202 [41] per Gaudron J.
218 Ibid., 220 [104] per McHugh J.
219 Ibid., 228 [124]–[126] per McHugh J. See *Esanda Finance Corporation v. Peat Marwick Hungerfords* (1997) 188 C.L.R. 241 at 263–4.
220 *Hill, Hawkins, Esanda*, and *Perre v. Apand*.
221 *Parramatta v. Lutz, Pyrenees*, and *Perre v. Apand*.

222 Levinas, *Totality and Infinity*, 202, 291.

223 Levinas, "Martin Buber and the Theory of Knowledge," in *Proper Names*, 17, 32.

224 *Burnie Port Authority.*

225 Levinas, *Otherwise than Being*, 100.

226 Thus, see the argument recently developed by Mason P in which he concluded that the law required him to establish "what, until recently, would have been termed 'proximity.'" *FA General Insurance v. Albert Lucre* (unreported, 2000) (N.S.W. Court of Appeal).

227 Levinas, *Otherwise than Being*, 114.

228 *Hill v. Van Erp*, 213 per McHugh J.

229 *Perre v. Apand*, 284 [283] per Kirby J.

230 Cohen, *Ethics, Exegesis and Philosophy.*

231 "The Approach to Al-Mu'tasim," in Borges, *Collected Fictions.*

232 Levinas, *Otherwise than Being*, 168.

233 Ibid., 143.

234 Ibid., 170.

235 Ibid., 168.

236 Coleman helpfully defends the discourse of tort law on just these grounds. "Tort Law and Tort Theory," 203.

237 Levinas, *Otherwise than Being*, 143.

238 Ibid., 139.

239 As I noted already, on this point I do not find myself in agreement with Diamantides, *The Ethics of Suffering*, 23.

240 "The debt increases in the measure that it is paid." Levinas, *Otherwise than Being*, 12.

241 Levinas, *Totality and Infinity*, 34.

242 "The Approach to Al-Mu'tasim," in Borges, *Collected Fictions.*

243 Gibbs, "The Other Comes to Teach Me," 219. Likewise, Roberts insists that the other is both the motivation for justice and an aspect of its content and its critique: "Rethinking Justice," 10.

CHAPTER SIX

1 The quotation is from the King James Version. I have made some minor editorial amendments.

2 Levinas, *Totality and Infinity*, 192.

3 Ibid., 278–80.

4 Levinas, *Otherwise than Being*, 170. For further on the implications of the accusative tense, see Peperzak, "The One for the Other," 445.

5 Ibid.
6 See Mandel and Novack, *The Marxist Theory of Alienation*; Marx, *Economic and Philosophic Manuscripts of 1844*.
7 Derrida, "Violence and Metaphysics."
8 Levinas, "Language and Proximity," in *Collected Philosophical Papers*, 109.
9 Levinas, *Otherwise than Being*, 143–9, 37–43.
10 Levinas, "Meaning and Sense," in *Collected Philosophical Papers*, 102–7.
11 Levinas, *Otherwise than Being*, 170.
12 Ibid., 56.
13 Levinas, "Language and Proximity," in *Collected Philosophical Papers*, 125.
14 *Hahn v. Conley* (1971) 126 C.L.R. 276 (hereinafter *Hahn*).
15 Ibid., 278 per Barwick CJ.
16 Ibid., 290 per Windeyer J; *Wrongs Act 1936* (SA), s. 25(c).
17 Ibid., 285 per Barwick CJ.
18 Ibid., per Barwick CJ.
19 Ibid., 291–2 per Windeyer J.
20 Ibid., 288 per Menzies J.
21 Ibid., 291 per Windeyer J.
22 Ibid.
23 Ibid., 285 per Barwick CJ.
24 Ibid., 294 per Windeyer J.
25 Ibid., 295 per Windeyer J. Justice McTiernan's short concurring judgment appears to make a similar argument.
26 Balkin and Davis, *The Law of Torts*, 215.
27 *Hedley, Bryne & Co v. Heller* [1964] A.C. 465.
28 Ibid., 599 per Lord Devlin.
29 *Shaddock & Associates Pty. Ltd. v. Parramatta City Council (No. 1)* (1981) 150 C.L.R. 225.
30 Ibid., per Gibbs CJ and Mason J.
31 Ibid., 242 per Stephen J.
32 (1985) 157 C.L.R. 424.
33 (1986) 162 C.L.R. 341.
34 Ibid., per Gibbs CJ, Mason, Wilson, and Dawson JJ.
35 Ibid., 360 [29].
36 *Hedley, Bryne & Co v. Heller* [1964] A.C. 465 per Lord Pearce.
37 Thus, see Luntz and Hambly, *Torts*, chap. 16; *San Sebastian v. The Minister*, 370 per Brennan J.

38 *San Sebastian v. The Minister*, 353 per Gibbs CJ, Mason, Wilson, and Dawson JJ.

39 See, especially, "Language and Proximity" (1967), in Levinas, *Collected Philosophical Papers*, 109–26.

40 Ibid., 115, 125.

41 Levinas, *Totality and Infinity*, 177.

42 Again, it is exactly on this point that the debate between Epstein and Perry unfolds: see above.

43 *Caltex Oil (Australia) Pty Ltd v. The Dredge "Willemstad"* (1976) 136 C.L.R. 529 at 555 per Gibbs J, cited in *Perre v. Apand* (1999) 198 C.L.R. 180 at 222 per McHugh J.

44 (1999) 198 C.L.R. 180.

45 Ibid., 228 [125] per McHugh J.

46 The great fire of Chicago, October 1871, was said to have been started when a cow kicked over a lantern. But see Richard Bayles, *The Great Chicago Fire*.

47 Bovine spongiform encephalopathy, or BSE.

48 (1999) 198 C.L.R. 180 at 227–8 [123–5]; see also Toohey and Gaudron JJ in *Esanda Finance Corporation Ltd v. Peat Marwick Hungerfords* (1997) 188 C.L.R. 241.

49 Levinas, "God and Philosophy" (1975), in *Collected Philosophical Papers*, 153–73, 167. Slight grammatical modifications to the Lingis translation.

50 Levinas, *Otherwise than Being*, 115–18.

51 Levinas, "No Identity" (1970), in *Collected Philosophical Papers*, 141–51, 146.

52 Levinas, *Time and the Other*, 69–80.

53 Levinas, *Otherwise than Being*, 141.

54 Levinas, *Totality and Infinity*, 257–8.

55 "The other is through and through a hostage, older than the ego, prior to principles": Levinas, *Otherwise than Being*, 117.

56 Levinas, *Totality and Infinity*, 27 and elsewhere.

57 Ibid., 26.

58 Ibid., 177.

59 Ibid., 244; see also 200.

60 *Québec Charter of Rights and Freedoms*, part 1, clause 2 (RSQC-12). Official translation: Every person must come to the aid of anyone whose life is in peril, either personally or by calling for aid, by giving him necessary and immediate physical assistance.

61 Levinas, *Otherwise than Being*, 13.

62 Levinas, "God and Philosophy," in *Collected Philosophical Papers*, 170.

63 *Kondis v. State Transport Authority* (1984) 154 C.L.R. 672.

64 Ibid., 687 per Mason J.

65 See the discussion by Mason J in *Sutherland Shire Council v. Heyman* (1985) 157 C.L.R. 424 and the criticism of Mason's analysis undertaken by the majority judgments in *Pyrenees Shire Council v. Day; Eskimo Amber v. Pyrenees Shire Council* (1998) 192 C.L.R. 330. But see also the strong remarks in defence of the concept by McHugh J (ibid). Even the use of the word "fictional" in this context is rather misleading, since it is one of the strengths of fiction that it strives to get behind social fictions – whether of race, class, nation, legal right, and so on – in order to better understand the actual lived experience of individuals. Fiction is far less fictional than law. See Manderson, "In the *Tout Court* of Shakespeare."

66 *Smith v. Leurs* (1945) 70 C.L.R. 256 at 262 per Dixon J (see also *Insurance Commissioner v. Joyce* (1948) 77 C.L.R. 39). In *Smith v. Leurs*, however, even this responsibility was limited, in circumstances in which parents of a child were not held liable for injury caused when their adopted son Brian put out the eye of another child with a shanghai (slingshot). There, however, the question was not whether the parents owed a duty of care but whether they had breached it. The High Court concluded that "the moderate course the defendants took of telling the boy to use the shanghai only on his own premises sufficed."

67 [1970] A.C. 1004 per Lord Morris of Borth-y-Gest (hereinafter *Dorset Yacht Company*). Lord Diplock speaks similarly of the "legal *right* to control" at 1063.

68 Ibid., 1070 per Lord Diplock.

69 (2000) 176 A.L.R. 411.

70 Ibid., 434 [91] per Kirby J.

71 Ibid., 420 [39] per Gleeson CJ.

72 Ibid., 447–8 [149–51] per Callinan J.

73 Ibid., 440 [117] per Hayne J.

74 Ibid., 438 [109] per Hayne J.

75 Ibid., 440 [117], and per Gleeson CJ at 418 [30].

76 Ibid., 434–5 [93–4] per Kirby J.

77 Ibid., 434 [93].

78 For example, ibid., 440 [116] per Hayne J.

79 Ibid., 439 [111] per Hayne J.

80 Ibid., 417 [25] per Gleeson CJ.

81 Ibid., 418 [29].

82 Ibid., 439 [113] per Hayne J.

83 Ibid., 438 [108].

84 Ibid., 440 [117].

85 In particular, ibid., per Callinan J., esp. 445 [141], 446–7 [146].

86 Ibid., 418 [29] per Gleeson CJ.

87 Ibid., 438 [109] per Hayne J (italics in original).

88 Ibid. 419 [36] per Gleeson CJ .

89 Ibid. 419 [134] per Callinan J.

90 For example, Levinas, *Otherwise than Being*, 117, 138–9.

91 Posner, "A Theory of Negligence," 45.

92 Commission of Inquiry into the Events at the Refugee Camps in Beirut, *Final Report* (Yitzhak Kahan, Aharon Barak, Yona Efrat, Commissioners), in Ebaan, *The Beirut Massacre*, 9–45.

93 Fisk, *Pity the Nation*.

94 Commission of Inquiry, in Ebaan, *The Beirut Massacre*, 67.

95 Speech to Knesset, 22 September 1982, ibid., 121, 126.

96 Ibid., 133.

97 Commission of Inquiry, in Ebaan, *The Beirut Massacre*, 22–7.

98 Ibid., 26.

99 Prime Minister Begin, ibid., 68.

100 Minister of Defence Sharon and Major General Drori, ibid., 46; see also 19, 22.

101 Commission of Inquiry, ibid., 69–73.

102 *Modbury Triangle Shopping Centre v. Anzil*, 440 [117] per Hayne J.

103 Ibid., 440 [117], and per Glesson CJ at 418 [30].

104 Emmanuel Levinas, transcript of interview on Radio Communauté, 28 September 1982, originally published in *Les Nouveaux Cahiers* 18 (1982–83) and reprinted as "Ethics and Politics," in *The Levinas Reader*, 289–97, 290–1.

105 Ibid.

106 Ibid., 292.

107 Ibid., 294.

108 Levinas, *Difficult Freedom*, 291.

109 Caygill, *Levinas and the Political*, 2–5, 85–8.

110 Ibid., 85–8, 162–76; Bernasconi, "Different Styles of Eschatology," 13–15. See Levinas, "Place and Utopia" and "The State of Israel and the Religion of Israel," in *Difficult Freedom*; "The State of Caesar and the State of David," 177; "Assimilation and New Culture," in *The Levinas Reader*. See also Perpich, "A Singular Justice."

111 Caygill, *Levinas and the Political*, 183–4, discusses, for example, "Space Is Not One Dimensional" (1961) and "The Russo-Chinese Debate and the Dialectic" (1960).

112 Ibid., 293.

113 Ibid., 296–7.

114 Derrida, *The Gift of Death/Donner la mort*, 68.

115 Levinas, "Ethics and Politics," 290. I have omitted the central phrase "– especially when it's somewhere close to you –" which indicates precisely that there are degrees of proximity and therefore degrees of responsibility. I do so not because the phrase is unimportant (as I will go on to argue, it is, on the contrary, absolutely central) but because Levinas appears to me in this sentence to treat it as an afterthought.

116 Ibid., 291.

117 Ibid., 293.

118 Ibid.

119 For a particularly interesting analysis of and ultimately insistence upon this incommensurability in a legal context, see Diamantides, "Ethics in Law" and *The Ethics of Suffering*.

120 Derrida, "Violence and Metaphysics," 185, 189.

121 Quoted in Simmons, "The Third," 97.

122 Caygill, *Levinas and the Political*, 144–5.

123 Farley, "Ethics and Reality," 216.

124 Ibid., 290.

125 Ibid.

126 Commission of Inquiry, in Ebaan, *The Beirut Massacre*, 21.

127 Levinas, *Totality and Infinity*, 192: "A light is needed to see the light."

128 Ebaan, *The Beirut Massacre*.

129 Indeed, it is frequently the case that spokesmen for the Israeli government complain that they are held to higher standards than other countries. This, for Levinas, was precisely the point. The State of Israel, through its supplement, the religion of Israel, was given a conscience as well as a government: see Levinas, "The State of Israel and the Religion of Israel"; Caygill, *Levinas and the Political*, 175–6.

130 Critchley, *The Ethics of Deconstruction*, 194–7.

131 See Kurzman, *Soldier of Peace*.

132 Levinas, *Otherwise than Being*, 158–9.

133 Levinas, *Totality and Infinity*, 21–4.

134 Newton, *The Fence and the Neighbor*.

135 Levinas, *Totality and Infinity*, 51.

CHAPTER SEVEN

1 Henry Moore (1898–1986), *Moon Head* (bronze, 1964).
2 Levinas, *Totality and Infinity*, 291.
3 Ibid., 179.
4 Ibid.
5 Ibid., 159.
6 Ibid., 194–7.
7 Ibid., 197.
8 Ibid., 199.
9 Ibid.
10 "Le visage du prochain," e.g., in Levinas, *Ethique comme philosophie première*, 101.
11 Levinas, *Totality and Infinity*, 199–200.
12 Ibid., 198.
13 Ibid. As in many places, the standard English translation is needlessly opaque.
14 Levinas, *Otherwise than Being*, 115.
15 Gibbs, "The Other Comes to Teach Me," 229.
16 See Derrida, "The Laws of Reflection."
17 Levinas, *Totality and Infinity*, 205.
18 Ibid., 257–8.
19 Ibid., 265.
20 Ibid., 50–1.
21 Ibid., 204.
22 Ibid. See also Levinas, *Otherwise than Being*, 61–3.
23 Levinas, "Language and Proximity," in *Collected Philosophical Papers*, 119–26.
24 Ibid., 119.
25 Levinas, *Otherwise than Being*, 115.
26 Levinas, *Totality and Infinity*, 294–7.
27 Defoe, *Robinson Crusoe*; and see Kasirer, *La solitude en droit privé*.
28 Levinas, *Totality and Infinity*, 254–80.
29 Derrida, *The Gift of Death / Donner la mort*, 68–70.
30 Ibid., chap. 4.
31 Derrida, "Violence and Metaphysics"; see especially Critchley, *The Ethics of Deconstruction*, 96–8. Further, see Derrida, "Force of Law."
32 Derrida, "Violence and Metaphysics," 79.

33 See Levinas, "Wholly Otherwise."
34 Levinas, *Otherwise than Being*, 157. I have retranslated the first sentence, which again seems to me needlessly difficult: see *Autrement qu'être*, 245.
35 See also Levinas, *Difficult Freedom*, 18.
36 Levinas, *Otherwise than Being*, 157.
37 Ibid., 158–9. (The original translation spells asymmetry in two different ways, but is wrong both times.)
38 Critchley, *The Ethics of Deconstruction*, 231.
39 Derrida, "Violence and Metaphysics," 185.
40 Levinas, *Otherwise than Being*, 159.
41 Ibid.
42 Roberts, "Rethinking Justice," esp. 7–8. See also Simmons, "The Third," 84–5.
43 In Angelique Chrisafis, "The Women Who Took On the IRA," *Guardian Weekly*, 18–24 March 2005, 20.
44 Roberts, "Rethinking Justice," 9.
45 Levinas, "Ethics and Politics," in *The Levinas Reader*, 293.
46 Lacan, *Écrits*.
47 See Derrida, *Limited Inc.*, and *Writing and Difference*, amongst other works. For more on the question of "closure" in the dialogue between Levinas and Derrida, see Critchley, *The Ethics of Deconstruction*.
48 (1947) 159 F. 2d. 173 (hereinafter *Carroll Towing*).
49 See Mason J. in *Wyong Shire Council v. Shirt* (1980) 146 C.L.R. 40 at 47–8.
50 *Carroll Towing* at 173 per Learned Hand J.
51 Thus see Posner, *Economic Analysis of Law*.
52 Levinas, *Totality and Infinity*, 36.
53 (1971) 126 C.L.R. 276.
54 Alphonso Lingis, introduction to Levinas, *Totality and Infinity*, 14.
55 Levinas, *Otherwise than Being*, 159.
56 Perry, "The Impossibility of General Strict Liability," 164–9.
57 [1951] A.C. 860.
58 Ibid., 863 per Lord Oaksey.
59 Ibid., 867 per Lord Reid.
60 Dowie, "Pinto Madness."
61 Ibid.
62 See also Birsch and Fielder, *The Ford Pinto Case*.
63 Levinas, *Otherwise than Being*, 157.

64 *Romeo v. Conservation Commission of the Northern Territory* (1998) 192 C.L.R. 431 (hereinafter *Romeo*).

65 Ibid.

66 *Nagle v. Rottnest Island Authority* (1993) 177 C.L.R. 423.

67 *Romeo* 480 [129] per Kirby J (footnotes omitted).

68 See *Geyer v. Downs* (1977) 138 C.L.R. 91, per Murphy and Aickin JJ.

69 See *Wyong Shire Council v. Shirt* (1980) 146 C.L.R. 40; *Nagle v. Rottnest Island Authority* (1993) 177 C.L.R. 423. In *Romeo*, of course, a warning sign would hardly have helped a girl, drunk, at night.

70 *Romeo*, 456–60 per Gaudron J and 460–3 per McHugh J.

71 *Sutherland Shire Council v. Heyman* (1985) 157 C.L.R. 424 per Mason J.

72 Levinas, foreword to *Difficult Freedom*, xiv.

73 Ibid.

74 *Bolton v. Stone* [1951] A.C. 860, per Lord Reid.

75 *Mercer v. Commissioner of Road Transport & Tramways (NSW)* (1936) 56 C.L.R. 580, per Rich, Evatt and McTiernan JJ.

76 Interestingly, the jury itself appears to have come to a middle position. In an odd "rider" affixed to their verdict, they concluded that "the defendant was not careless in the ordinary meaning of the word in not fitting the device but on the contrary, he was justified in taking the remote risk of claims for damages that might arise for accidents." No doubt the jury is reflecting a general view that financial responsibility is more easily acknowledged than moral responsibility. But clearly the rider is no support for Learned Hand's position, for on that reasoning, the Tramways Authority had done nothing wrong, and there would be no need to speak of "claims for damages" at all. The remark is not just "quite consistent" with a finding of negligence, as the majority note, but in fact dependent on it; dependent, therefore, on negligence amounting to something other than a cost-benefit analysis See ibid., per Rich, Evatt and McTiernan JJ.

77 See Levinas, "Martin Buber and the Theory of Knowledge," in Levinas, *Proper Names*.

78 Levinas, *Totality and Infinity*, 294.

79 See Levinas, "Ethics and Spirit," in *Difficult Freedom*, 3–10.

80 "My responsibility for the other is the *for* of the relationship." Levinas, *The Levinas Reader*, 90.

81 Levinas, *Difficult Freedom*, xiv.

82 The failure to understand the difference, and thus the failure to appreciate what Levinas means by infinity, lies at the heart of the some

of the most careless criticism of his work, as I trust I have elsewhere shown.

83 Critchley, *The Ethics of Deconstruction*, 229; see also 233–5.

84 Levinas, "Jacques Derrida: Wholly Otherwise," in *Proper Names*, 59.

85 See Beardsworth, *Derrida and the Political*, 133.

86 Levinas, "Reality and Its Shadow" (1948), in *Collected Philosophical Papers*, 1–13.

87 Levinas, "Wholly Otherwise," in *Proper Names*, 61.

88 Ibid.

89 Levinas, *Otherwise than Being*, 117.

90 Ibid.

91 See, for example, *Perre v. Apand* (1999) 198 C.L.R. 180 per McHugh J.

92 Ibid., 216 [91].

93 *Leigh & Sullivan v. Aliakmon Shipping* [1985] A.B. 350, 397 per Robert Goff LJ; *Caparo v. Dickman* [1990] 2 A.C. 605, 618 per Lord Bridge.

94 Discussed in Simmons, "The Third," 93–7.

95 Roberts, "Rethinking Justice," 5.

96 Derrida, "Violence and Metaphysics," 157–9, 181–5.

97 Derrida, "Force of Law," 947.

98 See also Sklar, *Legalism*.

99 Ibid., 959.

100 See also Roberts, "Rethinking Justice," 8–10.

101 Kelsen, "The Pure Theory of Law."

102 For a further discussion and defence of the position, see Manderson and Sharp, "Mandatory Sentences and the Constitution."

103 Derrida, "Force of Law," 961.

104 See Perpci, "A Singular Justice."

105 An additional discussion of the suspension and deferral in law, which again transforms this paradox into a vital, ethical, and progressive aspect of law, can be found in Derrida, "Before the Law."

106 Bernasconi, "The Trace of Levinas in Derrida," 18–25.

107 Bernasconi, "Deconstruction and the Possibility of Ethics," 130; Derrida, "Violence and Metaphysics," 142–3.

108 Rose, *The Broken Middle*.

109 The argument is brilliantly made and carefully developed in Beardsworth, *Derrida and the Political*.

110 Levinas, *Otherwise than Being*, 116, 159.

111 Derrida, *Specters of Marx*, 28.

112 Roberts, "Rethinking Justice," 8. See also Caputo, "Hyperbolic Justice"; Cohen, "The Privilege of Reason and Play"; Llewelyn, "Levinas, Derrida and Others vis-à-vis."

113 McHugh, "Neighbourhood, Proximity and Reliance"; *Perre v. Apand*, 210 [74] per McHugh J; *Hill v. Van Erp* (1995–96) 188 C.L.R. 159, per Gummow J. See Stone, *Legal System and Lawyers' Reasonings.*

114 Llewellyn, *Jurisprudence.*

115 Tushnet, "An Essay on Rights"; Kennedy, "The Structure of Blackstone's Commentaries"; Gordon, "Critical Legal Histories"; Kelman, "Trashing."

116 Derrida, *Of Grammatology.*

117 Derrida, "Force of Law," 955.

118 Ibid., 945. See Kearney, "Derrida's Ethical Re-Turn."

119 Balkin, "Transcendental Deconstruction, Transcendent Justice."

120 Levinas, *Otherwise than Being*, 165–71.

121 Simmons, "The Third," 84. See also Roberts, "Rethinking Justice," 7–8.

122 *Hill v. Van Erp*, per Gummow J quoting McHugh, "Neighbourhood, Proximity, and Reliance," n106.

123 Levinas, *Otherwise than Being*, 165–71.

124 Ibid., 170.

125 Ibid.

126 For further on contemporary theories of legislative drafting, see Horn, "Black Letters."

127 Levinas, *Otherwise than Being*, 170.

128 See "A Religion for Adults," in Levinas, *Difficult Freedom*, 11–23, esp. 19–21. See the critique of positivism as "infantile" in Frank, *Law and the Modern Mind.*

129 Piaget, *The Moral Judgment of the Child*. And see a detailed discussion of this question in Manderson, "From Hunger to Love."

130 Levinas, "Ideology and Idealism," quoted in Simmons, "The Third," 99.

131 I am echoing here an argument that has been made on more than one occasion, drawing on the conflict between law and justice in Sophocles' *Antigone*. See Douzinas and Warrington, "Antigone's *Dike*"; Manderson, "The Care of Strangers." See Levinas, *Totality and Infinity*, 213–14.

132 Levinas, *Éthique comme philosophie première*; Levinas, *Totality and Infinity*, 304.

133 Cohen, *Ethics, Exegesis and Philosophy*, 243–45.

134 (1998) 192 C.L.R. 330.

135 (2000) 176 A.L.R. 411.

136 (1998) 192 C.L.R. 431.
137 See Peperzak, "The One for the Other," 440–4.
138 Levinas, *Totality and Infinity*, 34.
139 Ibid., 244.
140 See, for example, Johnson, *Our Liability Predicament*.
141 Atiyah, *Accidents, Compensation and the Law*; *Accident Rehabilitation and Compensation Insurance Act* 1992 (NZ). See also Blair, *Accident Compensation in New Zealand*.
142 Gibbs, "The Other Comes to Teach Me."
143 *Perre v. Apand*, 209–10 [74–6] per McHugh J; "It is tolerably clear that proximity's reign ... has come to an end": *Pyrenees Shire Council v. Day* (1998) 192 C.L.R. 330 at 414 [238] per Kirby J.
144 See Levinas, *Le visage de l'autre*.
145 Levinas, *Éthique comme philosophie première*.
146 Thus, see Levinas, *Otherwise than Being*, 108; Levinas, *Totality and Infinity*, 268–70; and see Derrida, "Bois," in Critchley, *The Ethics of Deconstruction*, 107–9. See also Caygill, *Levinas and the Political*, 85–6; Bernasconi, "Deconstruction and the Possibility of Ethics," 131.
147 Levinas, *Totality and Infinity*, 270.
148 Levinas, *Otherwise than Being*, 108–14.
149 Ibid., 49.
150 For further on these themes in Levinas, see Farley, "Ethics and Reality," and Diamantides, "Ethics in Law."
151 See Hart, *The Concept of Law*; Dworkin, *Law's Empire*; Lucy, *Understanding and Explaining Adjudication*.
152 Despite his hostility to the observation: see the discussion in an earlier chapter and see also Bennington, "Mosaic Fragment"; Peperzak, "Jewish Experience and Philosophy"; Cohen, *Ethics and Exegesis*.
153 Levinas, *Difficult Freedom*, 22.
154 Derrida, "Violence and Metaphysics," 191. See also MacDonald, "Jewgreek and Greekjew"; Llewellyn, "Jewgreek or Greekgew"; Srajek, *The Margins of Deconstruction*.
155 Kelsen, "The Pure Theory of Law."
156 Levinas, *Otherwise than Being*, 141: "the soul, the very pneuma of the psyche"; ibid., 191: "The soul is the other in me."
157 Cane, *Responsibility in Law and Morality*; Stapleton, "Duty of Care Factors"; Vines, "Fault, Responsibility and Negligence in the High Court."
158 Duncan, *The Pre-Text of Ethics*, 159.
159 Levinas, *Totality and Infinity*, 197, 303.

Bibliography

LEGAL CASES

Albrighton v. Royal Prince Alfred Hospital [1980] 2 N.S.W.L.R. 542.

Andrewartha v. Andrewartha (No. 1) [1987] 44 S.A.S.R. 1.

Anns v. London Borough of Merton [1978] A.C. 728.

Arthur Hall v. Simons [2000] 3 W.L.R. 543.

Blyth v. Birmingham Waterworks Co. (1856) 11 Exch. Rep. 781.

Bolton v. Stone [1951] A.C. 860.

Bottomley v. Bannister [1932] 1 K.B. 458.

Bourhill v. Young [1943] A.C. 92.

Bryan v. Maloney (1995) 182 C.L.R. 609.

Burnie Port Authority v. General Jones Pty Ltd. (1994) 179 C.L.R. 520.

Caltex Oil (Australia) Pty. Ltd. v. The Dredge "Willemstad" (1976) 136 C.L.R. 529.

Campbelltown City Council v. Mackay (1989) 15 N.S.W.L.R. 501.

Candlewood Navigation Corporation v. Mitsui OSK Lines [1986] A.C. 1.

Caparo Industries PLC v. Dickman [1990] 2 A.C. 605.

Cattle v. Stockton Waterworks Co. [1875] LR 10 Q.B. 453.

Chadwick v. British Railways Board [1967] 1 W.L.R. 912.

Chapman v. Hearse (1961) 106 C.L.R. 112.

Charter of Human Rights and Freedoms, R.S.Q. c. C-12.

Chester v. Waverley Municipal Council (1939) 62 C.L.R. 1.

Cook v. Cook (1986) 162 C.L.R. 376.

Coultas v. Victorian Railway Commissioners (1886) 12 V.L.R. 895; (1888) 13 App. Cas. 222.

Demarco v. Ungaro (1979) 95 C.L.R. 385.

Donoghue v. Stevenson (1932) A.C. 562.

Dorset Yacht Co. Ltd v. Home Office [1970] A.C. 1004.

Esanda Finance Corporation v. Peat Marwick Hungerfords (1997) 188 C.L.R. 241.

Eskimo Amber Pty Ltd v. Pyrenees Shire Council (1998) 192 C.L.R. 330; [1998] 72 A.L.J.R. 152.

FA General Insurance v. Albert Lucre (unreported, 2000) (NSW Court of Appeal).

Frost v. Chief Constable [1997] 1 All E.R. 540.

Gala v. Preston (1991) 172 C.L.R. 243.

Geyer v. Downs (1977) 138 C.L.R. 91.

Giannarelli v. Wraith (1988) 165 C.L.R. 543.

Gray v. Brodribb Sawmilling Company (1986) 160 C.L.R. 16.

Hahn v. Conley (1971) 126 C.L.R. 276.

Hall v. Hebert (1993) 101 D.L.R. (4th) 129; 2 S.C.R. 159.

Hargrave v. Goldman (1963) 110 C.L.R. 40.

Hawkins v. Clayton (1988) 164 C.L.R. 539.

Hedley, Byrne & Co. Ltd v. Heller & Partners Ltd. [1964] A.C. 465.

Henwood v. Municipal Tramways Trust (1938) 60 C.L.R. 438.

Hill v. Chief Constable of West Yorkshire [1989] A.C. 53.

Hill v. Van Erp (1995–6) 188 C.L.R. 159.

Insurance Commissioner v. Joyce (1948) 77 C.L.R. 39.

Jackson v. Harrison (1978) 138 C.L.R. 438.

Jaensch v. Coffey (1984) 155 C.L.R. 549..

Kondis v. State Transport Authority (1984) 154 C.L.R. 672.

Leigh & Sullivan v. Aliakmon Shipping Co. Ltd. [1985] Q.B. 350.

Lowns v. Wood [1996] Aust Torts Rep ¶81–376.

McGinty v. Western Australia (1996) 136 C.L.R. 140.

McLoughlin v. O'Brien [1983] 1 A.C. 410.

Medical Practitioners Act, 1938 (N.S.W.).

Mercer v. Commissioner of Road Transport & Tramways (NSW) (1936) 56 C.L.R. 580.

Modbury Triangle Shopping Centre v. Anzil (2000) 176 A.L.R. 411.

Mount Isa Mines v. Pusey (1970) 25 C.L.R. 383.

Nader v. Urban Transit Authority of NSW (1985) 2 N.S.W.L.R. 501.

Nagle v. Rottnest Island Authority (1993) 112 A.L.R. 393; 177 C.L.R. 423.

Nelson v. Nelson (1995) 184 C.L.R. 538.

Ogwo v. Taylor [1988] A.C. 431.

Overseas Tankship v. Morts Dock & Engineering (The Wagon Mound (No. 1)) [1961] A.C. 388.

Palsgraf v. Long Island R.R. Co. [1928] 248 N.Y. 339.

Parramatta City Council v. Lutz (1988) 12 N.S.W.L.R. 293.

Perre v. Apand Pty. Ltd. (1999) 198 C.L.R. 180.

Preston v. Gala [1990] 1 Qd. R. 170.

Progress and Properties v. Craft (1976) 135 C.L.R. 651.

Prohibitions Del Roy (1607) 12 Co. Rep.

Pyrenees Shire Council v. Day; Eskimo Amber v. Pyrenees Shire Council (1998) 192 C.L.R. 330; [1998] 72 A.L.J.R. 152.

Re. Polemis [1921] 3 K.B. 560.

Riggs v. Palmer [1889] 22 N.E. 188.

Robertson v. Swincer (1989) 52 S.A.S.R. 356.

Romeo v. Conservation Commission of the Northern Territory (1998) 192 C.L.R. 431.

San Sebastian v. The Minister (1986) 162 C.L.R. 341.

Shaddock & Associates Pty. Ltd. v. Parramatta City Council (No. 1) (1981) 150 C.L.R. 225.

Smith v. Jenkins (1970) 119 C.L.R. 397.

Smith v. Leurs (1945) 70 C.L.R. 256.

Spence v. Percy [1992] 2 Qd. R. 299.

Stevens v. Brodribb Sawmilling Company (1986) 160 C.L.R. 16.

Sutherland Shire Council v. Heyman (1985) 157 C.L.R. 424.

The Commonwealth v. Introvigne (1982) 150 C.L.R. 258.

United States v. Carroll Towing Co. (1947) 159 F. 2d. 173.

Vaughan v. Menlove (1837) 3 Bing. N.C. 467; 132 E.R. 490.

Wagner v. International Railway Co. (1921) 133 N.E. 437; 232 N.Y. Rep. 176.

White v. Jones [1995] 2 A.C. 207.

Wilmot v. South Australia [1993] Aust Torts Rep ¶81–259.

Wyong Shire Council v. Shirt (1980) 146 C.L.R. 40.

WRITINGS OF EMMANUEL LEVINAS

Autrement qu'être ou au-delà de l'essence. Paris: Kluwer 1974.

"Beyond Intentionality." In A. Montefiore, ed., *Philosophy in France Today.* Cambridge: Cambridge University Press 1983.

Beyond the Verse: Talmudic Readings and Lectures. Trans. Gary D. Mole. London: The Ahtlone Press 1994.

Collected Philosophical Papers. Trans. Alphonso Lingis. Dordrecht & Boston: Martinus Nijhoff 1987.

De l'existence à l'existant. Paris: Editions de la Revue Fontaine 1947.

Difficile liberté. Paris: Editions Albin Michel 1976.

Difficult Freedom: Essays on Judaism. Trans. Sean Hand. London: Athlone Press 1990.

En découvrant l'existence avec Husserl et Heidegger. Paris: Vrin 1988 [1949].

Éthique comme philosophie première. Paris: Rivages Poches 1998.

Éthique et Infini: Dialogues avec Philippe Nemo. Paris: Fayard/Radio-France 1982.

Existence and Existents. Trans. A. Lingis. Hague: Martinus Nijhoff 1978.

Humanisme de l'autre homme. Paris: Fata Morgana 1972.

In the Time of the Nations. trans. Michael B. Smith. Bloomington: Indiana University Press 1994, 174.

"La Proximité." *Archives de Philosophie* 34 (1971): 373–91.

The Levinas Reader. Ed. Sean Hand. Oxford: Basil Blackwell 1989.

Le visage de l'autre. Dessins de Martin tom Dieck. Paris: Editions Seuil 2001.

Noms Propres. Paris: Fata Morgana 1978.

Otherwise than Being, or Beyond Essence. Trans. Alphonso Lingis. The Hague: Martinus Nijhoff 1981.

"The Paradox of Morality: An Interview with Emmanuel Levinas." In R. Bernasconi and D. Wood, eds., *The Provocation of Levinas: Rethinking the Other.* London: Routledge 1988.

Proper Names. Trans. M. Smith. London: Athlone Press 1996.

"State of Caesar and the State of David, The." In *Beyond the Verse: Talmudic Readings and Lectures,* trans. Gary D. Mole. London: The Athlone Press 1994.

Théorie de l'intuition dans la phénmonénologie de Husserl. Paris: Vrin 1963 [1930].

Time and the Other. Trans. Richard A. Cohen. Pittsburgh: Duquesne University Press 1987.

Totalité et Infini. The Hague: Martinus Nijhoff 1961.

Totality and Infinity. Trans. Alphonso Lingis. The Hague: Martinus Nijhoff 1969.

"Wholly Otherwise." Trans. Simon Critchley. In R. Bernasconi and S. Critchley, eds., *Re-Reading Levinas.* Bloomington: Indiana University Press 1982.

SECONDARY MATERIALS

American Psychiatric Association. *Diagnostic and Statistical Manual of Mental Disorders: DSM-IV.* 4th ed. Washington: American Psychiatric Press 1994.

Amirthalingam, K., and T. Faunce. "Patching up 'Proximity': Problems with the Judicial Creation of a New Medical Duty to Rescue." *Torts Law Journal* 5 (1997): 22–44.

Aristotle. *Nichomachean Ethics.* Harmondsworth, England: Penguin 1955.

Atiyah, P.S. *Accidents, Compensation and the Law.* London: Weidenfeld and Nicholson 1970.

Atterton, P. "Levinas and the Language of Peace: A Response to Derrida." *Philosophy Today* 36, no. 1 (1992): 59–70.

Awerkamp, D. *Emmanuel Levinas: Ethics and Politics.* New York: Revisionist Press 1977.

Baker, B., and D. Manderson. "*Boland v. Yates* Re-opens Case against Counsel's Immunity." *Law Society Journal* 39, no. 11 (2001): 74–8.

Balkin, J. "Transcendental Deconstruction, Transcendent Justice." *Michigan Law Review* 92 (1994): 1131–1201.

Balkin, R., and J.L.R. Davis. *The Law of Torts.* 2d ed. Sydney: Butterworths 1996.

Bartol, C. *Criminal Behavior: A Psychosocial Approach.* 4th ed. Englewood Cliffs, NJ: Prentice-Hall 1995.

Bauman, Z. *Postmodern Ethics.* Oxford: Blackwell 1993.

Bayles, R. *The Great Chicago Fire and the Myth of Mrs. O'Leary's Cow.* Jefferson, NC: MacFarland & Co. 2002.

Beardsworth, R. *Derrida and the Political.* New York: Routledge 1996.

Bennington, G. "Mosaic Fragment." In D. Wood, ed., *Derrida: A Critical Reader.* Blackwell: Oxford 1992.

Benso, S. "Of Things Face-to-Face with Levinas Face-to-Face with Heidegger: Prolegomena to a Metaphysical Ethics of Things." *Philosophy Today* 40, no. 1 (1996): 132–41.

– *The Face of Things: A Different Side of Ethics.* Albany, NY: SUNY Press 2000.

Benson, P. "The Basis of Corrective Justice and Its Relation to Distributive Justice." *Iowa Law Review* 77 (1992): 515.

Bentham, J. *An Introduction to the Principles of Morals and Legislation.* London and New York: Methuen 1982 [1832].

Bernasconi, R. "Deconstruction and the Possibility of Ethics." In J. Sallis, ed., *Deconstruction and Philosophy: The Texts of Jacques Derrida.* Chicago: University of Chicago Press 1987.

– "Different Styles of Eschatology: Derrida's Take on Levinas' Political Messianism." *Research in Phenomenology* 28 (1998): 3–19.

– "Levinas and Derrida: The Question of the Closure of Metaphysics." In R. Cohen, ed., *Face to Face with Levinas.* Albany, NY: State University of New York Press 1986.

– "The Third Party: Levinas on the Intersection of the Ethical and the Political." *Journal of the British Society for Phenomenology* 30 (1999): 76.
– "The Trace of Levinas in Derrida." In D. Wood and R. Bernasconi, eds., *Derrida and Différance*. Evanston: Northwestern University Press 1988.
Bernasconi, R., and S. Critchley, eds. *Re-Reading Levinas*. Bloomington: Indiana University Press 1982.
Bernasconi, R., and D. Wood, eds. *The Provocation of Levinas: Rethinking the Other*. London: Routledge 1988.
Birsch, D., and J. Fielder, eds. *The Ford Pinto Case: A Study in Applied Ethics, Business, and Technology*. Albany, NY: State University of New York 1994.
Blackshield, A., M. Coper, and G. Williams. *The Oxford Companion to the High Court*. Melbourne: Oxford University Press 2001.
Blackshield, T. "The 'Murphy Affair.'" In J.A. Scutt, ed., *Lionel Murphy: A Radical Judge*. McCulloch: Carlton, Victoria 1987.
Blair, A.P. *Accident Compensation in New Zealand: The Law Relating to Compensation for Personal Injury by Accident in New Zealand*. Wellington: Butterworths 1978.
Bloechl, J. *Emmanuel Levinas and the Religion of Responsibility*. Pittsburgh: Duquesne 2000.
Borges, J.L. *Collected Fictions*. Trans. Andrew Hurley. New York: Penguin 1998.
– *Labyrinths: Selected Stories and Other Writings*. Trans. Donald A. Yates and James E. Irby. Harmondsworth, England: Penguin 1970.
Burggraeve, R. "Violence and the Vulnerable Face of the Other: The Vision of Emmanuel Levinas on Moral Evil and Our Responsibility." *Journal of Social Philosophy* 30 (1999): 29–45.
Cane, P. "Responsibility and Fault: A Relational and Functional Approach to Responsibility." In P. Cane and J. Gardner, eds., *Relating to Responsibility: Essays for Tony Honoré on His Eightieth Birthday*. Oxford: Hart 2001.
– *Responsibility in Law and Morality*. Oxford: Hart 2002.
Cane P., and P. Atiyah. *Atiyah's Accidents, Compensation, and the Law*. 6th ed. Cambridge: Cambridge University Press 1999.
Cane, P., and J. Gardner, eds. *Relating to Responsibility: Essays for Tony Honoré on His Eightieth Birthday*. Oxford: Hart 2001.
Caputo, J. *Against Ethics: Contributions to a Poetics of Obligation with Constant Reference to Deconstruction*. Bloomington: Indiana University Press 1993.
– "Hyperbolic Justice: Deconstruction, Myth and Politics." *Research in Phenomenology* 21 (1999): 3–20.
Caygill, H. *Levinas and the Political*. New York: Routledge 2001.

Chanter, T. *Feminist Interpretations of Emmanuel Levinas.* Pittsburgh: Pennsylvania State University Press 2001.

– *Time, Death, and the Feminine: Levinas with Heidegger.* Stanford: Stanford University Press 2001.

Coase, R. "The Problem of Social Cost." *Journal of Law and Economics* 1 (1960): 1.

Cohen, R. *Ethics, Exegesis and Philosophy: Interpretation after Levinas.* Cambridge: Cambridge University Press 2001.

– "The Privilege of Reason and Play: Derrida and Levinas." *Tijdschrift voor Filosofie* 45, no. 2 (1983): 242–55.

– "What Good Is the Holocaust? On Suffering and Evil." *Philosophy Today* 43, no. 2 (1999): 176.

– ed. *Face to Face with Levinas.* Albany: State University of New York Press 1986.

Coleman, J. "Corrective Justice and Wrongful Gain." *Journal of Legal Studies* 11 (1982): 421–40.

– "The Mixed Conception of Corrective Justice." *Iowa Law Review* 77 (1992): 427–44.

– "Moral Theories of Torts: Their Scope and Limits: Part II." *Law and Philosophy* 2 (1983): 5–36.

– "The Practice of Corrective Justice." In D.G. Owen, ed., *Philosophical Foundations of Tort Law.* Oxford: Clarendon Press 1995.

– "Property, Wrongfulness, and the Duty to Compensate." *Chicago-Kent Law Review* 63 (1987): 451–70.

– *Risks and Wrongs.* Cambridge: Cambridge University Press 1992.

– "Tort Law and the Demands of Corrective Justice." *Indiana Law Review* 67 (1992): 349–79.

– "Tort Law and Tort Theory: Preliminary Reflections on Method." In Gerald Postema, ed., *Philosophy and the Law of Torts.* New York: Cambridge University Press 2001.

Commission of Inquiry into the Events at the Refugee Camps in Beirut. *Final Report* (Yitzhak Kahan, Aharon Barak, Yona Efrat, Commissioners). In A. Ebaan, *The Beirut Massacre: The Complete Kahan Commission Report.* Princeton and New York: Karz-Cohl 1983.

Cooper-Stephenson, K., and E. Gibson, eds. *Tort Theory.* Toronto: Captus Press 1993.

Cover, R. "*Nomos* and Narrative." *Harvard Law Review* 97 (1983): 4–68.

Critchley, S. *The Ethics of Deconstruction: Derrida and Levinas.* Oxford: Basil Blackwell 1992.

– *The Ethics of Deconstruction: Derrida and Levinas.* 2nd ed. Oxford: Basil Blackwell 1999.

Davis, C. *Levinas: An Introduction.* Cambridge: Polity Press 1996.

Defoe, D. *The Life and Strange Surprizing Adventures of Robinson Crusoe.* Oxford: Oxford University Press 1999.

Derrida, J. *Adieu to Emmanuel Levinas.* Stanford: Stanford University Press 1999.

- "At This Very Moment in This Work Here I Am," trans. Ruben Berezdivin. In Robert Bernasconi and Simon Critchley, eds. *Re-Reading Levinas.* Bloomington: Indiana University Press 1991, 11–48.

- "Before the Law." In D. Attridge, ed., *Acts of Literature.* Routledge: New York 1992.

- "Declarations of Independence." *New Political Science* 15 (1986): 7–15.

- "*Différance.*" In *Margins of Philosophy.* Trans. Alan Bass. New York: University of Chicago Press 1972.

- *Dissemination.* Trans. Barbara Johnson. Chicago: University of Chicago Press 1972.

- "Force of Law: The Mystical Foundation of Authority." *Cardozo Law Review* 11 (1990): 919–1045. Reprinted in D. Cornell, M. Rosenfeld, and D.G. Carlson, eds., *Deconstruction and the Possibility of Justice.* New York: Routledge 1992.

- *The Gift of Death/Donner la mort.* Trans. David Wills. Chicago: University of Chicago Press 1995.

- "The Law of Genre." In D. Attridge, ed., *Acts of Literature.* Routledge: New York 1992.

- "The Laws of Reflection: Nelson Mandela, in Admiration." In J. Derrida and M. Tlili, *For Nelson Mandela.* New York: Seaver Books 1987.

- *Limited Inc.* Ed. Gerald Graff. Evanston: Northwestern University Press 1988.

- *Of Grammatology.* Trans. Gayatri Chakravorty Spivak. Baltimore: Johns Hopkins University Press 1967.

- *The Politics of Friendship.* London: Verso 1999.

- *Positions.* Trans. Alan Bass. Chicago: University of Chicago Press 1981.

- *Specters of Marx: The State of the Debt, the Work of Mourning, and the New International.* Trans. Peggy Kamuf. London: Routledge 1994.

- "Violence and Metaphysics: An Essay on the Thought of Emmanuel Levinas." In *Writing and Difference.* Trans. Alan Bass. London: Routledge 1978, 97–192.

- *Writing and Difference.* Trans. Alan Bass. Chicago: University of Chicago Press 1967.

Derrida, J., and A. Dufourmantelle. *Of Hospitality.* Trans. R. Bowlby. Stanford: Stanford University Press 2000.

Descartes, R. *Le Discours de la Méthode*. Paris: Vrin 1966 [1637].

Diamantides, M. "The Ethical Obligation to Show Allegiance to the Unknowable." In D. Manderson, ed., *Courting Death: The Law of Mortality*. London and Sterling: Pluto Press 1999, 181–93.

– "Ethics in Law: Death Marks on a Still Life." *Law and Critique* 6 (1995): 209–28.

– *The Ethics of Suffering: Modern Law, Philosophy and Medicine*. Dartmouth: Ashgate 2000.

– "In the Company of Priests: Meaninglessness, Suffering and Compassion in the Thoughts of Nietzsche and Levinas." *Cardozo Law Review* 24, no. 3 (2003): 1275–1307.

– "The Subject May Have Disappeared but Its Suffering Remains." *Law and Critique* 11, no. 2 (2000): 137–66.

Dixon, O. "The Law and the Constitution." *Law Quarterly Review* 51 (1935): 590.

Douzinas, C. *The End of Human Rights: Critical Legal Thought at the Turn of the Century*. Oxford: Hart Publishing 2000.

– "Human Rights at the 'End of History': Justice between the Symbolic and the Ethical." *Angelaki: Journal of the Theoretical Humanities* 4, no. 1 (1999): 99–114.

– "Justice, Judgment and the Ethics of Alterity." In Kim Economides, ed., *The Deontology of Law*. Oxford: Hart Publications 1997.

Douzinas, C., and R. Warrington. "Antigone's *Dike*." In *Justice Miscarried: Ethics, Aesthetics and the Law*. New York and London: Harvester Whestsheaf 1994.

Dowie, M. "Pinto Madness," *Mother Jones*, September/October 1977.

Duncan, D.M. *The Pre-Text of Ethics: On Derrida and Levinas*. Peter Lang 2001.

Dworkin, R. *Law's Empire*. Cambridge, MA: Belknap Press 1986.

Ebaan, A. *The Beirut Massacre: The Complete Kahan Commission Report*. Princeton and New York: Karz-Cohl 1983.

Eliot, T.S. *Old Possum's Book of Practical Cats*. London: Faber and Faber 1962 [1939].

Englard, I. *The Philosophy of Tort Law*. Aldershot, England: Dartmouth 1993.

Epstein, R. "A Theory of Strict Liability." *Journal of Legal Studies* 2 (1974): 151–204.

Farley, W. "Ethics and Reality: Dialogue between Caputo and Levinas." *Philosophy Today* 36, no. 3 (1992): 210.

Fish, S. "Dennis Martinez and the Uses of Theory." *Yale Law Journal* 96 (1987): 1773.

- *Doing What Comes Naturally: Change, Rhetoric and the Practice of Theory in Literary and Legal Studies.* Durham, NC: Duke University Press 1989.

Fisk, R. *Pity the Nation: The Abduction of Lebanon.* New York: Atheneum 1990.

Fitzpatrick, P. *Modernism and the Grounds of Law.* Cambridge: Cambridge University Press 2001.

- *The Mythology of Modern Law.* London: Routledge 1992.

Foucault, M. *The Birth of the Clinic.* Trans. A.M. Sheridan Smith. New York: Vintage 1975.

- *Discipline and Punish: The Birth of the Prison.* Trans. Alan Sheridan. New York Vintage Books 1979.

- *The Order of Things: An Archaeology of the Human Sciences.* New York: Pantheon Books 1970.

- *Power/Knowledge: Selected Interviews and Other Writings, 1972–1997.* Colin Gordon, ed. New York: Pantheon 1980.

Frank, J. *Law and the Modern Mind.* New York: Brentano's 1930.

Freud, S. *Civilization and Its Discontents.* Trans. D. McLintock. London: Penguin Books 2002 [1930].

Gardner, J. "Obligations and Outcomes in the Law of Torts." In P. Cane and J. Gardner, eds., *Relating to Responsibility: Essays for Tony Honoré.* Oxford: Hart Publishing 2001.

Gawunde, A. "The Learning Curve," *The New Yorker,* 28 January 2002.

Geertz, C. "Local Knowledge: Fact and Law in Comparative Perspective." In *Local Knowledge: Further Essays in Interpretive Anthropology.* New York: Basic Books 1983.

Gibbs, R. "Height and Nearness: Jewish Dimensions of Radical Ethics." In A. Peperzak, ed., *Ethics as First Philosophy: The Significance of Emmanuel Levinas for Philosophy, Literature and Religion.* Routledge: New York 1995.

- "The Other Comes to Teach Me: A Review of Recent Levinas Publications." *Man and World* 24 (1991): 219–33.

Goodhart, A.L. "The *Ratio Decidendi* of a Case." *Modern Law Review* 22 (1959): 117–24.

Goodrich, P. *Reading the Law: A Critical Introduction to Legal Method and Techniques.* Oxford and Cambridge, MA: Basil Blackwell 1986.

Gordon, R. "Critical Legal Histories." *Stanford Law Review* 36 (1984): 57–125.

Gormley, A. *Field for the British Isles.* British Museum: Terracotta, overall size variable 1993.

Green, L. "Foreseeability in Negligence Law." *Columbia Law Review* 61 (1961): 1401–24.

Haberfield, L. "*Lowns v. Woods* and the Duty to Rescue." *Tort Law Review* 6, no. 1 (1998): 56–80.

Habermas, J. *The Philosophical Discourse of Modernity.* Trans. Frederick Lawrence. Cambridge, MA: MIT Press 1991.

Hambly, D., and H. Luntz. *Torts: Cases and Commentary.* 4th ed. Sydney: Butterworths 1995.

Hand, S. *Facing the Other: The Ethics of Emmanuel Levinas.* Richmond, England: Curzon 1996.

– ed. *The Levinas Reader.* Oxford: Basil Blackwell 1989.

Hare, R.D. *Psychopathy: Theory and Research.* New York: Wiley Press 1970.

Hart, H.L.A. *The Concept of Law.* Oxford: Clarendon Press 1960.

Hegel, G.W.F. *Phenomenology of Spirit.* Trans. A.V. Miller. Oxford: Oxford University Press 1977.

Heidegger, M. "The Origin of the Work of Art." In *Poetry, Language, Thought,* trans. A. Hofstadter. New York: Harper & Row 1971.

Hendley, S. *From Communicative Action to the Face of the Other: Levinas and Habermas on Language, Obligation, and Community.* Maryland: Lexington Books 2000.

Hobbes, T. *Leviathan.* Ed. C.B. Macpherson. Harmondsworth, England: Penguin 1968 [1651].

Hocking, J. *Lionel Murphy: A Political Biography.* Cambridge: Cambridge University Press 2000.

Honoré, T. "Are Omissions Less Culpable?" In P. Cane and J. Stapleton, eds., *Essays for Patrick Atiyah.* Oxford: Clarendon Press 1991.

– *The Foundations of Tort Law.* Oxford: Clarendon Press 1995.

– *Responsibility and Fault.* Oxford: Portland 1999.

Horn, N. "Black Letters: Epistolary Rhetoric and Plain English Laws." *Griffith Law Review* 9 (2000): 7.

Horwitz, M. *The Transformation of American Law.* Cambridge: Harvard University Press 1977.

Hutchison, A. *Critical Legal Studies.* Totowa, NJ: Rowman and Littlefield 1989.

Johnson, J.T.H. *Our Liability Predicament: The Practical and Psychological Flaws of the American Tort System.* Lanham, MD: University Press of America 1997.

Kafka, F. "The Parable of the Law." In *Collected Stories,* trans. W. Muir and E. Muir. Harmondsworth, England: Penguin 2000.

Kant, I. *Religion within the Limits of Reason Alone*. Trans. T. Greene. New York: Harper's 1960 [1793].

Kasirer, N. "Le droit robinsonien." In N. Kasirer, ed., *La solitude en droit privé*. Montreal: Éditions Thémis 2002.

Katz, C. *Levinas, Judaism, and the Feminine: The Silent Footsteps of Rebecca*. Bloomington: Indiana University Press 2003.

Kearney, R. "Derrida's Ethical Re-Turn." In G. Madison, ed., *Working through Derrida*. Evanston, IL: Northwestern University Press 1993.

Keating, G. "Social Contract Concept of the Tort Law of Accidents." In G. Postema, ed., *Philosophy and the Law of Torts*. New York: Cambridge University Press 2001.

Kelman, M. *A Guide to Critical Legal Studies*. Cambridge, MA: Harvard University Press 1987.

– "Trashing." *Stanford Law Review* 36 (1984): 293–348.

Kelsen, H. *General Theory of Law and State*. New York: Russell & Russell 1945.

– "The Pure Theory of Law." *Law Quarterly Review* 50 and 51 (1934–35): 1.

Kennedy, D. "The Structure of Blackstone's Commentaries." *Buffalo Law Review* 28 (1978): 205.

Kennedy, D., and Klare, K. "A Bibliography of Critical Legal Studies." *Yale Law Journal* 94 (1984): 461–505.

Kevelson, R. *Peirce, Science, Signs*. New York: Peter Lang 1996.

Kosky, J. *Levinas and the Philosophy of Religion*. Bloomington: Indiana University Press 2001.

Kostal, R. "Currents in the Counter-Reformation." *Tort Law Review* 3 (1995): 100–16.

Kramer, A. "Proximity as Principles: Directness, Community Norms and the Tort of Negligence." *Tort Law Review* 11, no. 2 (2003): 70–103.

Kundera, M. *The Unbearable Lightness of Being*. New York: HarperCollins 1984.

Kurzman, D. *Soldier of Peace: The Life of Yitzhak Rabin, 1922–1995*. New York: HarperCollins 1998.

Kymlicka, W. *Liberalism, Community, and Culture*. Oxford: Clarendon Press 1991.

Lacan, J. *Écrits: A Selection*. Trans. Alan Sheridan. New York: Norton 1977.

Lawton, P. "Love and Justice: Levinas's Reading of Buber." *Philosophy Today* 20 (1976): 77–83.

Levi-Strauss, C. *Myth and Meaning*. Toronto: University of Toronto Press 1978.

Libertson, J. *Proximity, Levinas, Blanchot, Bataille and Communication*. Phaenomenologica 87. The Hague: Martinus Nijhoff 1982.

Llewellyn, J. *Emmanuel Levinas: The Genealogy of Ethics*. London: Routledge 1995.

– "Jewgreek or Greekjew." In John Sallis, ed., *The Collegium Phenomenologicum: The First Ten Years*. Dordrecht: Kluwer Academic Publishers 1988, 273–87.

– "Levinas, Derrida and Others vis-à-vis." In John Llewelyn, ed. *Beyond Metaphysics*. Atlantic Highlands: Humanities Press, 1985, 185–206.

Llewellyn, K. *Jurisprudence: Realism in Theory and Practice*. Chicago: University of Chicago Press 1962.

Locke, J. *Two Treatises of Government*. 2d ed. London: Cambridge University Press 1970.

Lucy, W. *Understanding and Explaining Adjudication*. Oxford: Oxford University Press 1999.

Luntz, H., and D. Hambly. *Torts: Cases and Commentary*. 4th ed. Sydney: Butterworths 1995.

MacDonald, M. "'Jewgreek and Greekjew': The Concept of the Trace in Derrida and Levinas." *Philosophy Today* 35, no. 3 (1991): 215–27.

Mackie, J.L. *Ethics: Inventing Right and Wrong*. Harmondsworth, England: Penguin 1979.

Macpherson, C.B. *The Political Theory of Possessive Individualism: Hobbes to Locke*. London: Oxford University Press 1962.

Maloney, P. "Levinas, Substitution, and Transcendental Subjectivity." *Man and World* 30 (1997): 49–64.

Mandel, E., and G. Novack. *The Marxist Theory of Alienation*. New York: Pathfinder Press 1973.

Manderson, D. "Apocryphal Jurisprudence." *Studies in Law, Politics and Society* 23 (2001): 81–111.

– "The Care of Strangers." *Res Publica* 10, no. 2 (2001): 1–4.

– "Et lex perpetua: Dying Declarations and the Terror of Süssmayr." In D. Manderson, ed., *Courting Death: The Law of Mortality*. London and Sterling: Pluto Press 1999.

– "From Hunger to Love: Myths of the Source, Interpretation, and Constitution of Law in Children's Literature." *Law and Literature* 15 (2003): 87–142.

– "In the *tout court* of Shakespeare: Interdisciplinary Pedagogy in Law." *Journal of Legal Education* 54 (2004): 283–302.

– "Modes of Law: Music and Legal Theory – An Interdisciplinary Workshop." Consulting editor. *Cardozo Law Review* Special Symposium Issue 20, nos. 5–6 (1999): 1326–1694.

– *Songs without Music: Aesthetic Dimensions of Law and Justice*. Berkeley, CA: University of California Press 2000.

Manderson, D., and N. Sharp. "Mandatory Sentences and the Constitution: Discretion, Responsibility, and Judicial Process." *Sydney Law Review* 22 (2000): 585–624.

Marlowe, C. *Doctor Faustus.* In Christopher Marlowe, *The Complete Plays.* J.B. Steane, ed. Harmondsworth, England: Penguin 1986 [1604].

Marquez, C. "The Curvature of Intersubjective Space: Sociality and Responsibility in the Thought of Emmanuel Levinas." *Analecta Husserliana* 22 (1987): 343–52.

Marx, K. *Economic and Philosophic Manuscripts of 1844.* Trans. Martin Milligan. New York: International Press 1964.

McHugh, M. "Neighbourhood, Proximity and Reliance." In P. Finn, ed., *Essays on Torts.* Sydney: Law Book 1989.

Melville, H. *Moby Dick.* Oxford: Oxford World Classics 2000 [1851].

Menlowe, M., and A. Smith, eds. *The Duty to Rescue: The Jurisprudence of Aid.* Aldershot, England: Dartmouth 1993.

Milchman, A., ed. *Postmodernism and the Holocaust.* Amsterdam: Rodopi 1998.

Mill, J.S. *Utilitarianism.* Indianapolis: Hackett 1979 [1861].

Mill, J.S., and J. Bentham. *Utilitarianism and Other Essays.* Alan Ryan, ed. London: Penguin Books 1987.

Moore, H. *Moon Head.* Singapore Art Museum: Bronze 1964.

Motha, S. "Mabo: Encountering the Epistemic Limit of the Recognition of 'Difference.'" *Griffith Law Review* 7 (1998): 79–96.

Motha, S., and T. Zartaloudis. "Law, Ethics and the Utopian End of Human Rights." *Social and Legal Studies* 12, no. 2 (2003): 243–68.

New, M., with R. Bernasconi and R. Cohen, eds. *In Proximity: Emmanuel Levinas and the Eighteenth Century.* Lubbock, TX: Texas Tech University Press 2001.

Newton, A.Z. *The Fence and the Neighbor: Emmanuel Levinas, Yeshayahu Leibowitz, and Israel among the Nations.* Albany: SUNY Press 2001.

Nozick, R. *Anarchy, State and Utopia.* Totowa, NJ: Rowman 1974.

Owen, D.G. "Philosophical Foundations of Fault in Tort Law." In D.G. Owen, ed., *Philosophical Foundations of Tort Law.* Oxford: Clarendon Press 1995.

Owens, W. "The Parable of the Old Man and the Young." In *War Poems and Others.* London: Chatto & Windus 1976 [1917].

Peperzak, A. *Beyond: The Philosophy of Emmanuel Levinas.* Evanston, IL: Northwestern University Press 1997.

– "Emmanuel Levinas: Jewish Experience and Philosophy." *Philosophy Today* 27 (1983): 297–306.

- "The One for the Other: The Philosophy of Emmanuel Levinas." *Man and the World* 24 (1991): 427–59.
- *To the Other: An Introduction to the Philosophy of Emmanuel Levinas.* West Lafayette, IN: Purdue University Press 1993.
- ed. *Ethics as First Philosophy: The Significance of Emmanuel Levinas for Philosophy, Literature and Religion.* New York and London: Routledge 1995.

Perelman, C. "Equity and the Rule of Justice." In C. Perelman, *Justice, Law and Argument: Essays on Moral and Legal Reasoning.* Dordrecht: D. Reidel 1980.

Perpich, D. "A Singular Justice: Ethics and Politics between Levinas and Derrida." *Philosophy Today* 42 (Supp.) (1998): 59–70.

Perry, S. "The Impossibility of General Strict Liability." *Canadian Journal of Law and Jurisprudence* 1 (1988): 147–71.

- "Responsibility for Outcomes, Risk, and the Law of Torts." In G. Postema, ed., *Philosophy and the Law of Torts.* New York: Cambridge University Press 2001.
- "Risk, Harm, and Responsibility." In D.G. Owen, ed., *Philosophical Foundations of Tort Law.* Oxford: Clarendon Press 1995.
- "On the Relationship between Corrective and Distributive Justice." In J. Horder, ed., *Oxford Essays in Jurisprudence.* Oxford: Clarendon Press 2000.
- "The Mixed Conception of Corrective Justice." *Harvard Journal of Law and Public Policy* 15 (1992): 917–38.
- "The Moral Foundations of Tort Law." *Iowa Law Review* 77 (1992): 449–514.

Pettit, P. "The Capacity to Have Done Otherwise." In P. Cane and J. Gardner, eds., *Relating to Responsibility: Essays for Tony Honoré on His Eightieth Birthday.* Oxford: Hart 2001.

Piaget, J. *The Moral Judgment of the Child.* New York: Free Press 1997 [1932].

Posner, R. "The Concept of Corrective Justice in Recent Theories of Tort Law." *Journal of Legal Studies* 10 (1981): 187–206.

- *Economic Analysis of Law.* 6th ed. New York: Aspen Publishers 2003.
- "Epstein's Tort Theory: A Critique." *Journal of Legal Studies* 8 (1979): 457–75.
- "A Theory of Negligence." *Journal of Legal Studies* 1 (1972): 29–96.
- "Utilitarianism, Economic, and Legal Theory" *Journal of Legal Studies* 8 (1979): 103–40.

Postema, G., ed. *Philosophy and the Law of Torts.* New York: Cambridge University Press 2001.

Raffoul, F. "On Hospitality, between Ethics and Politics: Review of *Adieu à Emmanuel Levinas* by Jacques Derrida." *Research in Phenomenology* 28 (1998): 274–82.

Rawls, J. *A Theory of Justice*. Cambridge: Belknap Press 1999.

Réaume, D. "Is Integrity a Virtue? Dworkin's Theory of Legal Obligation." *University of Toronto Law Journal* 39, no. 4 (1989): 380.

Robbins, J. *Altered Reading: Levinas and Literature*. Chicago: University of Chicago Press 1999.

Roberts, S. "Rethinking Justice: Levinas and Asymmetrical Responsibility." *Philosophy in the Contemporary World* 7 (2000): 5–12.

Rose, G. *The Broken Middle: Out of Our Ancient Society*. London: Blackwells 1992.

– *Judaism and Modernity: Philosophical Essays*. Oxford: Blackwells 1993.

– *Mourning Becomes the Law: Philosophy and Representation*. Cambridge: Cambridge University Press 1996.

Sandel, M. *Democracy's Discontent: America in Search of a Public Philosophy*. Cambridge, MA: Belknap Press 1997.

Schneider, B. *Daniel Libeskind: Jewish Museum Berlin, between the Lines*. Berlin: Prestel Press 1999.

Schrit, A. ed. *The Logic of the Gift*. New York: Routledge 1997.

Schwartz, G. "The Ethics and Economics of Tort Liability Insurance." *Cornell Law Review* 76 (1990): 313–65.

– "Mixed Theories of Tort Law: Affirming Both Deterrence and Corrective Justice." *Texas Law Review* 75 (1997): 1801–34.

Shakespeare, William. *The Riverside Shakespeare*. Boston: Houghton Mifflin 1997.

Shapo, M. *The Duty to Act*. Dallas: University of Texas Press 1978.

Shavell, S. "Strict Liability versus Negligence." *Journal of Legal Studies* 9 (1980): 1.

Shils, E. *Tradition*. Chicago: University of Chicago Press 1981.

Silverman, H., ed. *Derrida and Deconstruction*. London: Routledge 1989.

Simmons, W.P. "The Third: Levinas's Theoretical Move from An-archical Ethics to the Realm of Justice and Politics." *Philosophy and Social Criticism* 25 (1999): 83–104.

– "Zionism, Place and the Other: Toward a Levinasian International Relations." *Philosophy in the Contemporary World* 7 (2000): 21–5.

Singer, J. "The Player and the Cards: Nihilism and Legal Theory." *Yale Law Journal* 94 (1984): 1–7.

Sklar, J. *Legalism*. Cambridge: Cambridge University Press 1964.

Smith, M. "Responsibility and Self Control." In P. Cane and J. Gardner, eds. *Relating to Responsibility.* Oxford: Hart 2001.

Sophocles. *Antigone.* Wiltshire: Aris & Phillips 1987.

Srajek, M.C. *The Margins of Deconstruction: Jewish Conceptions of Ethics in Emmanuel Levinas and Jacques Derrida.* Dordrecht: Kluwer 1998.

Stapleton, J. "Duty of Care Factors: A Selection from the Judicial Menus." In P. Cane and J. Stapleton, eds., *The Law of Obligations: Essays in Celebration of John Fleming.* Oxford: Oxford University Press 1998.

Stolle, J. "Levinas and the Akedah: An Alternative to Kierkegaard." *Philosophy Today* 45, no. 2 (2001): 132–43.

Stone, J. *Legal System and Lawyers' Reasonings.* Stanford: Stanford University Press 1964.

– *Social Dimensions of Law and Justice.* Sydney: Maitland 1966.

Strajek, M. *The Margins of Deconstruction: Jewish Conceptions of Ethics in Emmanuel Levinas and Jacques Derrida.* Dordrecht: Kluwer 1998.

Sturgess, G. "Murphy and the Media." In J.A. Scutt, ed., *Lionel Murphy: A Radical Judge.* McCulloch: Carlton, Victoria 1987.

Taylor, C. *Hegel.* Cambridge: Cambridge University Press 1975.

Tushnet, M. "An Essay on Rights." *Texas Law Review* 62 (1984): 1363–1403.

Vines, P. "Fault, Responsibility and Negligence in the High Court." *Tort Law Review* (2000): 130–45.

– "The Needle in the Haystack: Principle in the Duty of Care in Negligence." *University of New South Wales Law Journal* 23, no. 2 (2000): 35–57.

– "Proximity as Principle or Category: Nervous Shock in Australia and England." *University of New South Wales Law Journal* 16 (1993): 458.

Visker, R. "Dis-Possessed: How to Remain Silent 'After' Levinas." *Man and World* 29 (1996): 119–46.

Weinrib, E. "The Case for a Duty to Rescue." *Yale Law Journal* 90 (1980): 247–93.

– "Causation and Wrongdoing." *Chicago-Kent Law Review* 63 (1987): 407–50.

– "Corrective Justice." *Iowa Law Review* 77 (1992): 403–25.

– "The Gains and Losses of Corrective Justice." *Duke Law Review* 44 (1995): 277–97.

– *The Idea of Private Law.* Cambridge: Harvard University Press 1995.

– "The Jurisprudence of Legal Formalism." *Harvard Journal of Law and Public Policy* 16 (1993): 583–96.

– "'Legal Formalism': On the Immanent Rationality of Law." *Yale Law Journal* 97 (1984): 949–1016.

– "Right and Advantage in Private Law." *Cardazo Law Review* 10 (1989): 1283–1309.
– "The Special Morality of Tort Law." *McGill Law Journal* 34 (1988): 403–13.
Williams, B. "What Has Philosophy to Learn from Tort Law?" In D.G. Owen, ed., *Philosophical Foundations of Tort Law*. Oxford: Clarendon Press 1995.
Williams, G. "The High Court and the People." In H. Selby, ed. *Tomorrow's Law*. Sydney: Federation Press 1995.
Windeyer, V. "A Birthright and Inheritance – The Establishment of the Rule of Law in Australia." *University of Tasmania Law Review* (1962): 635–69.
Wood, D., and R. Bernasconi, eds. *Derrida and Difference*. Evanston, IL: Northwestern University Press 1988.
Wright, R., "The Standards of Care in Negligence Law." In D.G. Owen, ed., *Philosophical Foundations of Tort Law*. Oxford: Clarendon Press 1995.
Yeats, W.B. "Before the World Was Made." In *Collected Works of W.B. Yeats*. 2d ed. New York: Scribner 1997.
Yeo, S., "Rethinking Proximity: A Paper Tiger?" *Tort Law Review* 5, no. 3 (1997): 174.

Index